CUBA:
The Logic of the Revolution

CUBA:
The Logic of the Revolution

Edited with an Introduction by
DAVID P. BARKIN
City University of New York
Lehman College
and
NITA R. MANITZAS
Ford Foundation
Santiago, Chile

WARNER MODULAR PUBLICATIONS, INC.
Eleven Essex Street
Andover, Massachusetts 01810

ACKNOWLEDGMENTS

The editors and publisher gratefully acknowledge the permission of the authors and editors of the journals to reprint the articles in this volume. Full citations appear on the first page of each selection.

Copyright © 1973 by Warner Modular Publications, Inc. All rights reserved. No part of this publication may be reproduced, stored in a retrieval system, or transmitted, in any form or by any means, electronic, mechanical, photocopying, recording or otherwise, without the prior written permission of the publisher. Printed in the United States of America.

Library of Congress Catalog Number 73-3872

10 9 8 7 6 5 4 3 2 1

The Developmental Economics Series is under the editorship of

DAVID P. BARKIN
City University of New York
Lehman College

GEORGE HARPOOTLIAN
Associate Publisher

Suggested Citation

David P. Barkin and Nita R. Manitzas (eds.), Cuba: The Logic of the Revolution, Warner Modular Publications, Andover, Massachusetts, (1973).

All original publications in this series appear first as separate modules. Most modules will appear in one collection; many will appear in several. To facilitate research use, all modules are numbered serially, and each module carries the same number and folio sequence in all incarnations.

About the authors...

DAVID P. BARKIN (City University of New York) is an economist specializing in Latin American affairs. He has published two books on regional development and is interested in the relationship between the distribution of income and strategies of economic development. He was a visiting professor at the Institute of Economics of the University of Havana.

FERNANDO HENRIQUE CARDOSO (Brazilian Center for Demographic Research) is a Brazilian sociologist who has published numerous books on problems of Latin American development. His contribution to this collection is based on his close collaboration with many Latin Americans working on the relationship between Cuba and the rest of the hemisphere.

RICHARD R. FAGEN (Stanford University) is a political scientist who has written several books about Latin America. The Transformation of Political Culture in Cuba is based on interviews and extensive visits to different parts of the island in recent years.

JORGE E. HARDOY is an Argentine urbanist with extensive publications in the area. He was president of the Interamerican Society of Planning. His contribution to this volume is the product of a visit to Cuba as an expert for the United Nations and is complemented by his book Reforma urbana en Cuba revolucionaria, which recently appeared in Venezuela.

MARVIN LEINER (City University of New York) is a specialist in teaching. After years of work in black communities in New York, he moved to Cuba with his family to study educational development on the island. His book, Children Are the Revolution: Day Care in Cuba, will appear shortly and he is presently working on another one on primary education.

NITA R. MANITZAS (Ford Foundation, Santiago, Chile) is a student of political science in Latin America and is finishing her dissertation on Cuba for Columbia University. Her work is based on her broad knowledge of development patterns in Latin America where she has lived for many years.

BERTRAM SILVERMAN (Hofstra University) is an economist specializing in labor affairs. His stay in Cuba allowed him to closely examine the system of moral incentives and he has edited a book: Man and Socialism in Cuba: The Great Debate.

Contents

	Editors' Introduction	E260
Chapter I	NITA R. MANITZAS: The Setting of the Cuban Revolution	M260
Chapter II	NITA R. MANITZAS: Social Class and the Definition of the Cuban Nation	M261
Chapter III	DAVID P. BARKIN: Cuban Agriculture: A Strategy of Economic Development	R261
Chapter IV	BERTRAM SILVERMAN: Economic Organization and Social Conscience: Some Dilemmas of Cuban Socialism	R262
Chapter V	DAVID P. BARKIN: The Redistribution of Consumption in Cuba	R263
Chapter VI	MARVIN LEINER: Major Developments in Cuban Education	M264
Chapter VII	JORGE E. HARDOY: Spatial Structure and Society in Revolutionary Cuba	M265
Chapter VIII	RICHARD R. FAGEN: Continuities in Cuban Revolutionary Politics	R266
Chapter IX	FERNANDO H. CARDOSO: Cuba: Lesson or Symbol?	M267

Editors' Introduction

In the last dozen years the Cuban Revolution has received prolific treatment at the hands of scholars, journalists, embittered exiles and ebullient admirers. While this literature ranges from hostile to the adulatory, most of the authors share a common disposition to treat Cuba as a special case, an unique phenomenon that has no other frame of reference than itself. Not since Professor Dudley Seers led a team of researchers to the island in 1962 has there been a serious, multidisciplinary attempt to examine the Cuban experience within its larger context, as a particular "type" within the family of developing nations.*

It is the purpose of this book to bring Cuba back into the mainstream of so-called "development literature." By using the tools of social science, the authors hope to shed new light and meaning on various facets of the Cuban revolutionary experience. Political and socio-economic development is described and basic problems are explored. Our purpose, however, is not only description; we also hope to contribute to an understanding of the modernization process and to the search for better approaches and policies relevant for other countries.

THE DEVELOPMENT CONUNDRUM

In the second half of the twentieth century the problems of development have emerged as a central issue for the international community. The more developed tier of nations has sent advisors, teachers, technicians, bankers, and builders across the globe to attempt to launch less affluent peoples into developmental orbit. A host of bilateral and multilateral agencies has sprung up to assist the quest. Major resources have been marshaled for development programs. And the poorer countries, whatever their political coloration or patterns of social hierarchy, have made development their common aspiration. The United Nations proclaimed the 1960s to be the "First Development Decade." Academia was not far behind; over the last dozen years, the body of scholarly writing on development has multiplied in abundance.

But if the development literature has flourished, the lot of the poorer countries has not commensurately improved. The dismal result of the "First Development Decade" has by now been well documented. The gap between rich and poor countries has widened, not closed. The absolute number of the world's ill-fed, ill-housed, and illiterate peoples continues to advance. The cities of the Third World are swollen with unemployed and with persons now fashionably referred to as "marginal populations." Even those countries that have managed to make respectable gains in average-per-capita income over the last ten years still find themselves grappling with the fundamental structural problems of underdevelopment. Significant increases in gross national product, once thought to be the mark and measure of national progress, have not necessarily brought in their wake the solutions to unemployment and poverty. Indeed, in such countries as Brazil and Mexico—the so-called "economic miracles" of the

---

* Dudley Seers, ed., <u>Cuba: The Economic and Social Revolution,</u> Chapel Hill: University of North Carolina Press, 1964.

last decade—there now is evidence that macro-growth has been accompanied by higher concentrations of income and greater social inequalities than before. In sum, the complacent assumptions and theories of the early 1960s have proved flawed and fallible. And the optimism that once underlay such ventures as the Alliance for Progress has been dissipated in the face of accumulating empirical evidence.

In much of the Third World today there is a questioning of old dogmas and a search for new alternatives. Nationalist elites in the developing countries are no longer willing to accept on faith the formulae and panaceae prescribed for them by their more affluent neighbors. Indeed, rather than looking to the developed nations as models to emulate, they now are suggesting that it is the developed world itself—with its entrenched patterns of international trade, overseas investment, and monetary controls—that helps prolong the stagnation and economic disadvantage of underdeveloped nation-states. They are increasingly wary of the traditional aid packages offered to them by the developed countries. And they are seeking new operational models and new, innovative responses to the problems posed by an unequal world. The climate, in sum, has shifted markedly since 1960, when most countries seemed willing to accept Mr. Rostow's orderly vision of a universe in which all nations, one after another, would progress down the same, predestined path to "takeoff."

With the benefit of hindsight, we would suggest that the development theories of the early 1960s, especially as they emerged in the United States, were basically astigmatic. To begin with they evolved against the backdrop of the Cold War; and the tendency of the time to see the world in stark, Manichean terms was reflected in the Western view of development. The only options considered open to developing countries were Western capitalism or Soviet communism. And, within this bipolar framework, the Soviet system was not seen as an alternative development model, but simply as a distasteful phenomenon.

Little or no thought was given to the possibility—now an obvious reality—that countries pursuing a capitalist trajectory might become enmeshed in various forms of new-colonialism or might evolve into corporate states; the common presumption was that any country willing to work diligently and to follow the model of "free enterprise" would eventually become a latter-day replica of the United States or the British Isles.

With similar myopia, there was little recognition of a possible pluralism within the Marxist universe or of the Third World's potential for building a rich variety of socialist edifices. The Marxian world was presumed to be monolithic. And the Yugoslav and Chinese cases, which clearly challenged this view, were simply ignored in the language and literature of development theorists; deemed irrelevant by the development Establishment, they were left to the purview of "area studies" and international relations. That development models might be numerous, that the options open to developing countries might be multiple, these were not generally accredited notions in the Western world at the outset of the "First Development Decade." And that Marxian socialism might be an alternative development strategy was a fact recognized only by Marxists—whose views had little hearing or credence in traditional development circles.

Paralleling this Cold War view of development matters was a series of presumptions, similarly hidebound and narrow, about the replicability of developmental processes. The common assumption of the early 1960s was that developing countries, to reach the point of "takeoff," had only to retrace the steps and stages of the already-developed nations. Accordingly, considerable space in the development literature was devoted to identifying the key causal variables at play in nineteenth-century England and the United States. The implicit notion was that one need simply reproduce such variables in the twentieth century to achieve the same results. Thus, if the privately owned, medium-sized family farm was diagnosed as the principal vehicle for rural development in North America, then it followed that today's Third World countries must perforce direct their agrarian reform efforts to creating such holdings. If the middle class was seen as the key to political stability and commercial expansion in last century's England, then contemporary development must be predicated on the emergence of an indigenous middle class. If stolid, Calvinist burghers had accumulated the capital for Europe's industrial advance, then it was clear that the first order of business for Third World governments was to facilitate and assist whatever entrepreneurial elements they might find in their societies. And so it went. That development in the contemporary world might be qualitatively different than anything that had gone before was not readily acknowledged. Nor was it generally recognized that the impact of the developed countries on their poorer neighbors had definitively altered the very nature of the development process.

This narrow view of development was typically accompanied by a strong dose of economic determinism. Western development theorists might criticize Marx for giving inordinate weight and attention to the "economic base." In their own fashion, however, they were equally, if not more, obsessed with economic variables. In their vision of the development process, they saw the economy as primary, as the fount from which all other good would ultimately flow. Economic growth would automatically and eventually bring in its wake social mobility, educational opportunity, greater equality, and political openness.

There were, of course, variations on the theme, some more sophisticated than others. But the underlying premise was essentially the same: the economy was the key to development and to other kinds of societal change. Irrational politics, gross social inequalities, and other flaws in the fabric of underdeveloped nation-states would be corrected once an economy was launched into the orbit of "self-sustaining growth." It was even argued that any attempt at an early stage of development to radically change the social balance and to distribute more broadly and equally the national total of wealth and services would be counterproductive; it would be a squandering of the resources needed for capital accumulation and economic growth. Once the economic pie was respectably large and once annual gross national product began to outdistance annual population growth by a wholesome margin, there would inevitably be a "trickle-down" to the more disadvantaged groups in society. The economy, in sum, was seen as the independent variable in the development process. Broad-scale social welfare, consensual political orders, and other attributes of a healthy, modern commonweal were seen, and treated, as derivative matters.

Such economic determinism was reflected in an overwhelming preoccupation with the indices of growth and macro-economic statistics as measures of development. Strategies of development were framed largely in terms of computable increases in national income. The quality of growth was generally ignored; and it was rarely recognized that "economic miracles" might be achieved at the cost of social inequity and political repression. The traditional growth models were not constructed to register such qualitative variables.

These traditional theories, strategies, and measurements are now being challenged in much of the Third World. And definitions of development are beginning subtly to shift. It is in such a context of renewed questioning that the Cuban case has more than intellectual interest.

THE CUBAN EXPERIENCE

The Cubans, by self definition, are fundamentally concerned with development. Like their counterparts in most other developing countries, Cuban planners over the last dozen years have sought solutions to basic development problems: poverty, illiteracy, unemployment, malnutrition, and disease. Here, however, the similarity ends, for the Cubans have rejected traditional development ideologies and strategies. Instead of partial, incremental reforms, they have opted for a strategy based on the total transformation of society and its structures. More importantly, instead of treating the economy as the key to improving the human condition, they have reversed the orthodox line of reasoning and postulated the human element—in its variety of attitudinal, behavioral, and institutional expressions—as the independent variable of development.

The Cuban disillusionment with traditional developmental strategies is, in part, the result of historical experience at home and elsewhere in the hemisphere. As the Cubans have been quick to point out, the developmental policies and tactics adopted by most Third World countries have thus far served mainly to increase the wealth and power of national minorities. Although neo-capitalist strategies may bring new national elites to the foreground and may even, in some instances, extend benefits and opportunities to a greater segment of the community, the fact remains that huge sectors of the population continue outside this modernized mainstream, denied any share in their national patrimony. Even though equality may be one of the goals verbalized by most development planners, it is, at best, an ideal lying far in the future; and, in the meantime, even the better development programs have led to increasing concentrations of wealth and political power in the hands of minority elites.

The Cubans have explicitly rejected developmental policies that tell the poor to await their reward in heaven, or in the next generations. Obviously, they were helped in their purpose by the mass exodus of upper- and middle-class Cubans to the North American mainland, a process that automatically opened up social space and opportunity for those left behind. But aside from such fortuitous a circumstance, the Cubans also embarked on a purposeful and interrelated set of strategies designed to bring the entire population, immediately and irrevocably, into the "modernizing" sector of society. To achieve this end, the Cuban revolutionary leaders rejected the piecemeal and evolutionary path to development. Instead of embarking on a series of gradual and essentially fragmented reforms of discrete national institutions, they have pursued the massive reorganization of their society as a whole.

For the Cubans, development strategies which attempt to retrace the incremental steps that characterized development in North America and Western Europe during the eighteenth and nineteenth centuries are doomed to failure. Technology, communications, and geopolitics have collapsed historical time for today's traditional societies. Reformist strategies in any single institutional area which do not recognize the intrinsic interrelation of all societal structures and institutions serve only to create greater internal distortions and contradictions for the country that attempts them. Development, in sum, in the Cuban frame of reference is postulated as a total process.

Although recognizing the totality of the Cuban experience, the several authors in this book have individually chosen to examine discrete aspects of the Cuban phenomenon. Time, space, and the differing methodologies of the social science disciplines have imposed such a framework on us. Nonetheless, although the material is organized as a series of sectoral analyses and no attempt has been made to construct a single theoretical edifice, the internal coherence of the Cuban revolutionary strategy has given rise to certain common themes that run, like a unifying thread, through all the individual essays. First, the Cubans explicitly recognize the complex nature of their development process. While they do not neglect the economic dimension, they have never treated the economy in isolation or to the exclusion—temporary or otherwise—of social and political variables. They understand the need for a fundamental restructuring of all institutions in order to reverse the inherited pattern of pyramiding privilege. Second, in contract to traditional approaches, the need for social change initially overrode the concern for economic growth in the Cuban order of development priorities. Third, mass mobilization and participation have been treated as essential elements in the search for and implementation of solutions to national problems. And, finally, the Cubans have never regarded development as a value-free enterprise, a technocratic craft that can be isolated from human ideology and values. The interrelated and logical coherence of sectorial strategies which contribute to the modernization of Cuban society underscores the dialectical nature of the efforts to achieve a unity of theory and practice in the evolution of practical policies.

The reconstruction of the institutional framework was the logical result of the Cuban interpretation of the causes of underdevelopment. Traditional institutions could not be used to solve inherited social and economic problems; these institutions themselves helped perpetuate or even exacerbate the social conflicts and inequities characterizing the neocolonial society. In order to break the self-reinforcing pattern of accumulating wealth and power, fundamental institutional changes were essential. Realizing, for example, the futility of attempting to achieve a thorough redistribution of income with isolated programs, they moved to reshape productive structures which in the past had created a highly stratified labor force and class structure. Better-trained workers were clearly needed for development, but educational efforts began with a massive literacy drive consistent with an egalitarian outlook and the need to communicate with the entire population and integrate it into the evolving political system. Elitist educational training programs for economic development, characteristic of many other countries, were never seriously considered.

The primary importance given to social problems in Cuban planning provides another contrast with other countries in which economic growth is unchallenged in the order of priorities. The first task the new government defined for itself when it came to power in 1959 was the elimination of the most striking inequities of the pre-revolutionary class structure. The peasants and rural proletariat suddenly found themselves in privileged positions as agricultural activity was stimulated and consumption subsidized. Production in all areas was increased but greater concern was shown for eliminating unemployment, especially the seasonal unemployment which had for decades been the scourge of Cuba. Even when resource scarcities became widespread and difficult choices were made to support investment programs, social and political considerations continually conditioned the way in which decisions relating to production and consumption were implemented.

Within this setting—egalitarian and developmental—new ways are being sought to ensure popular participation at all levels. Not only are local groups taking greater responsibility for the management of their own lives—as is evidenced by the growth of people's courts and the added importance of neighborhood organizations—but, as Fidel Castro and other Cuban leaders have pointed out, many problems which elsewhere might be expected to be solved by planners are being handed to unions and other local groups for resolution. Production and consumption targets are established nationally but local participation in their implementation is a key and often ignored aspect of social and political organization in Cuba.

The choice of the path of conciencia (morale incentives)—and the abandonment of an exclusive dependence on material incentives—must also be viewed as part of the program to encourage popular participation. In Cuba modernization is expected to proceed on the basis of individual comprehension and acceptance of national efforts. Furthermore, it necessarily requires changes in attitudes as well as individual sacrifices of material objects for a new conception of collectivistic well-being. Rather than acceding to the ever-rising demands for consumption characteristic of workers in most countries, the Cubans are creating a new consumption pattern and structure of rewards based on group participation and identification with national achievements. Individual consumption of more material goods is being restricted while collective participation in social services is rapidly expanding. As an essential step in this process, individual motivation must be related to national goals.

This strategy has not been easy. Cuba cannot ignore external pressures to abandon its present trajectory. The country has received large amounts of aid from the socialist world and continues to depend on it for most of its foreign trade. Its national development program, however, differs markedly from theirs. As a result, strong criticisms of this route have been offered and Cuba has modified its policies. It is true that the Cubans have paid dearly for their hard-won experience; low labor productivity is a serious problem, as are other problems related to the coordination and administration of economic and social planning. The elimination of some tensions and contradictions produced—dialectically—new pressures and contradictions which still persist. Other difficulties arise from foreign pressures, both from the capitalist world and from the "sister republics" of the socialist world. The former, for obvious reasons, has contributed in varying degrees to the strengthening of the political and economic blockade imposed by the United States of America. The latter group clearly sees the Cuban deviations with some disquiet and is exerting its influence to convince the Cubans to follow a more orthodox (and, in this sense, less egalitarian) path. But it would be too simplistic to place all the blame for Cuba's problems on its international relations, without recognizing that the Cuban revolutionary process requires sacrifices that the society continues to pay in its battle to overcome underdevelopment.

Underdevelopment, of course, is the centuries-old yoke which Cuba is trying to shed. It is much more than a struggle to produce more goods. The Cubans reorganized their economy, redesigned their cities, provided education and medical care, and restructured social relations in an attempt to modernize. In the light of international experience the results are noteworthy: illiteracy has been virtually erased, participation has increased, and involuntary unemployment eliminated. At the same time, substantial resources were freed for investment; and structural changes in the economy promise large increases in production in the coming years. Many adjustments are still needed to take full advantage of the economy's productive potential and to construct a new social order. But the goal of "development" is still far off; the meaning of this task is examined at length in this book as the authors analyze various crucial aspects of the Cuban revolutionary process. We hope that it serves not as a guide but rather as an illustration of an experience which will contribute to the almost desperate search for better policies to achieve the <u>total development</u> of other societies.

March 15, 1973
Santiago de Chile

NITA R. MANITZAS
Ford Foundation, Santiago, Chile

The Setting of the Cuban Revolution

"To see Castro's Revolution only in its Marxist dimension is to miss much of the meaning in the current Cuban phenomenon. It is like examining only that part of an iceberg which protrudes above the surface of the water. Submerged beneath the surface in the Cuban case is a complex set of elements that are generally obscured by the emotionally charged fact of Cuba's Communist commitment."

The bulk of North American literature on Castro's Cuba—both scholarly and journalistic, Marxist and non-Marxist—starts from the premise that Cuba is, above all else, a member of the Soviet camp. Whatever may be its variations on the Marxist theme, it is treated essentially as a Communist "case." For certain purposes, most notably the study of comparative Communism, this approach is obviously useful. In terms of explaining the internal dynamics of the Cuban Revolution, however, it leads to something of a blind alley. It tends to highlight a particular, limited set of variables in the revolutionary process; and it has given rise over the past ten years to a welter of theories about contemporary Cuba that are in general one-dimensional and in the worst cases patently biased.

To see Castro's Revolution only in its Marxist dimension is to miss much of the meaning in the current Cuban phenomenon. It is like examining only that part of an iceberg which protrudes above the surface of the water. Submerged beneath the surface in the Cuban case is a complex set of elements that are generally obscured by the emotionally charged fact of Cuba's Communist commitment.

What is all too often forgotten is that Cuba, whatever its present ideological course, falls within a particular category in the international community of nations. Marxist or not, Cuba is, in essence, an underdeveloped country. Its underdevelopment is, indeed, a condition of which the Cubans themselves are acutely aware. Despite their important ties to the Soviet Union, the Cubans tend to identify more with those countries that together comprise the "Third World." Thus, to understand contemporary Cuba, it is necessary first to understand the fact of Cuban underdevelopment and, second, to recognize those features that are typical of underdevelopment everywhere and those that would appear to be unique to Cuba. To make this distinction, the logical starting point is not January 1, 1959, when Fidel and his fellow rebels descended triumphant from the Sierra Maestra. Rather, the roots of the contemporary Cuban condition must first be sought in the sweep of prerevolutionary history that anteceded Fidel Castro's appearance on the scene.

A LATIN AMERICAN CASE

To begin, within the Third World Cuba belongs to a particular subset of developing countries. In important respects the Latin American region

A WARNER MODULAR PUBLICATION

Copyright © 1973 by Warner Modular Publications, Inc.

All rights reserved. No part of this publication may be reproduced, stored in a retrieval system, or transmitted, in any form or by any means, electronic, mechanical, photocopying, recording, or otherwise, without the prior written permission of the publisher. Printed in the United States of America.

Library of Congress Catalog Card Number 73-5214

10 9 8 7 6 5 4 3 2 1

The Developmental Economics Series is under the editorship of

DAVID P. BARKIN
City University of New York
Lehman College

SUGGESTED CITATION

Nita R. Manitzas, "The Setting of the Cuban Revolution," Warner Modular Publications, Module 260 (1973), pp 1–18

All original publications in this series appear first as separate modules. Most modules will appear in one collection; many will appear in several. To facilitate research use, all modules are numbered serially, and each module carries the same number and folio sequence in all incarnations.

must be distinguished from the general run of countries wrestling in this century with problems of economic development, modernization, and nation-building. First, according to the usual indices of development—gross national product, industrialization, access to education, etc.—Latin America is much more advanced than most countries in Africa and Asia. Second, as a result of its special colonial history which lasted more than three centuries, the Latin American countries are more closely tied to the culture and traditions of Western Europe; Spanish hegemony in the area lasted more than the colonial regimes in any other part of the world. And when the Spaniards were finally expelled, their descendants remained as citizens of the new republics; a heritage further enriched by successive waves of European immigration. Lastly, for over one hundred years, Latin American history has been continually affected by the colossus to the north. There is no doubt that the culture and economy of the United States of America have weighed more heavily on the Latin American republics than on the more distant lands of the Third World.[1]

These distinguishing characteristics were more blatant in prerevolutionary Cuba than anywhere else in Latin America (with the special exception of Puerto Rico). Spanish dominion lasted a full three-quarters of a century after the other countries of the region had become independent. And the United States' presence was nowhere more visible or pervasive, actually including governance on occasion. Indeed, many of the features that set Cuba apart from the rest of the Latin American family can be traced to the sheer weight of North American involvement in the island's affairs.

The Economic Heritage

In the structure of its economy, prerevolutionary Cuba displayed a variety of characteristics typical of the Latin American brand of underdevelopment. Like most countries of the region, Cuba was basically a monoculture. From the beginning of the twentieth century—and even into the revolutionary period—sugar was the country's ineluctable fact of life. Internationally it earned Cuba the dubious title of "sugar plantation of the world," and domestically it dictated the shape of Cuba's principal social and economic institutions. Although sugar rarely amounted to more than a fifth of total national output, it monopolized more than half the cultivable land and employed almost a quarter of the labor force. More importantly, it regularly accounted for 80 per cent of Cuba's export earnings. Like bananas in Panama, copper in Chile, and tin in Bolivia, sugar dictated Cuba's ability to marshal foreign exchange and thus to purchase from abroad the commodities needed for domestic growth.*

The annual sugar cycle determined the rhythm of railway traffic, banking transactions, internal trade, and employment. In the last analysis, sugar dominated not only the national economy but also the national psyche. And it left Cuba prey to the full range of problems commonly associated with monoculture and dependence on a primary good, including seasonal fluctuations, extreme sensitivity to external market forces, and, especially after World War II, deteriorating terms of trade. As a British economist, Dudley Seers, has pointed out:

> Cuba was not, of course, unique in this respect. Every exporter of agricultural products experiences seasonal fluctuations. Practically without exception, primary producers have suffered severely from recessions and depressions. They were all affected to a greater or lesser extent by the slowing up of growth in North America, and more recently in Western Europe, and by the failure of exports of primary products even to keep pace with this growth rate in the industrial countries. Among the main reasons for this lag in commodity sales were the low income-elasticities of demand for primary products, especially foodstuffs, and the increasing tendency of industrial countries to subsidize their own farmers. These depressing tendencies on demand also influenced prices, so the problems of underdeveloped countries have been aggravated by a downward trend in the terms of trade in the last decade.[2]

Cuba also had much in common with other Latin American countries in the internal structure of its industry and agriculture. The industrial sector was underdeveloped, employing less than 20 per cent of the labor force (well under half the number engaged in agriculture). The few large, modern industrial plants that were operating in prerevolutionary Cuba were almost without exception foreign-controlled; the bulk of indigenous industry was small-scale and technologically backward. Low productivity, excess productive capacity, and a marked bias toward low-volume, high-priced manufacture were the predominant characteristics of Cuban industry. Local entrepreneurs and modern managers were few and far between. And domestic capital gravitated more to real estate or investments abroad than to native industry. In these respects Cuba closely paralleled the rest of Latin America.

Similarly, Cuban agriculture resembled to a significant extent the general Latin American model. The latifundium, a typical feature of the Latin American rural landscape, was prominent in Cuba. Overall, the pattern of land tenure followed the Latin American norm. Thirteen thousand farms, representing less than 8 per cent of the total farm units, extended over 70 per cent of the cultivable land area. At the other end of the spectrum, approximately 70 per cent of the farm units were crowded onto a little over 11 per cent of the country's farmland.[3] Even these figures, however, do not fully reveal the striking degree of land concentration in prerevolutionary Cuba. Perhaps a more telling statistic is that when Batista fled the country, the twenty-eight largest sugar-cane producers together owned or rented more than 20 per cent of all farmland—thus controlling, in effect, almost one-fifth of the national land area.

As in most of Latin America, the characteristic pattern of land cultivation in Cuba was extensive, rather than intensive. Also, the land was flagrantly underutilized, with vast tracts held in reserve for sugar or left to natural pasture. It

---

* Most of the data contained in this chapter is derived from a few basic sources. Unless otherwise noted, the statistical data cited are from: Dudley Seers, ed., Cuba: The Economic and Social Revolution (Chapel Hill: The University of North Carolina Press, 1964); International Bank for Reconstruction and Development, Report on Cuba (Baltimore: The Johns Hopkins Press, 1951); U.S. Department of Commerce, Investment in Cuba (Washington, D.C.: Government Printing Office, 1956); Lowry Nelson, Rural Cuba (Minneapolis: University of Minnesota, 1950); and Michel Gutelman, L'agriculture socialiseé à Cuba (Paris: Francois Maspero, 1967).

has been estimated that at least half of the cultivable land was perennially idle. Although successive Cuban governments for over thirty years had declared agricultural diversification a national necessity, very little of substance was done about it. Private sugar growers, enjoying sizeable profits with only a minimal input, were unwilling to make the capital investments required to diversify their crop. From their point of view, it made more economic sense in the short run to leave much of their landholdings idle; among other things, the internal quota system protected them from the worst effects of such inefficient land use. One result was that Cuba, with land resources sufficiently abundant and fertile to supply most of its domestic needs, was forced to import more than $200 million in agricultural commodities each year by the end of Batista's reign. Even more telling, almost three-quarters of these imports were foodstuffs, most of which could readily have been produced on the island itself.

The infrastructure for modern agriculture also was lacking. In the typical Latin American mold, Cuba in the 1950s had only 294 agricultural engineers while boasting 6,560 lawyers. Agricultural research and extension were minimal. Although some progress was made in irrigation and mechanization after World War II, the general level of agricultural technology was deficient. The backwardness of Cuban agriculture in this area is perhaps best illustrated by the fact that during the fifty years preceding the Revolution cane yields remained static and may even have declined slightly.

Aside from the structural features of the economy, the economic psychology that predominated in prerevolutionary Cuba was, with variations in degree and intensity, common to Latin America. The distortions and fluctuations inherent in an agricultural monoculture combined with the inherited attitudes and values of the Spanish colonial past to produce a pattern of economic behavior that, from the standpoint of the country's developmental needs, was basically counterproductive. For the Cuban of means, as for his counterpart elsewhere in Latin America, tangible property, especially land, had particular value. Investment in real estate, accordingly, was more attractive than capital investment. In similar style, short-term speculation promising rapid and high returns was preferred to long-term investment in improving productive capacity. A tendency for private savings to flow abroad also hindered the mobilization of domestic capital for economic growth. In 1955, for example, it was estimated that Cuban citizens had $150 million tied up in Florida real estate alone.

The corollary to this kind of economic psychology was that Cubans tended to look increasingly to the government to undertake the capital investments and capital risks that in North America and much of Western Europe have normally been assumed by the private sector. The trend reached its peak in the mid-1950s under the Batista regime. By 1957 the public sector accounted for 40 per cent of the total investment in Cuba. Nor was the role of the state in economic matters confined to capital expenditure. Although the Batista government never created new industries or nationalized old ones and ran them outright, as many other Latin American governments have done, its activities were sufficiently wide-ranging to give it a major hand in the overall direction of the economy. Tax concessions, subsidies, loans, a variety of protectionist measures, price stabilization policies, and the like—although designed to help the private businessman and to stimulate economic development—in actual fact gave to the state a preeminent role in economic matters. Thus, for Cuban citizens, as for most Latin Americans, direct and extensive intervention by the state in all aspects of the economy was an accepted fact of life well before Fidel Castro made his Revolution.

Also typical of general Latin American conditions were the extremes of wealth and poverty that coexisted in prerevolutionary Cuba and the striking imbalance between the rural and urban areas of the island. It is true, of course, that by the standards of the underdeveloped world as a whole Cuba's situation bordered on the affluent. Even within Latin America, Cuba ranked in the top quarter in terms of per capita GNP, physicians per thousand inhabitants, automobiles and television sets per capita, and most other indicators of relative well-being.* Nonetheless, what-

---

* Reliable statistics for the prerevolutionary period, especially accurate economic data, are relatively hard to come by. Estimates, for example, of average per capita income in the late 1950s range from $353 per annum, as calculated by the Cuban National Bank, to $500 or even more.
(footnote continued...)

ever the comparative advantage, the absolute indices of poverty and rural-urban imbalances still remained.

In 1956, the rural per capita annual income was estimated at $91.25, less than one-third the national average. Only 11 per cent of rural families regularly drank milk, only 4 per cent ate meat, and only 2 per cent ate eggs. Rural health standards were similarly deficient, with an estimated 36 per cent of the population suffering from intestinal parasites, 14 per cent from tuberculosis, and 13 per cent from typhus. While Havana boasted one physician for every 420 inhabitants, rural Oriente, at the other end of the scale, had only one for every 2,550 people. Whereas, by the early 1950s, 87 per cent of all urban dwellings had electricity, only 9.1 per cent of rural housing was similarly supplied. Further, 66 per cent of all rural homes had dirt floors, only 2.3 per cent had running water, and 96.5 per cent had no refrigeration of any kind.

One could continue to quote such figures ad infinitum. They would only serve to underscore further the essential point—namely, that while the aggregate statistics might place Cuba comfortably near the top of the developing world, the country nevertheless exhibited the typical extremes and inequalities found in other underdeveloped countries. The difference was one of degree, not of kind. As one observer has remarked, "If not underdeveloped in the overall sense, Cuba was unevenly and inharmoniously developed in the manner characteristic of many other Latin American nations."[4] At the same time, despite these marked resemblances to the prevailing Latin American model, there were also significant departures from the norm that made Cuba's economy decidedly a typical case.

Sugar. While Cuba's exaggerated dependence on a single primary product gave rise to many of the same problems characteristic of all economic monocultures, the intrinsic nature of the Cuban monoculture was in many ways distinctive. Perhaps most important in terms of subsequent developments is the fact that Cuban sugar production was fundamentally capitalistic, rather than patrimonial. As one author has observed, "Cuban latifundia . . . had nothing in common with the big, almost self-sufficient haciendas of the other Latin American countries which hardly come into the money economy and are worked by serf-like peasants."[5] Under the prevailing system of sugar cultivation, the typical rural laborer in prerevolutionary Cuba was a wage earner rather than a peon or a subsistence farmer. According to the last census before the revolution, in 1952 paid workers comprised 63.6 per cent of the total agricultural labor force. In other words, Cuba had a sizeable rural proletariat, outnumbering by a goodly margin the subsistence peasantry that, in most other Latin American countries, makes up the bulk of the rural population.

In this sense the majority of Cuba's rural inhabitants were more "modern" than most of their counterparts elsewhere in Latin America. And the rank order of rural aspirations differed accordingly. The thirst for land characteristic of the peasant was subordinate to demands for better living and working conditions, higher wages, job security, better educational opportunities for children, and the like. Logically, this distinctive aspect of the Cuban rural scene would be an important factor at such time as any government decided to embark on a program of agrarian reform; the range of options would be different than in a more traditional setting. Among other things, the pressure to distribute little parcels of land to masses of peasant families would be, in the Cuban case, minimized.

Like the structure of the rural labor force, the structure of land ownership and management was also atypical, again reflecting the capitalistic nature of Cuba's sugar economy. Less than one-third of the farm units were run directly by their owners. On the larger plantations, management was in the hands of hired administrators. Moreover, the owners of the major sugar holdings were corporate enterprises, often representing foreign capital, rather than individual families. The indigenous, landed aristocracy typical of most Latin American countries was conspicuously absent. (Also absent, then, would be the inter-

---

(continued...)
Despite the discrepancies, however, virtually all analysts are agreed that Cuba ranked high in the Latin American region, well within the upper quarter. For one of the better discussions and estimates of national income in prerevolutionary Cuba, see Harry Oshima, "A New Estimate of the National Income and Product of Cuba in 1953," Food Research Institute Studies II, no. 3 (November 1961): 213-227.

personal and power relationships inherent in a patrimonial, agrarian establishment.) The consequences of this phenomenon would work to the benefit of a revolutionary government seeking to dislodge the landowners from the position of preeminence. The bonds that tied them to their estates would be more readily broken than in a more traditional society.

Another feature of the sugar monoculture was the degree of unemployment that it generated. All underdeveloped countries typically display a high level of underemployment and marginal employment. In Cuba—thanks to the capitalistic form of sugar cultivation and the organization of the prerevolutionary economy—the problem was compounded by a high rate of absolute unemployment. Even during the sugar harvest, when employment levels hit their peak, the unemployment level fluctuated around 9 per cent of the labor force. In the so-called "dead season" between harvests, a minimum of one-fifth of the labor force was unemployed. The principal results were twofold: first, there was a significant pool of unemployed labor that could be called upon when the appropriate occasion arose; second, those persons who were steadily employed were psychologically conditioned to oppose any labor-saving development that might put their jobs in jeopardy.

> The sugar industry was itself affected: mechanized cutting and bulk loading were successfully opposed, although with other sugar producers they had become common practice. Tobacco workers also resisted mechanization. Cuba's exports became therefore less competitive and correspondingly more dependent on the special position afforded by U.S. quotas.[6]

Foreign domination. This special position was a final, unique feature of Cuba's sugar monoculture. Unlike most underdeveloped countries, Cuba was protected by the umbrella of the U.S. sugar quota, together with its preferential price, from the full impact of world market forces on its principal export crop. This relative advantage, however, was purchased at the price of overwhelming dependence on a single buyer. The U.S. sugar quota, while in theory shielding Cuba from the worst extremes of international price fluctuations, in practice still left the island at the mercy of external agencies—namely, the U.S. Congress and the Secretary of Agriculture, who annually determined the fate of the Cuban sugar crop.

It was not only sugar cultivation per se that was affected by the U.S. quota, but the general dynamics of the Cuban economy. The quota and the preferential tariffs accorded Cuban tobacco and a few other agricultural products were not achieved cheaply. Under the terms of the Reciprocal Trade Agreement of 1934, Cuba's comparative advantage in the U.S. market was balanced by a series of measures designed to open the Cuban market to a wide range of U.S. commodities. Cuba agreed, among other things, to lower substantially the duties on a long list of U.S. products, to remove quantitative restrictions on many U.S. imports, and to reduce internal taxes on goods originating on the mainland. This arrangement had a profound effect on the pattern of economic and, in particular, industrial growth in Cuba over the next twenty-five years. Precluded from employing protective tariffs and other discriminatory measures against U.S. goods, Cuba was thus unable to follow any rigorous policy of import substitution to stimulate indigenous industry and general economic development. When Batista attempted to redress the balance by instituting protectionist measures, it was already too little and too late. When Castro arrived on the scene, there was no strong domestic manufacturing base in Cuba. Infant industry had generally been suffocated under the flood of competitive U.S. products. The results of the Reciprocal Trade Agreement were another atypical feature of the prerevolutionary economy. Unlike the other Latin American republics, for whom import substitution was a basic component of economic strategy for many years, Cuba's advance toward industrialization was subordinated to the seemingly easier course of living off the mainland economy.

Until the revolution, the United States supplied 80 per cent of Cuba's imports. But U.S. dominance of the Cuban economy is only partially explained by external trade statistics. The strategic importance of the United States in the internal economy was equally, if not more, significant. As Dudley Seers has remarked:

> The Cuban economy was so wedded to the U.S. economy that the country was in many ways an appendage of it—though without enjoying, as a poor state in the United States does, federal social services or access to U.S. sources of employment.[7]

In the mid-1950s, U.S. capital controlled 40 per cent of Cuba's raw sugar production, 90 per cent of telephone and electric light and power services, and 50 per cent of the public railways. Cuban branches of U.S. banks held a quarter of all bank deposits. United States corporations played a preponderant role in the refining and distribution of petroleum and a virtually exclusive role in the exploitation of Cuba's most important mineral resources. Also, U.S. capital figured prominently in retail merchandising and manufacturing, cattle ranching, production of cement, chemicals, and rubber, and the tourist industry. It was, indeed, no less than Meyer Lansky who was responsible for most of Havana's famed tourist hotels and gambling casinos (a fact that may go far to explain why, although tourism appeared to be a major Cuban industry, it contributed surprisingly little to the Cuban national product and to Cuba's foreign exchange reserves).*

The extraordinary weight of U.S. investment in the Cuban economy was greater, by far, than in any other country, whether in Latin America or elsewhere. Whether one subscribes to the thesis that this investment made a healthy contribution to the Cuban economy, or whether one adopts the alternative thesis that it was basically injurious, one conclusion can probably be drawn without argument: given the experience elsewhere in Latin America in recent years, it is hardly to be doubted that such extensive foreign economic domination could only produce a reservoir or national sentiment that would be, on balance, negative. Even Ambassador Philip Bonsal, certainly no apologist for Fidel Castro, remarked in 1967 about U.S. business interests in Cuba, "taken as a whole . . . their impact was irritating, stifling, and frustrating to the rising sense of Cuban nationalism."[8]

Under these circumstances it is not illogical to assume that any Cuban government that moved to nationalize the large spread of U.S. holdings would encounter little opposition among the mass of the native population. Such an assumption, if valid, would go far toward explaining the relative ease and rapidity with which Castro and his associates were able to transform the Cuban economy in the first two years of the Revolution. In a country in which native investors and entrepreneurs held a larger share of economic power, the transition would have been more difficult. It would also have been more difficult in a country in which the government had not already assumed such a large role in the management of economic affairs.

Two other distinctive features of the economy also had an influence on the subsequent evolution of events. First, for at least a full thirty years before the Revolution the Cuban economy was stagnant. The rapid growth of sugar production in the first quarter of the twentieth century came to an abrupt halt when world markets weakened. Output during the next thirty years fluctuated around the level of the 1920s, with only occasional cyclical swings corresponding to surges in demand during World War II and the Korean war. These peaks, however, did not compensate for the troughs; the result over the long term was a minimal rate of growth. Compared to the growth rates registered by most other Latin American countries, Cuba—in terms of production, crop yields, exports, and income—was for three decades at a virtual standstill. Real per capita income barely held its own from 1925 to 1955.

Erratic growth curves and periods of serious depression are not, of course, unique in Latin America; but the extent and duration of Cuba's economic paralysis were atypical. Only in the smallest and poorest of Latin American countries, such as Haiti, might one find a comparable phenomenon. Elsewhere in the region, even in those countries where growth rates since 1929 have been laggard, per capita income has certainly risen. And where the export sector has been sluggish, as in Argentina and Chile, other sectors have undergone significant expansion nonetheless. In contrast, Cuba's economic stagnation was virtually absolute.

The final noteworthy characteristic of the Cuban economy was the consistent and extreme underutilization of resources. Underutilized capacity is, of course, a typical feature of an underdeveloped economy. But in Cuba the phenomenon was peculiarly blatant. Reporting on the Cuban economic picture in 1956, the U.S. Department of Commerce concluded that "few countries carry a heavier overhead of underutilized produc-

---

* For an interesting insight into this aspect of the prerevolutionary Cuban setting, see Nicholas Gage's article on Meyer Lansky, "The Little Big Man Who Laughs at the Law," The Atlantic 226, no. 1 (July 1970): 62-69. According to Gage, Lansky, rebuffed in his attempt to do business with the revolutionary government, at one time put a bounty of $1 million on Castro's head.

tive facilities."[9] Neither the sugar mills nor the ports, the railroads nor the mining and manufacturing sectors were operating at anywhere near full capacity. An important result was that a government intent on revolutionizing the country would find itself with considerable room to maneuver. Not only were idle land and labor available for immediate mobilization, but productivity levels were also so low that national leaders launching an effective development drive would be able to count on substantial increases in output from what had hitherto been underutilized productive capacity. If such a development effort also shifted demand from luxury consumption goods to more basic products, additional resources would be at once available for productive purposes. In other words, the underutilization of resources in prerevolutionary Cuba would open up for the Castro government a range of options that, in a country with significantly less surplus capacity, might well have been foreclosed.

The Social Order

This discussion of the prerevolutionary economy has revealed a mixture of traits, some closely paralleling the common Latin American model and others markedly distinctive. In the structure of society, however, the mix was less evenly balanced; Cuba's departures from the Latin American norm were far more manifest than any apparent similarities. Cuba displayed, it is true, the typical cleavage between a small, lavishly wealthy class at the top of society and a large, indigent mass at the bottom. But the pattern of stratification was more fluid than in other Latin American countries. And neither the upper class nor the lower class were in their nature typical of the general Latin American norm.

Two factors would seem to have been of overriding weight in determining the distinctive characteristics of the prerevolutionary social order. There was, in the first instance, the play of peculiar historical forces and, secondly, the special and unremitting exposure of Cuban society for more than half a century to the cultural influence of the United States.

Cuban history after the 1820s followed a course markedly different from the rest of Latin America. Spanish colonial rule, which had ended elsewhere in the region before 1825, continued in Cuba almost until the turn of the twentieth century. The struggle for independence, moreover, was more protracted and intense than in any other Latin American country, beginning with the Grito de Yara that launched the Ten Years' War in 1868 and culminating some thirty years later in the Spanish-American War. Even then, Cuba was to have four years of U.S. occupation before finally achieving sovereign independence in 1902. This set of historical occurrences did much to shape the subsequent nature of Cuban nationalism. It also had a profound effect on the evolution of the social order.

In effect, the lateness of independence in Cuba collapsed historical time; the same train of events that took place in the rest of Latin America in the course of almost a century was compressed in Cuba into the space of less than a decade. The ouster of the Spanish oligarchy, the assumption of power by the criollo conservative factions, and, finally, the classical liberal revolution—a three-step process that everywhere else in Latin America took several decades to complete—took place in Cuba within a ten-year span. This circumstance, coupled with the fact that the world into which Cuba emerged independent was significantly different from the world into which the other Latin American countries had been born, qualitatively affected the development of the Cuban social order.

The upper class. In the first place, it left Cuba without a traditional upper class. The Spanish landed aristocracy, displaced by the war of 1898, left a vacuum that was never filled—as it was elsewhere in Latin America—by a criollo aristocracy. Instead, within less than two decades of independence the pattern of sugar cultivation had hardened into a capitalistic mold, and the patrimonial agrarian order that became entrenched in most other Latin American countries in the century following independence never appeared in Republican Cuba. One result was that Cuba's upper class, as it evolved in the decades before the Revolution, came to be defined differently than in the rest of Latin America—by money rather than by inherited social status. Its ranks were filled not by a seignorial gentry but by businessmen, bankers, merchants, and anyone else with sufficient wherewithal to live affluently.

The emergence of this kind of upper class, rather than a traditional landed aristocracy, was not without significance in the prerevolutionary setting. In a certain sense it meant that the social order was more "modern" than in most other Latin American countries. Certainly it was more open and fluid; while entry into the upper social strata was not necessarily based on merit, neither was it determined by ascription. Rather, as Richard Fagen has remarked elsewhere, "money and the concomitant capacity to buy and consume were the key bases of human differentiation."[10]

Under these circumstances, it is not illogical to suppose that the Cuban upper class would have less moral legitimacy in the eyes of the population at large than the upper class in a more rigidly stratified, traditional social order. Unlike a traditional aristocracy, it was new; its ranks were not sealed off; and its claim to status was based purely on secular considerations. There was no element of sacred inviolability, of inherent "rightness," attached to its position in society.

The claim to legitimacy was weakened even further by another distinctive characteristic of the Cuban upper class, namely, its intrinsic identification with foreign interests. Much of the wealth generated in prerevolutionary Cuba depended in one way or another on the United States. The fortunes of a large segment of the upper class were thus inextricably linked to the mainland business community. This close economic connection was reinforced by the weight of U.S. cultural influence in Cuba. Members of the upper class copied U.S. life styles at home and surrounded themselves with U.S. luxury goods. They invested their money in U.S. enterprises and sent their children off for schooling on the mainland. In a word, Cuba's upper class was not intimately meshed into the fabric of national society. Not surprisingly, then, a revolutionary government could dislodge it relatively easily without producing either social or psychic cataclysm in the rest of the social order.

The lower class. At the other end of the social spectrum, the lower classes in prerevolutionary Cuba also were in many respects atypical. While the indices of poverty might bear much in common with the rest of Latin America, the intrinsic character of the lower classes was distinctive. Once again, the lateness of Cuban independence and its location in historical time were among the conditioning factors.

Elsewhere in Latin America, independence preceded the industrial revolution and came couched in the rhetoric of the Enlightenment and the French Revolution. The criollo aristocracy was thus mobilized, but the lower classes were left largely unaffected and, to all intents and purposes, outside the pale of national society. Once crystallized, this pattern would prove difficult to change. Well into the twentieth century, the urban labor force in most Latin American countries was politically feeble and only sporadically organized; the peasantry tended to remain outside the national framework altogether. Precapitalist modes of production, entrenched patterns of stratification, and even, in some countries, profound cultural and linguistic barriers all militated against the incorporation of the lower classes into the national power structure. Even in those countries where an organized labor movement eventually was able to establish a significant foothold, such as in Argentina and Uruguay, it generally failed to extend its roots into the countryside.

In contrast, the particular set of historical, economic, and ideological factors that converged in Cuba at the time of independence gave the new republic from the outset the nucleus of a "modern" lower class or, to use the classical Marxist idiom, of a genuine proletariat rather than a lumpenproletariat. In the first place, Cuban independence postdated the industrial revolution in Europe and the United States by a goodly number of years. Secondly, the time lag between the collapse of the Iberian economic order in 1898 and the introduction of capitalism into the cities and countryside was so brief as to be inconsequential; it left no opportunity for an intervening economic system to entrench itself as the patrimonial system did elsewhere in Latin America. Finally, in place of the Enlightenment, Cuba's independence coincided with the arrival in the New World of anarcho-syndicalist doctrine, followed within two decades by the ideological currents of the Russian Revolution. The birth of the republic and the birth of an organized, articulate labor movement were virtually simultaneous occurrences.

Facing a social order that was relatively fluid and an economic structure that was essentially capitalistic, organized labor expanded and flourished in Cuba over the next six decades with only occasional setbacks. For an agricultural country, the size of union membership was remarkable, amounting to slightly over 1.2 million in 1955, or roughly one-fifth of the entire Cuban population.* Politically, this was not a negligible force, a fact explicitly recognized by all governments after 1933 when labor was instrumental in bringing about the downfall of President Machado. Thus, well before the Revolution a significant segment of Cuba's lower classes was already mobilized and to some extent integrated—if not directly, at least through the union leadership—into the national power structure.

Nor was the influence of the labor movement confined to the cities and mining communities, as has typically been the case elsewhere in Latin America. Instead, it extended directly into the countryside, where industrial workers and agricultural labor commingled in the large sugar complexes. Unionization, the admixture of industrial and agricultural wage-workers, and, finally, the fact that the Communist party was active in the union leadership for many years, gave a coloration to the Cuban lower classes that was largely lacking in other Latin American countries. In essence it exposed them to values and norms of behavior that were secular, rationalistic, and fundamentally modern in stamp.

There were, of course, pockets of subsistence peasants living outside the sugar complexes and clusters of unemployed, urban slum-dwellers who fell outside the circumference of the organized labor movement. But neither by geography, culture, nor language were they sufficiently isolated from the mainstream of the Cuban community to form the kind of separate, almost foreign, enclave that can be found in many other Latin American countries. However profound might be the social and economic cleavages dividing these groups from the rest of society, there were no insuperable obstacles that would thwart a revolutionary government intent on absorbing them into the national collectivity. Richard Fagen has neatly catalogued this aspect of prerevolutionary Cuban society as follows:

> There were no obdurate tribal minorities, no separatist territorial factions, no language enclaves, no paralysing racial problems, no premodern Indian communities. Living on an island without great climatic extremes, no insurmountable geographical barriers, and no overpopulation problem on the horizon, the more than 7 million Cubans presented a striking contrast to countries such as Indonesia or Mexico. Batista's Cuba exhibited a greater degree of national integration than did Mexico after 50 years of "integrative revolution." Such was the sociocultural legacy inherited by Castro.[11]

The existence of a mobilized lower class, coupled with the relative homogeneity of the population at large, set prerevolutionary Cuba apart from most other underdeveloped countries, whether in Latin America, Africa, or Asia. It would subsequently prove an important advantage to a revolutionary government having to marshal human resources on a broad scale for development or, as demonstrated at the time of the Bay of Pigs assault, for defense.

The middle class. The middle class in prerevolutionary Cuban society was less readily definable than either the lower or upper classes. Indeed, it is questionable whether the broader concept of "class"—implying not only economic and occupational status, but also a certain collective consciousness and a cluster of shared values and attitudes—was in any sense applicable to Cuba's middle groups. By economic standards alone they formed a substantial sector in prerevolutionary Cuba; in fact, it is generally conceded that the Cuban middle stratum was among the largest in Latin America. But what evidence there is suggests that in behavior, aspirations, and attitudes, the Cuban middle class defied the classical paradigms of both Marxists and non-Marxists alike. Rather than any commonality of interests, the distinguishing trait of the Cuban middle groups would seem to have been the depth and diversity of their internal divisions. Collectively, the middle class bore no resemblance to the cohesive, self-conscious bourgeoisie of standard Marxist theory,

---

*   Victor Alba, Historia del movimiento obrero en America Latina (Mexico City: Libreros Mexicanos Unidos, 1964), appendix, table 42. See also James O'Connor, The Origins of Socialism in Cuba (Ithaca, N.Y.: Cornell University Press, 1970), p. 181. In absolute numbers, Cuba's union membership—including white-collar and blue-collar workers—was surpassed in Latin America in the 1950s only in Brazil, Argentina, and Mexico, all countries with exceedingly larger populations than in Cuba.

unremittingly pursuing its class interests; nor did it approximate the idealized image of the non-Marxist theorists, who see the middle class everywhere as the mainstay of progress and stability and the embodiment of all the entrepreneurial virtues required for economic development.

On the contrary, members of the Cuban middle class followed no collective model at all. They figured prominently among the supporters of the Batista regime and were equally prominent in the leadership of the anti-Batista guerrilla forces. Among their numbers were apolitical shopkeepers and urban terrorists, extreme nationalists and enthusiastic pro-Americans, socialists and conservatives, the engagé and the apathetic. In short, there was to be found among the middle strata no common ideology, no distinguishing set of attitudes or virtues, and no collective self-identification. Fragmented rather than united, the Cuban middle groups, although numerically significant, would pose no important threat to a government such as Castro's. Even when they deserted the Revolution, they could find no common ground for opposing it; their intra-class cleavages were part of the baggage they carried with them into exile, an encumbrance that became all too apparent at the time of the Bay of Pigs.

In its lack of internal coherence the Cuban middle class was not unlike the middle groups emerging elsewhere in Latin America. Where it departed importantly from the Latin American norm, however, was in the extent to which its fortunes were determined, for better or for worse, by foreign economic interests. Directly or indirectly, much of the Cuban middle class—especially those sectors engaged in business or commerce—was dependent on the United States for its livelihood. Whether it was a sugar grower adjusting his production to the U.S. quota, a small businessman relying on mainland suppliers for equipment and spare parts, a salaried manager or technician making a better wage with a U.S. company, or a shopkeeper selling imported consumer goods, the net effect was the same. With the exception of certain professionals and employees of the government bureaucracy, few middle-class Cubans were unaffected by the U.S. presence in the economy. Thus in the orthodox Marxist idiom, there was no "national bourgeoisie" of any consequence operating independently of the mainland business establishment. This fact would have bearing on the policies of a revolutionary government bent on reordering the class structure. The role assigned to the national bourgeoisie in the standard Marxist-Leninist scheme of things could go largely unheeded by the Cuban leadership.

Culture and Religion

With regard to society as a whole, three distinctive features of the prerevolutionary setting are of special relevance to the subsequent course of Cuban events. First, unlike most other Latin American countries, Cuba did not have a strong ecclesiastical establishment. The power of the Roman Catholic church elsewhere in the region was not duplicated in Cuba after independence. The Cuban clergy was foreign in complexion, predominantly Spanish-born, and its clientele was drawn almost exclusively from the middle and upper classes. Also, the Cuban church was urban-based: the small adobe chapels that dot the rural landscape in most of Latin America were not a familiar feature of the Cuban countryside. Therefore, the influence of the church among the mass of the population, especially in the rural areas, was of little moment. As a result, once a revolutionary government came to power, it would not find a formidable opponent in the Cuban church; whatever power base the church had was limited to the very groups a revolutionary leadership would seek to displace. In sum, the Cuban church, unlike the church in many other Latin American countries, was in no position to offer serious moral or ideological competition to a revolutionary movement.

A second important feature of prerevolutionary society was its relative level of culture. By the standards of the developed countries, Cuba, with approximately 25 per cent of its adult population illiterate, was an uneducated backwater. By the standards of the underdeveloped world, however, it was uncommonly advanced. Moreover, because of its relatively small population, the absolute number of Cuban illiterates was less than one might find in some countries having a better percentile ranking.

Similarly, the Cuban educational establishment, while woefully deficient on all qualitative and quantitative counts, was nevertheless relatively advantaged when compared with that of most other countries in the Third World. With only 53 per cent of its primary-age population actually enrolled in school in 1955, Cuba lagged well behind such nations as Argentina and Uruguay in its educational performance, but it was still ahead of most Latin American countries. A revolutionary government determined to transform Cuba into a modern, educated nation would have to make a prodigious effort, but the problem would not appear insuperable. To put the matter is some comparative perspective, one need only contrast the effort involved in teaching a million or so Cuban adults to read and write with trying to do the same job in a country such as Brazil, where some 30 million people above school age are classified as illiterate. The difference in the orders of magnitude is too great to be simply numerical.

In educating and mobilizing the population, a revolutionary leadership in Cuba also would be assisted by geography; the island is small, easily traversed, and without any insurmountable natural barriers preventing access to remote sections of the country. Furthermore, prerevolutionary society would leave as part of its legacy a sophisticated system of communications. Cuba, at the time of the Revolution, boasted a television set for every 25 inhabitants, a ratio unmatched anywhere else in Latin America; it was an advantage that Fidel Castro would exploit to the fullest. In sum, both natural and man-made conditions would combine to facilitate a revolutionary government's penetration of Cuban society.

A final, unique ingredient in the prerevolutionary social mix was the pervasive cultural influence of the United States. All Latin American countries, to one degree or another, feel the weight of North American culture on their societies. In Cuba, however, the exposure was more intense and intimate than anywhere else. And because Cuba's post-colonial society was of later vintage and less crystallized than the social order elsewhere in the region, one can logically suppose that its resistance to external currents would have been weaker.

In its more obvious manifestations, the U.S. impact on Cuban society was readily apparent in the movie theaters, in the widespread use of Madison Avenue advertising techniques, in the sale of Coca Cola and Cadillacs, in the Cuban passion for baseball, and the like. In Havana, particularly, the influence of U.S. culture—reinforced by the 200,000 U.S. tourists who annually left their imprint on the city's style of life—was everywhere physically in evidence.

Subliminally, however, more subtle forms of cultural transfer were also undoubtedly at work.

While there are no means of measuring the net impact of U.S. values, attitudes, and mores on Cuban society, there is good reason to assume that in six decades of close and continuous association, the United States would have had a significant secularizing effect on the social order left behind by the Spaniards. In some areas the result was direct and visible, as in the separation of church and state, written into the Cuban constitution at the turn of the century with the overt encouragement of the U.S. occupation authorities. Elsewhere, in more intangible areas such as individual values, the data available permit no more than educated guesses about the probable impact of the U.S. presence in Cuba. It is perhaps sufficiently telling simply to note that for over half a century the Cuban populace was submitted to a cultural bombardment that was, in its essence, technologically oriented, rationalistic, antitraditional, and, superficially at least, egalitarian in its world view. Distasteful as this cultural penetration may have been to certain Cubans, one nonetheless can presume that it would ultimately prove something of a benefit to a revolutionary government: Fidel and his fellow rebels would find in Cuba a society that, if it had not fully absorbed its dose of antitraditional values, had at least been closely exposed to the full cultural baggage of a modern nation-state.

In its class structure and in the overall character of national society, the distinctive features of the prerevolutionary Cuban setting far outweighed any points of resemblance to the general Latin American model. Indeed, it is possible to speculate that it was the special nature of the Cuban social order rather than any particular set of economic indices that was the strongest factor in determining the options available to the Castro government. In a more isolated, rigidly stratified, and traditional society, the manouverability of a revolutionary regime would have been considerably less.

The Political Dimension

In its political dimension, prerevolutionary Cuba more closely approximated the typical Latin American case. Like most other Latin American countries, Cuba modelled its original constitution after the U.S. document. And, again like other Latin American states, it honored its constitution more in the breach than in the observance. The institutional underpinnings of orderly succession and political legitimacy never took firm root in Cuban society. Within four years of the withdrawal of the U.S. occupation forces in 1902, armed revolt had broken out in the provinces, with the liberals contending that their conservative opponents had used fraud to assure their success in the presidential elections. Peace was restored only with a second round of U.S. military occupation, this time lasting a little over two years. Before departing, the U.S. authorities reorganized the electoral system and scheduled new elections. Conducted under the supervision and scrutiny of the North Americans, the balloting was free of scandal and resulted in the victory of the liberal candidate.

With the U.S. withdrawal in 1909, however, the Cubans found themselves unable to sustain a workable constitutional order. Armed uprisings in 1912 and 1916, ostensibly in protest against government corruption and electoral fraud, again brought the U.S. marines to Cuba. Another electoral crisis in 1920, while not precipitating a further foray by the Marines, was settled only with the intervention of President Wilson's special emissary, General Enoch Crowder.

What precisely were the proximate causes of political corruption and electoral fraud in the early years of the Cuban republic, and whether the United States was justified in its repeated interventions—these are not the crucial questions a half-century after the fact. Stuffed ballot boxes and U.S. marines were, rather, the details embellishing a more significant drama that was being played in Cuba. What happened, in essence, in the first two decades after independence was that the political processes defined in the constitution failed to acquire the force of moral authority in the Cuban political culture. Moreover, as the twentieth century wore on, the concept of due political process grew progressively weaker until it had virtually no relation to the actual practice of politics. In North America and much of Western Europe, formalized political process and political legitimacy are opposite sides of the same coin; in Cuba, by the time of the Revolution, there was little or no connection between the two. As in much of Latin America, palace coups, military dictatorship, and widespread governmental corruption were familiar features of the Cuban political landscape. And even on those occasions when the trappings of electoral democracy were brought into play, the accompanying fraud and the persistence of a politics that benefited only certain groups of society eroded whatever faith there might have been in traditional democratic processes.

The weakening of the political process was a phenomenon that had been increasingly in evidence in many Latin American countries. Where Cuba departed from the general Latin American pattern was in the fact that the deterioration of the constitutional order was more rapid, compressed into a time span of only five decades or so. It was thus more radical and more total, as later events were to demonstrate.

The North American legacy. An even more distinctive and important aspect of the prerevolutionary political order was the degree to which it was influenced by the interests and actions of a foreign power. In the twentieth century, it is fair to say, no Latin American country has fully escaped the magnetic pull of the United States in political affairs. But the political fortunes of Cuba were bound to the mainland with an intimacy unequalled anywhere else in the region.

The interest of the United States in Cuba antedated by several decades the Cuban war of independence. Indeed, during the first half of the nineteenth century the possibility of annexing Cuba was a recurring theme in U.S. government circles. In 1848, for example, under President James Polk, the United States attempted to purchase the island outright, an offer that was rejected by the Spaniards. Subsequently, although annexationist sentiment waned, the U.S. continued to evince a more than passing interest in Cuban affairs. In an age of sea power, Cuba's geographic location had considerable strategic importance. The island was a major source of sugar for the United States and, moreover, represented a potential market of some magnitude for U.S. manufacturers. And, finally, the Cuban struggle for independence, frustrated for more than thirty years, struck a sympathetic chord among many North Americans.

The crucial turning point in Cuba's relations with the United States came in 1898, with U.S. entry into the Cuban conflict against Spain. To most North Americans, if they happen to think about it at all, U.S. military involvement was the deciding factor in Cuba's liberation from Spain. To many Cubans, however, rightly or wrongly, U.S. intervention had a different flavor. According to their reading of history, rather than helping the Cuban rebels, who by then had an army of some fifty thousand men in the field, the United States stole from them the fruits of a victory that was already within their grasp. The United States "found a pretext to enter the war," as one Cuban author has put it, "and at war's end three months later took over control of the island, disbanded the rebel army, and dictated the terms of peace."[12] In terms of understanding the subsequent course of Cuban events, the question of whether or not the Cubans could have freed themselves from Spanish rule without U.S. assistance is largely immaterial. The essential point is that sufficient Cubans believed a certain version of history to make it, if not a reality, at least a part of national mythology.

The termination of hostilities with Spain was followed by four years of U.S. military occupation. Cuba had been decimated in the course of its three-year struggle; the country was beset by economic difficulties, severe health problems, and general disorganization; and, finally, there was some suspicion on the North American side that the Cubans were not yet ready for self-governance. Accordingly, under the stewardship of General Leonard Wood, the United States administered the island's affairs until 1902, introducing a large body of new legislation, constructing sanitary facilities, schools, and other public works, supervising the drafting of a national constitution, and, for good measure, eradicating yellow fever.

Whatever may have been the actual course of events at the time, the retrospective view of the military occupation varies broadly: the common U.S. assumption is that the occupation government conferred a multitude of benefits on the infant republic; the Cuban view is less charitable. To appreciate the depth of difference between the North American and Cuban interpretations after the fact, one need only contrast the following two judgments. Writing in 1935, a U.S. scholar asserted: "Wood will undoubtedly rank as one of the greatest colonial administrators in history, comparable to Britain's Curzon or France's Lyautey."[13] A Cuban now in exile in the United States has more recently characterized the Wood administration as follows:

> Wood was arbitrary, cynical, unscrupulous, and adept at intrigue. He employed all these qualities in his corruption of the island and in creating problems among the Cubans. Our historians are agreed that he planted a swarm of evil habits in the bloodstream of the new nation. Like all dictators, he created the public works that give them the glitter they need to distract the public's attention, as well as the opportunity to rob great sums of money under cover of huge budgets, inflated bills, and non-existent costs. He did all he could to obstruct the advent of the Cuban republic.[14]

Again, in terms of understanding subsequent events and, in particular, the development of Cuban nationalism, the actual historical fact would not be as important as the meaning with which it was imbued.

The initial involvement of the United States in Cuba's political life would in later years be far overshadowed for most Cubans by the impact of the Platt Amendment. Originally tacked onto the U.S. Congressional Army Appropriation Bill for 1901 and 1902 and subsequently included in the Cuban constitution at the instance of the United States, the Platt Amendment for the next thirty years was the tangible symbol of Cuba's special relationship with the mainland. The key provision was the famous Article III:

> The government of Cuba consents that the United States may exercise the right to intervene for the preservation of Cuban independence, the maintenance of a government adequate for the protection of life, property, and individual liberty, and for discharging the obligations with respect to Cuba imposed by the treaty of Paris on the United States, to be assumed and undertaken by the Government of Cuba.[15]

Article III provided the juridical justification for the military occupation from 1906 to 1909 and for the subsequent marine landing parties in 1912 and 1916. Later, when the United States became less directly interventionist in its policy toward Latin America, the Platt Amendment's other provisions still gave the U.S. government broad latitude for intermeddling in the political concerns of Cuba. General Enoch Crowder's unofficial suzerainty over Cuban governmental affairs in the early 1920s—including his hand in the selection of President Alfredo Zayas' cabinet, which was subsequently known in Cuba by the popular title of "Crowder's Cabinet"—was proof of the influence the United States could exert over the Cuban political order even when it no longer chose to resort to military intervention.* So, also, was the role of Ambassador Sumner Welles during the cataclysmic political events of 1933 and 1934.

If any year can be designated the crucial one in terms of the future course of Cuban history, it was probably 1933. The national upheaval that toppled the dictatorship of Gerardo Machado and, after a brief interregnum, brought Ramón Grau San Martín and his Auténtico party to power had all the earmarks of a true revolution, as distinct from a traditional palace coup. Claiming the mantle of José Martí, the martyred father of Cuban independence, and basing his program on a three-pronged platform of "nationalism, socialism, and anti-imperialism,"[16] Grau promised the Cubans a radical, but explicitly non-Communist, transformation of national society. As it happened, he did not have the opportunity to deliver. Distrusted, if not personally disliked, by the American Ambassador, Sumner Welles, Grau and his administration were refused recognition by the United States. With the Plàtt Amendment still in force, the U.S. action—or, more accurately, nonaction—sounded the death knell for the Grau regime. Within four months he was out of office. His replacement, hand-picked by Fulgenico Batista, leader of the Cuban military establishment, with the tacit approval of Welles' successor, Ambassador Jefferson Caffrey, was a traditional politician of conservative stripe. A chapter in Cuban history was thus effectively closed.

To later generations of Cubans, the Platt Amendment and the abortive revolution of 1933 would become the crucial symbols of Cuba's frustrated nationhood. Tangible rather than abstract, they could be a focal point for the accumulated resentments of Cuban nationalists. Later, for a revolutionary government, they would serve importantly as ready-made national symbols, at one and the same time defining the external enemy and absorbing much of the collective guilt for past national failures. They could, in short, be manipulated by the leadership to evoke support for a broad range of political actions, even, ultimately, direct confrontation with the United States.

The abrogation of the Platt Amendment in 1934 removed an immediate irritant, but it did not essentially alter the special political relationship between Cuba and the mainland. Although the explicit policy of the United States was one of nonintervention and the U.S. profile was somewhat lower than it had been earlier, it was the tone rather than the crux of the relationship that had changed. Describing the situation after 1934, two North American observers have written:

> In practice, the level of United States investments in Cuba, the volume of trade between the two countries, and the pervasive influence of American publications, opinions, and values were such that the United States, by simply failing to associate itself with internal forces tending to change, exerted a powerful conservative influence. It was strongly encouraged in this direction by the ruling political cliques and by American and Cuban businessmen who sought guarantees of political stability.
>
> Although there was no major example of direct United States intervention during this period, the power to intervene did not lapse. According to Earl Smith, Ambassador to Cuba from June 1957 to January 1959, "The United States, until the advent of Castro, was so overwhelmingly influential in Cuba that . . . the American ambassador was the second most important man in Cuba; sometimes even more important than the president." Many Cubans, aware of this influence, held the United States directly responsible for the actions of the Cuban government and accused it of intervention; others attacked it for not intervening to correct abuses.[17]

Thus, in the minds of many Cubans, the pre-revolutionary political order was inextricably identified with a foreign power. This factor would later be of benefit to a revolutionary government. The destruction of existing political institutions would imply no special rupture with an indigenous

---

* Article II of the Platt Amendment placed certain limitations on the Cuban government's ability to incur public debt. Broadly interpreted, as it was during the course of General Crowder's mission, this clause could give the United States considerable leeway for intervening in Cuba's financial affairs.

past. In this respect Cuba probably approximated more closely those underdeveloped countries that have emerged from colonial status during the twentieth century than the other Latin American countries, which began to evolve their political orders in the relative peace and independence of the early 1800s.

The pre-revolutionary left. A final distinguishing feature of prerevolutionary Cuban politics was the early and utter bankruptcy of the democratic left. The Cuban Auténticos, organized by Grau San Martín in the early 1930s, were forged in the mold of the so-called "popular" parties of Latin America, of which the Apristas in Peru are generally considered the prototype. Although officially tracing their inspiration to José Martí, the Auténticos, like the other popular parties of the region, also were influenced by Marxist thought; but their Marxism was closer to European social democracy than to the Soviet variant. Indeed, the Auténticos and the official Communist party of Cuba were normally at loggerheads. Distilled to its essence, the Auténticos program was one of nationalism and radical social and economic reform within a democratic political framework. Their nationalism basically comprised a vision of Cuba as a developed and fully independent country. Their reformism, had it been implemented, would probably have approximated the policies of a moderately socialistic welfare state. The leadership of the Auténtico party was drawn almost exclusively from the Cuban middle class, but from a particular substratum of that class. They were intellectuals and professionals, rather than businessmen, shopkeepers, or landowners. Grau San Martín himself had been a university professor. And much of his early support had come from university students.

In 1944, ten years after Grau's brief presidential career was abruptly terminated, the Auténticos were returned to power by the electorate in one of Cuba's few experiences with a free and honest ballot. Carrying five of the island's six provinces, Grau and his administration were initially greeted with a popular enthusiasm bordering on euphoria. Once in office, however, Grau and his elected successor, Carlos Prio Socarras, proved totally ineffective in dealing with Cuba's more pressing social and economic problems. Moreover, their administrative ineptitude was compounded by the extraordinary degree of corruption that flourished under their governance. As one Cuban exile has succinctly observed, Grau "was one of the very worst presidents we have ever had."[18] By the time they were turned out of office some eight years later by Batista's coup d'etat, the Auténticos had managed to dissipate most of their widespread popularity, as well as to fracture their party. More significantly for the future course of events, they had succeeded in eroding whatever faith was left in Cuba in the efficacy of electoral democracy and, futher, had bankrupted the democratic left as a force in Cuban politics.

In 1947, appalled by the graft under Grau's administration and the little that had been accomplished by way of genuine social reform, a splinter party, known as the Ortodoxos, split off from the Auténticos under the leadership of Eduardo Chibas, a former student leader of the 1930s. The program of the Ortodoxos varied little from the Auténtico platform, except in its rigorous commitment to honest government. It, too, drew for its inspiration on the writings of José Martí and was strongly nationalist in orientation. It was as an Ortodoxo candidate for congressional office that Fidel Castro was to make his initial entry into Cuban politics in early 1952. By then, however, it was late in the day for the democratic left: Chibas had committed suicide the year before, shooting himself at the end of a nationwide radio speech denouncing the continuing corruption in Cuban political life; Batista was preparing his coup d'etat; and the Cuban population had lost much of their faith in the promises of social reformers. Batista's ouster of the elected Prio Socarras government on March 10, 1952—signalling the end of due constitutional process in Cuba—was accomplished virtually without bloodshed and with extraordinary ease. It caused little reaction among the mass of the population and, in short order, both business and organized labor fell into line behind the new government. The erosion of formal political process in Cuba had gone sufficiently far that a coup d'etat—and, by logical extension, the government it installed—was by now a generally tolerable phenomenon.

It is this political background that goes far to explain the ease with which a revolutionary leadership would later be able to overturn the existing political order. In terms of ideology, the bankruptcy of the democratic left meant that there was no persuasive alternative to whatever ideology Castro might choose to follow. He might alienate many middle-class citizens as his pronouncements became increasingly radical, but he would find among the mass of the people no competing ideology sufficiently strong to challenge his own. In terms of formalized political institutions, a revolutionary government would also have considerable freedom of action. Castro and his lieutenants would find few enshrined political shibboleths, few ingrained political processes, that they would have to respect in reordering the country. The political forms associated with the prerevolutionary order had been sufficiently abused that they had no universal validity in the political culture. Thus, the Castro government could dispense with the electoral process because, as a legitimating device, it had lost much of its meaning in Cuba. And it could experiment with a variety of new political forms without running afoul of any entrenched, traditional ways of conducting political business.

Nationalism. A final, critical factor in terms of the subsequent unfolding of fidelismo would be the nature of Cuban nationalism and nationalist ideology in the prerevolutionary period. Like all other Latin American countries, Cuba through the 1950s lacked many of the attributes of a modern nation-state. The Cuban population, though more homogeneous than the population of most underdeveloped countries, nevertheless did not form a genuine national community. The boundaries between social classes, for example, while more fluid than elsewhere in the Latin American region, were nevertheless palpable and important. And identification with class, or at least with a certain subset within the class hierarchy, more often than not overrode any identification with the broader community of the nation. The essential fragmentation of the national community was evidenced by the conduct of politics. Whatever might be the rhetoric employed by any given government, Cuban politics in the prerevolutionary period was basically subnational politics, reflecting the interests of a particular class or of particular sectors allied together, rather than the interests of the national community at large. In the early years of the twentieth century, Cuban politics was the private preserve of the upper-class liberals and conservatives. Later, in the 1930s, the middle class gained access to the reins of political power, buttressed by the support of the more powerful urban labor unions. But the rural laborer, the unemployed, the unskilled nonunion worker, and the indigent in general were still written out of the effective political community.

Against this reality, however, the essence of Cuban nationalist thought, traceable as far back as the war of independence, was inclusive rather than exclusive. In the writings of José Martí, the boundaries of the national community encompassed all Cubans equally. Further, Martí not only posited the nation as the ultimate claimant of citizen loyalty, superceding all other allegiance, but he explicitly proclaimed the ideal of a state in which no class would have dominion over any other and the goods of the nation would be for the benefit of all. In essence, his view of a future Cuba, at times almost religious in its fervor, came remarkably close to the political definition of a modern nation-state. All subsequent Cuban nationalists, claiming Martí as their inspiration, paid lip service to this vision of the nation. If the ideal was never realized in practice, it was nonetheless expressly present in the main currents of nationalist ideology. A revolutionary government, egalitarian in outlook and intent upon drawing into full national participation the most disenfranchised and disadvantaged sectors of society, would not need to break new ideological ground to justify its actions. It could rest its case on an indigenous tradition of thought extending back to the founding fathers of the Cuban republic.

The constructive content of Cuban nationalism was, however, far overshadowed by its negative bias during most of the prerevolutionary period. In its overt manifestations, Cuban nationalism was more frequently concerned with what it defined as the external enemy than with the internal processes of national integration and nation building. Anti-Americanism was, in a word, a hallmark of Cuban nationalism from the first days of independence.

In this respect the Cubans were not unlike other Latin American nationalists of the mid-twentieth century. But the Cuban brand of anti-Yankee sentiment was of longer standing and, if anything, more virulent. Although Martí himself, during his years of exile in the United States, wrote much that was favorable about the country, Cubans were fond of quoting what they considered his definitive judgment: "I know the monster, I have lived in its entrails."[19] Subsequent events—foremost among them the imposition of the Platt Amendment on the Cuban body politic—exacerbated rather than alleviated whatever negative feelings there were. By 1922 a Cuban newspaper, La

Nación, would be moved to exhort its readers, "The day will have to arrive when we will consider it the most sacred duty of our life to walk along the street and eliminate the first American we encounter."[20] If later expressions of anti-American sentiment were more restrained in language, they were nevertheless deep-seated. In the long run, they gave a particular cast to Cuban nationalism that would ultimately prove useful to a revolutionary government. Fidel Castro would not have to invent an external enemy in order to mobilize and unify the population; the enemy had long before been identified by the political culture.

This, then, was the Cuba inherited by Fidel Castro and his companions. It displayed many of the standard features of underdevelopment, especially the particular brand of underdevelopment endemic to the Latin American region. Yet, at the same time, there were also unique variables in the prerevolutionary setting that distinguished Cuba from the general run of countries in the underdeveloped world. It is in the pattern of relationships between these variables, between the typical and the unique, that one can trace the roots of the Cuban Revolution and find the beginnings of a social explanation for much of its subsequent evolution. In sum, the prerevolutionary setting provided the conditions that permitted Castro to mount the revolution he did. It is with the effects of this revolution on certain aspects of Cuban development that subsequent chapters will be concerned.

REFERENCES

1. Kalman H. Silvert, The Conflict Society: Reaction and Revolution America (New York: American Universities Field Staff, 1966) p. 11.

2. Dudley Seers, ed., Cuba: The Economic and Social Revolution (Chapel Hill: The University of North Carolina Press, 1964) p. 4.

3. Documentación Básica (República de Cuba, Documento IP-7, Segundo Seminario de la FAO Sobre Problemas de la Tierra, Montevideo, 1959 [mimeographed]), as adapted by Thomas F. Carroll, "The Land Reform Issue in Latin America" in Albert O. Hirschman, ed., Latin American Issues: Essays and Comments (New York: The Twentieth Century Fund, 1961) p. 181, table 5.

4. Richard R. Fagen, The Transformation of Political Culture in Cuba (Stanford: Stanford University Press, 1969) p. 23.

5. Boris Goldenberg, The Cuban Revolution and Latin American (New York: Frederick A. Praeger, 1965) p. 129.

6. Seers, op. cit., p. 15.

7. Ibid, p. 20.

8. "Cuba, Castro, and the United States," Foreign Affairs 45, no. 2 (January 1967): 265.

9. Ibid, p. 6.

10. Ibid, p. 145

11. "Revolution—For Internal Consumption Only," Trans-Action 6, no. 6 (April 1969): 10.

12. Teresa Casuso, Cuba and Castro (New York: Random House, 1961) p. 26.

13. Russell H. Fitzgibbon, Cuba and the United States, 1900-1935 (Menasha, Wisc.: George Banta Publishing Company, 1935) p. 31.

14. Casuso, op. cit., pp. 44-45.

15. Quoted by Bryce Wood, The Making of the Good Neighbor Policy (New York: W. W. Norton & Company, 1967) p. 49.

16. Ramón Grau San Martín, La Revolución Cubana ante América, Ediciones del Partido Revolucionario Cubano (Mexico City, 1936) p. 104.

17. Wyatt MacGaffey and Clifford R. Barnett, Cuba: Its People, Its Society, Its Culture (New Haven, Conn.: HRAF Press, 1962) pp. 313-314.

18. Casuso, op. cit., p. 85.

19. As quoted by MacGaffey and Barnett, op. cit., p. 215.

20. Quoted in Fitzgibbon, op. cit., p. 177.

NITA R. MANITZAS
Ford Foundation, Santiago, Chile

70¢

Social Class and the Definition of the Cuban Nation

"The profoundly egalitarian commitment of the Cuban leadership extends well beyond the simple question of income differentials. It is reflected in a broad array of tactics and policies, including their strong emphasis on moral over material incentives as a means of stimulating productivity; their preoccupation, reflected in their investment priorities, with erasing the most glaring differences between rural and urban life styles; and their penchant for sending urban office workers out to the cane fields for a round of voluntary labor."

Much has been written about the class origins and orientation of the Cuban Revolution. To cite only a few examples, to Theodore Draper it appeared essentially as "a middle-class revolution that has been used to destroy the middle class."[1] For Paul Sweezy and the late Leo Huberman, the Revolution owed its greatest debt to "the vanguard role of the peasants," and Fidel Castro was himself "the embodiment of the revolutionary will and energy of the peasantry."[2] To Jacques Arnault, examining the Cuban Revolution through a more orthodox Marxist lens, it fit within the classical Marxist-Leninist tradition: a revolution of "national liberation" led by the "small and medium urban bourgeoisie," followed by a socialist phase in which "the working class is to be the decisive instrument, supported by the poor peasantry."[3] And, finally, running counter to all such attempts to categorize the Revolution in terms of class, are those writers who see the Revolution essentially as a mass phenomenon drawing support across class boundaries, or as a movement basically divorced from social class, led by intellectuals and other "rootless" members of society. As Boris Goldenberg, an exponent of the latter view, has remarked, "any analysis framed in terms of social classes is utterly misleading and befogs the character of the Cuban Revolution."[4]

Aside from the fact that people tend to see only what they want to see, much of the inconsistency among these varying interpretations of the Cuban Revolution arises from the fact that social class, as a theoretical construct, is one of the more difficult social-science concepts to handle satisfactorily. Perhaps one means of cutting the Gordian knot is to leave aside questions concerning the theoretical meaning of social class and to focus on the empirical effects of class within the particular historical context. There is little argument about the fact that in developing countries the nature of social hierarchy has an explicit relationship to the pace and direction of the modernization process. With respect to the economy, it is now widely accepted as a truism that a rigid, traditional class order will impede the emergence of certain conditions—most notably occupational mobility—that are essential for industrialization and general economic growth. It is no less the case that, at the level of nationhood writ large, social class, crystallized in a particular mold, can be a direct and major obstacle to national integration and the emergence of a cohesive national community.

A WARNER MODULAR PUBLICATION

Copyright © 1973 by Warner Modular Publications, Inc.

All rights reserved. No part of this publication may be reproduced, stored in a retrieval system, or transmitted, in any form or by any means, electronic, mechanical, photocopying, recording, or otherwise, without the prior written permission of the publisher. Printed in the United States of America.

Library of Congress Catalog Card Number 73-5215

The Developmental Economics Series is under the editorship of

DAVID P. BARKIN
City University of New York
Lehman College

SUGGESTED CITATION

Nita R. Manitzas, "Social Class and the Definition of the Cuban Nation," Warner Modular Publications, Module 261 (1973), pp 1–17

All original publications in this series appear first as separate modules. Most modules will appear in one collection; many will appear in several. To facilitate research use, all modules are numbered serially, and each module carries the same number and folio sequence in all incarnations.

In its essence, modern nationhood implies the blurring of class divisions under the weight of an overarching loyalty to the nation as a whole. When, as in most of the developing world, class boundaries cut more deeply than national boundaries, when empathy with one's fellow citizens stops short at the frontiers of class, and when loyalty to class overrides any larger loyalty to the national community, then the fundamental conditions for modern nationhood—at least, according to the standards of modernity current in the mid-twentieth century—are lacking. The absence of a complete supra-class identification with the society as a whole will inevitably result in subnational identifications, subnational politics, and, finally, incomplete or distorted nationhood.

By this yardstick, prerevolutionary Cuban society lacked the essential qualifications of a modern national polity. Although the Cuban social hierarchy was neither as rigidly structured nor as traditional in character as the class orders in many other countries of the developing world, it nevertheless acted as an effective counterweight to the emergence of a fully integrated national community. Substantial segments of the population, especially among the rural lower class, were excluded from the mainstream of national society. And at the upper reaches of the social scale, the claims of nationality were more often than not subordinate to more parochial considerations. As the political scientist Russell H. Fitzgibbon has commented, "It can scarcely to denied—though obviously the generalization is not limited to Cuba among Latin American states—that wealthy persons were more loyal to class than to country."[5]

It would be erroneous to suggest, as some authors have, that prerevolutionary Cuba was carved up among monolithic class groupings, each with its clearly defined class interests and loyalties. On the contrary, the pattern of stratification was reasonably complex and the cleavages within major classes were as deep, if not deeper, than the boundary lines drawn between classes. An Havana laborer, insulated by protective legislation and by his union membership, did not tend to make common cause with an unemployed guajiro in the countryside. Nor were the middle sectors any more cohesive. Loyalty and shared interests tended to coalesce below the level of class, within and around subclass groupings. At the same time—and this is perhaps the crucial fact of the prerevolutionary social order—there was no overriding identification superseding class and welding together the various strata of society in a coherent national community.

THE SOCIAL ORIENTATION OF THE REVOLUTIONARY MOVEMENT

It was against this background that Fidel Castro, in 1953, first defined the class orientation of the Cuban Revolution. Facing his judges after the abortive attack of July 26 on the Moncada Barracks in Santiago de Cuba, Fidel, in his famous defense speech, explicitly catalogued the people included within his rebel universe. Given the importance of social class in the subsequent evolution of events, it is worth quoting Castro's roll call in its entirety:

> The people we counted on in our struggle were these:
>
> Seven hundred thousand Cubans without work, who desire to earn their daily bread honestly without having to emigrate in search of a livelihood.
>
> Five hundred thousand farm labourers inhabiting miserable shacks, who work four months of the year and starve during the rest, sharing their misery with their children; who have not an inch of land to till, and whose existence would move any heart not made of stone.
>
> Four hundred thousand industrial labourers and stevedores whose retirement funds have been embezzled, whose benefits are being taken away, whose homes are wretched quarters, whose salaries pass from the hands of the boss to those of the moneylender, whose future is a pay reduction and dismissal, whose life is eternal work and whose only rest is in the the tomb.
>
> One hundred thousand small farmers who live and die working on land that is not theirs, looking at it with sadness as Moses looked at the promised land, to die without ever owning it; who, like feudal serfs, have to pay for their use of their parcel of land by giving up a portion of its products; who cannot love it, improve it, beautify it, nor plant a lemon nor an orange tree on it, because they never know when a sheriff will come with the rural guard to evict them from it.
>
> Thirty thousand teachers and professors who are so devoted, dedicated and necessary to the better destiny of future generations and who are so badly treated and paid.
>
> Twenty thousand small business men, weighted down by debts. ruined by the crisis and harangued by a plague of grafting and venal officials.
>
> Ten thousand young professionals, doctors, engineers, lawyers, veterinarians, school teachers, dentists, pharmacists, newspapermen, painters, sculptors, etc., who come forth from school with their degrees, anxious to work and full of hope, only to find themselves at a dead end with all doors closed, and where no ear hears their clamour or supplication.
>
> These are the people, the ones who know misfortune and, therefore, are capable of fighting with limitless courage.[6]

Despite the flights of rhetoric, the message is unequivocal. Certainly, one thing is abundantly clear: in no sense was Castro at his Moncada trial predicating a classical bourgeois revolution. Although he described his constituency in terms of occupation rather than class *per se*, the populist orientation is unmistakable. It can be discerned not only in the list of those groups explicitly included in the sweep of his concern; even more telling in terms of class bias is the roster of those omitted. Conspicuously absent from the universe Fidel defined for his Revolution were such occupational groups as landowners, bankers, rentiers, industrialists: in sum, all those who together comprised the upper class and the topmost layers of the middle class in prerevolutionary Cuba. By extrapolation, the population included within the revolutionary boundaries drawn by Fidel Castro in 1953 were the lower classes, the petite bourgeoisie, and a final subgenus—personified by Castro himself—of disaffected, middle-class intellectuals.

Although the fidelista position on social class was subsequently honed and refined and, especially after the Revolution was in power some years, tended to become more restrictive, the populist content of Castro's original program has remained over time a consistent thread in his ideological formulations. Distilled to its essence, the Moncada speech made plain Fidel's conscious alignment with the underprivileged sectors of Cuban society—with the perennial "outs." Whatever transmutations his ideology may have undergone since then, this orientation has not changed.

Aside from its clearly populist bias, the ideological position of the Cuban revolutionary leadership on matters of social class was, in the immediate flush of victory, uncrystallized and occasionally self-contradictory. From early on, it was evident that the upper class was not counted a part of Castro's constituency, but the stance of the leadership vis-à-vis the other classes in society was less clearcut. At times the audience they addressed was defined vaguely and globally as "the people." At other times they divided their world into two simple categories, the "rich" and the "poor." On April 18, 1959, some three months after the fidelistas came to power, Ché Guevara, the Revolution's chief ideologist, remarked in an interview:

> The Cuban Revolution is not a class revolution, but a liberation movement that has overthrown a dictatorial, tyrannical government. The people detested the American-supported Batista dictatorial government from the bottom of their hearts and so rose up and overthrew it. The revolutionary government has received the broad support of all strata of people because its economic measures have taken care of the requirements of all and have gradually improved the livelihood of the people. The only enemies remaining in the country are the latifundistas and the reactionary bourgeoisie.[7]

Ten days later, on the television program "Telemundo Pregunta," he stated, seemingly in disregard of his earlier assertion, "The revolutionary government has two essential allies: the peasants and the workers. It is a mistake to think that a Revolution benefits all social classes." But in clarifying who would not benefit, he confined himself to the upper class:

> The rich who have inherited their wealth and have large landholdings do not have much of a chance, these will feel the weight of the Revolution. The foreign rich who invested from abroad and stole land with the consent of the state will also be hurt by the Revolution.[8]

The fate of the middle class was left hanging.

Meanwhile, in his speeches and writings, Guevara was beginning to lay the groundwork for yet another and more elaborate interpretation of the Revolution, a construct which placed all social groups—including the urban worker—in subordinate status and ascribed to the peasantry the key, catalytic role in the early stages of the revolutionary process. In accordance with this ex post facto explanation of the Revolution's genesis, the original band of middle-class guerrilla fighters were gradually transformed into agrarian revolutionaries, radicalized by the peasant masses and ultimately uniting with them under the banner of agrarian reform. Thus:

> The people in the Sierra grow like wild flowers, untended and without care, and they wear themselves out rapidly, working without reward. During those consultations we began to grow more conscious of the necessity for a definitive change in the life of the people. The idea of agrarian reform became clear and oneness with the people ceased being theory and was converted into a fundamental part of our being.
> The guerrilla group and the peasantry began to merge into one single mass, without our being able to say at which moment on the long revolutionary road this happened, nor at which moment the words became profoundly real and we became a part of the peasantry.[9]

These ideological peregrinations of the revolutionary leadership have been used to support a variety of theories about the original class matrix of the Cuban Revolution and, indeed, about the motives of the revolutionaries themselves. Especially in the immediate aftermath of Castro's public embrace of Marxism-

Leninism, it became something of a fashionable pastime to comb through the early declarations of the rebel leaders looking for threads with which to weave a convincing explanation of what had occurred.

Viewed from a longer perspective, it seems unnecessary to put too fine a point on the matter. While they might conveniently be described as "intellectuals," the revolutionary leaders who descended from the Sierra Maestra were certainly not schooled and disciplined social theorists. If one accepts their own statements at face value, they arrived in Havana in 1959 with nothing approaching a full-blown philosophical or ideological system. Their ideological utterance, starting with Castro's "History Will Absolve Me" speech and continuing on into their first years in office, was something of a potpourri, reflecting the influence of Jose Martí, of the programs of the Auténtico and Ortodoxo parties in the 1930s and 1940s in Cuba, of more general currents of Latin American thought, especially of the aprista variety, and, finally, of certain populist and egalitarian theories that have been prevalent for much of the present century in the international marketplace. They were conditioned, in sum, by a particular strain of Western thought, filtered through the web of Cuban historical experience and Cuban nationalist sentiment.

Eclectic and unsystematized, this convergent stream of thought did not constitute a coherent doctrine. It gave vague shape to the deep-rooted concern of the rebel leaders for "social justice" and for the dispossessed, the disadvantaged, and the generally alienated sectors of society; and it painted in broad, rough strokes the vision of a nation in which all citizens would have equal claim to happiness and to the basic benefits that their society could bestow. Thus, it defined a general posture toward society and social class that opened certain ideological options and foreclosed others. But it did not provide the Cuban leadership with any rigorous analytical framework for explaining to themselves and to others the exact workings of their Revolution, nor did it give them any sharp and tested tools for fully measuring the class implications of their basically egalitarian vision. Hence, their apparent vacillations in the early stages of their term in power as they set about defining their constituency and, by extension, the new Cuban community.

In another aspect, the lack of a coherent class doctrine and the progressive shifts of the leadership on the question of social class also reflected the ebb and flow of real circumstance. The Agrarian Reform Law of May 1959, for example, crystallized the opposition of certain subgroups in society against the regime, causing them to be read out of the accepted, global definition of "the people." Again, the escalating level of controversy with the United States led to the progressive elimination from the revolutionary constituency of those persons whose fortunes were tied to the North American economy or who saw their interests linked to the mainland.

Aside from the upper class, with whom Castro had never been especially concerned anyway, the bulk of these early defections from the Revolution was concentrated in the middle social strata—particularly in the landowning, commercial, and professional sectors. This circumstance was reflected in the progressive hardening of the revolutionary attitude toward the middle and upper reaches of the middle class. The original definition of the class composition of the Cuban Revolution, blurred and relatively broad in outline when the rebel army came to power, was sharpened and refined by its testing in reality.

THE DEFINITION OF CLASS IN THE NEW GOVERNMENT

By the end of their first year in office, the revolutionaries' reference to "the people" could increasingly be seen to center on the lower class. The role of middle-class individuals in the overthrow of Batista, for example, which had been readily acknowledged in the early days of the new regime, was now minimized or ignored altogether. Speaking on the anniversary of Jose Marti's birth in January, 1960 Ché Guevara reflected this growing bias:

> This is a revolution made for the people through the people's efforts. The Revolution began from below and its ranks were filled by peasants and workers; it demanded the sacrifice of workers and peasants in the countryside and cities of the island. It has not forgotten them after victory.

"With the poor of the earth I will cast my lot," Martí said, and that is what we have done. We have been put in our posts by the people and here we shall remain as long as they want, destroying all injustice and establishing a new social order.[10]

Whether or not one unquestioningly accepts Guevara's description of a revolution "from below," there is no mistaking the general drift of his thinking. To be sure, he and others of the leadership made it plain that the revolutionary ranks included, in addition to the lower class, such categories of persons as intellectuals and students. And even as late as March 1960 Fidel Castro would be willing to admit that "a considerable part of the middle class supports the Revolution."[11] But in the sentences that followed, he made it clear that he did not consider the middle class generally to be a reliable mainstay of the Revolution; and, moreover, while the lower class was collectively defined within the revolutionary boundaries, the middle class, qua class, was not. Rather, its members were granted their badges of admission on an individual basis or, occasionally, in an occupational group, and always with the implicit assumption that within the Revolution they would make common cause with the lower strata of society.[12] Those who were unable or unwilling to submerge their class interests—or, indeed, their individual interests—under the greater weight of the Revolution and to identify themselves with the mass of workers and peasants were simply read out of the global definition of "the people."

Although this evolving definition of the revolutionary community tended to leave increasing numbers of people outside the pale—and, in the case of the exiles, physically outside Cuba—it nevertheless still embraced the majority of the Cuban populace. As is typically the pattern of underdevelopment everywhere, in the Cuba that Castro inherited the socially and economically disadvantaged sectors of society far outnumbered the combined group of middle- and upper-class persons who had formally occupied prominent niches in the social hierarchy.

Interestingly, during this period in which the revolutionary ideology was progressively hardening, Castro and Guevara, the two chief spokesmen for the fidelistas, found themselves more often than not on the opposite side of the fence from the orthodox Cuban Communists in matters of class analysis. Steeped in the traditional formulas of Soviet Marxism, the Partido Socialista Popular (PSP), in its plenum held in May 1959, examined the Revolution, diagnosed it as a movement of "national liberation," and concluded that it rested on a four-class alliance involving the workers, the peasants, the petite bourgeoisie, and the national bourgeoisie.[13] (In this scheme of things, Castro was himself by inference dumped into the petit bourgeois category, a distinction that he may or may not have appreciated fully.)

Even when, by the end of 1959, the fidelista leaders gave clear indication of abandoning any thought of counting the so-called national bourgeoisie among their allies, the PSP stuck to its guns. As late as August 1960, at their Eighth Congress, the PSP leadership, in the person of Blas Roca, was still talking of a four-class coalition.[14] On this issue, as on so many others in the first two years or so of the Revolution in power, the PSP was lagging far behind Castro and his coterie. While the orthodox Communists continued to conduct their elaborate, multi-class analyses, Fidel was already beginning to reduce Cuban society to a simple dichotomy: on the one hand, the working masses and whosoever else, breaking free of class, made common cause with them; and, on the other side, all those who—for whatever reason—failed to unite themselves unconditionally with this populist mass. This dichotomy, in varying guises, was a thread running through many of Castro's speeches. Time and again he projected an image of the Cuban world divided between two polar camps, between those who were for the Revolution and those who were against it, between patriots and gusanos, between the poor and the rich, the exploited and the exploiters. There was in this dichotomy no middle road and, certainly, little room for the complex class analyses of the PSP.

In the end it was the PSP, rather than Castro, who capitulated on the point. Years later, Régis Debray, presumably with Castro's blessing, wrote the ultimate epitaph for the PSP notion of the four-class alliance, describing it as "outworn, discredited, eroded by failure."[15] And in all fidelista statements on revolution, the idea of support from a national bourgeoisie is expressly excluded. Nonetheless, the concept is still part of the ideological baggage carried by the Soviet-oriented Communist parties elsewhere in Latin America.

At the time, this running confrontation between the PSP and the fidelistas on the issue of social class was submitted to rigorous scrutiny by various observers of the Cuban scene who attempted to find in each detail and nuance evidence that Castro either was or was not a bona fide Communist or, from the Marxist side, that the Cuban Revolution either was or was not a genuinely Marxian case. With the advantage of ten years' hindsight, the issues involved take on a different coloration. It is now possible to suggest that the debate had a more complex meaning than appeared on the surface.

Although they were using basically the same vocabulary, the PSP and the fidelistas were not, in the final analysis, addressing the same set of issues. The PSP leaders were applying their traditional class formulas to a new social case in order to determine how and where it fit within their established theoretical model. This was not simply an academic exercise, for the outcome of their analysis would be the basis for formulating their tactical position vis-à-vis the Revolution. But it was, nonetheless, at considerable distance from the level at which the fidelistas were operating.

While the heat generated by the Revolution's increasingly radical measures obscured at the time the underlying nature of the fidelista position, in the relative calm of retrospection it appears that Fidel and his associates were engaged in quite a different ideological undertaking than the PSP. Whether consciously or not, they were embarked on no less an enterprise than the redefinition of the Cuban national community. Their initial ideological concern with "social justice" and with the underprivileged and alienated sectors of the Cuban community, explicitly affirmed in Castro's Moncada speech, was translated, once they were in power, into a political imperative that had as its goal the incorporation into the national mainstream of all those groups that had previously been excluded, starting with the most disadvantaged and outcast segments of prerevolutionary society.

It is in this context that Guevara's thesis of the Revolution's agrarian roots, which was not an especially accurate reflection of reality, takes on logical meaning. As many critics have been quick to point out, the peasant of the Sierra Maestra, about whom Ché tended to wax almost lyrical on occasion, was not representative of the Cuban agrarian population-at-large, most of whom were wage earners and thus inherently proletarian rather than peasant in character. But the Sierra Maestra inhabitant, eking out his living from a barren and unyielding terrain, was indeed the most disadvantaged and neglected of the Cuban populace. By placing him in the center of this theoretical construction, Guevara was actually saying little about Cuban reality and quite a bit about the ideological inclinations of the fidelistas. That he subsequently succumbed to his own theory and assigned a similar role to the Bolivian peasant very likely proved his own undoing in the end.

The concern of the fidelistas with bringing into the national mainstream the more deprived sectors of society was concretely reflected in much of the early social and economic legislation of the revolutionary regime, most notably in the first agrarian reform and in the amount of investment that was funneled into the rural areas of the country. That these measures, expressly designed to benefit the lower classes, would in turn alienate other groups in the Cuban community was something that may or may not have entered into Castro's initial calculations. In any case, once it materialized as palpable fact, he accepted this consequence and adjusted his ideological definitions accordingly.

In this process the rigorous and explicit class categories employed by the PSP were largely irrelevant, if not antithetical, to what the fidelistas were about. Engaged essentially in a massive effort of national integration, their purposes were best served not be accentuating the welter of class divisions in society, as the PSP was naturally prone to do, but by submerging them within the larger concept of "the people." Hence, in place of the PSP's intricate class constructions, they tended to employ dichotomies that were actually the definition of who was and who was not within the national community. This sense of nationhood, underlying and conditioning the ideological stance of the fidelistas on matters of social class, was brought vividly into focus in Castro's May Day address in 1961, shortly after the defeat of the Cuban exile forces at the Bay of Pigs. Contrasting prerevolutionary Cuba with the new Cuban order, Castro declared:

> It was the custom to talk about the motherland; there were some who had a wrong idea of the motherland. There was the motherland of the privileged ones, of a man who has a large home, while the others live in hovels. What motherland did you have in mind? . . . A motherland where a small group lives from the work of others? A motherland of the barefoot child who is asking for alms on the street? What kind of motherland is this?
>
> A motherland which belonged to a small minority? Or the motherland of today? The motherland of today . . . where we have learned to decide our own destiny, a motherland which will be, now and forever—as Marti wanted it—for the well-being of everyone and not a motherland for a few.
>
> The motherland will be a place where such injustices are eliminated. Now we have a real concept of motherland. We are willing to die for a motherland that belongs to all Cubans. . . .
>
> The people gain the real concept of motherland only when the interests of the privileged classes are liquidated, and when a nation with its wealth becomes a nation for everyone, and opportunity and happiness for everyone.[16]

By this time, of course, the *fidelista* concept of "everyone" had been considerably refined and narrowed. It had, indeed, hardened to the point that when, later in the same year, Castro publicly announced his conversion to Marxism-Leninism, his definition of the Cuban revolutionary community was not inherently incompatible with a Marxist view of society. What Castro took from Marxism was, in effect, a scientific rationalization of the position that he had already adopted. Among other things, Marx's vision of the last stage of capitalist society—a confrontation between two implacably opposed social classes—provided theoretical justification for Castro's essentially dichotomous portrayal of the Cuban world—even though Castro's two opposing social camps were not, on close inspection, exact replicas of Marx's proletariat and bourgeoisie. Again, Marx's concept of class conflict explained away the opposition of certain groups in society to Fidel Castro's increasingly radical and egalitarian measures by defining it as inevitable. And, in addition, Marx's philosophical system postulated an ultimate and inevitable utopia, sufficiently vague in definition so as not to be unduly constraining, but explicitly predicating a future in which class divisions would be totally erased. In turn, what Castro did to Marxism was to take what originally had been a supranational vision and fit it within the framework of a national community.

The ultimate implications of this marriage of Marxism to Castro's admixture of populism and nationalism were not immediately apparent. In the first flush of his conversion Fidel's formal ideological prose tended to display a rigid orthodoxy that followed closely the Soviet version of Marxian reality. He paid public obeisance to the PSP, increasingly peppered his speeches with some of the more stock phrases from the Marxist-Leninist lexicon, and generally appeared to have adopted the standard Soviet position on matters of social class and social organization.

It was no more than a temporary illusion. Underneath the surface a process of ideological evolution and refinement was beginning that would culminate eventually in a Cuban version of Marxism that departs in important respects from the Soviet model. The telltale signs were not long in coming. Indeed, as early as 1963 Ernst Halperin, an experienced observer of the Communist scene, would remark that "in spite of [Castro's] vociferous professions of adherence to the Marxist-Leninist creed, he is no orthodox Communist of the Moscow—or, for that matter, the Peking—mold."[17] Some four years later, speaking at the University of Havana, Castro himself underscored this ideological independence of mind:

> We proclaim it to the world: This Revolution will hold true to its path, this Revolution will follow its own line, this Revolution will never be anybody's satellite or yes-man. It will never ask anybody's permission to maintain its own position either in matters of ideology, or on domestic or foreign affairs. . . .[18]

EGALITARIANISM IN CUBA

The Cuban sense of self-determination, and the extent to which it has set Cuba apart from the

Soviet Marxist model, has found vivid reflection in matters of social structure and organization, especially in Fidel Castro's extreme and uncompromising egalitarianism. In their interpretation of Marx's vision, the Soviets, at least since Stalin's day, have carefully distinguished between egalitarianism and a "classless" social order. Thus, while they now proclaim the abolition within their own society of social classes, as defined by Marx, they nonetheless have maintained a complicated structure of differential wage scales, bonuses, and other material incentives that at least imply a considerable variation in life styles and perhaps even of life chances among their population. Nowhere has this matter received more eloquent treatment than in Milovan Djilas' The New Class, written over a decade ago.

In contrast to the Soviet model, the Cubans seek to eliminate not only social classes but all traditional lines of cleavage that may cut through the fabric of a national community. Thus, for example, above and beyond the abolition of class divisions, their egalitarian interpretation of Marx leads them also to predicate as an ultimate goal the end of any and all material differentials that can separate man from man in gradations of relative rank or privilege. This utopian vision already finds some reflection in Cuban reality, most notably in the increasing number of services that are provided free to the population-at-large and, somewhat in reverse fashion, in the strict system of rationing that limits on an equal basis the access of Cubans to those basic goods that are in shortest supply. It also is mirrored in the concern of the Cuban leadership with progressively lessening wage differentials, with the express aim of eventually achieving, as Castro has publicly stated, total "income egalitarianism."[19] Nowhere, perhaps, has this goal received more explicit definition than in Fidel's speech of July 26, 1968, celebrating the fifteenth anniversary of the Moncada Barracks attack. It is worth quoting at length, not only for the insight it offers into the basic ideological reasoning of the leadership, but also because it provides a vivid example of the essentially didactic quality that characterizes much of Castro's seemingly interminable oratory. While admitting that the Cuban position might well leave them open to charges from certain orthodox quarters of being petit bourgeois and idealistic, the Prime Minister nonetheless declared:

Some day we will all have to receive the same. Why? Some will ask: will a cutter earn as much as an engineer? Yes. Does that mean that an engineer will receive less? No. But some day a cane cutter—and I say cane cutter symbolically, because in the future we won't have any—let us say, the driver of a harvest combine or a truck, will earn as much as an engineer today.

And why? The thing is clear, very logical. The Revolution has thousands of young students in the universities. The Revolution has thousands of young people studying abroad, dedicated to studying, to becoming engineers, chemists, specializing in different fields. Who pays for their expenses? The people.

If the Revolution needs to send many young people to study in Europe and others in universities, all right; we ask them to study, and they do it in a disciplined way, but that doesn't mean they are privileged. It is important to the Revolution that they study, that they prepare themselves. But at the same time that thousands of our young people study abroad, thousands of others have to go into the fields to plant cane, to weed cane, to do very hard work. Within a few years there will be much more wealth in our country. The former will have finished three, five years of studies and will have become technicians, engineers; and the latter will have been working those years in the fields, and they will not become engineers, but they will develop our economy, they will be building the future of our country.

Under what concept and in what way would it be just for us to tell these young people after a few years, in a more prosperous country, in a country with much more wealth, you are earning one-fourth of an engineer's wages? Would it be just, would it be basically just, that those whom the country called on not to go to the university but to work to win the battle of the economy, to make the effort which at this time we cannot make with chemistry or with the machines that we do not have, but must make with our hands, with our sweat—would it be just whenever the nation is able to enjoy the riches which they are creating now, for us to treat them as fourth- or fifth-class citizens, entitled to receive from society an insignificant part of what in the future will be received by those who are in the universities, those who are studying abroad?...

No! Not at all. Communist conscience means that in the future the wealth that we create through everybody's effort should be equally shared by all. That is communism, that is communist conscience! And there will not be a single honest citizen . . . there will not be a single person in this country with human sensitivity who will not be able to understand how just this concept is which our people defend, which our Revolution proclaims and which our students have made their watchword.[20]

Among the several strands of the argument, there looms prominently the concern of the Cuban leadership with some abstract and absolute standard of what is "just," a theme that has been a consistent thread in the fidelista ideology since its initial expression some fifteen years earlier in Fidel Castro's Moncada speech. As interpreted by Castro, this concept of ultimate social justice goes well beyond the triad of basic equalities on which Western democracy has traditionally rested: equality before the law, equality before the marketplace, and equality before God. It equalizes, in addition, the intrinsic worth of each individual as it is expressed in his work and, through his work, in his contribution to the common weal. Thus, it implies a definition of national community in which all persons, regardless of occupation, have equal commitment and make equal contribution and, therefore, share equally in the benefits the community can bestow. It is, of course, a vision that Castro and his colleagues acknowledge to lie at some indeterminate point in the future. But it nonetheless conditions many of their present policy decisions, which frequently fly in the face of traditional Soviet practice and, presumably, of the advice the Cubans receive from their Soviet and East European technical advisors.

The profoundly egalitarian commitment of the Cuban leadership extends well beyond the simple question of income differentials. It is reflected in a broad array of tactics and policies, including their strong emphasis on moral over material incentives as a means of stimulating productivity; their preoccupation, reflected in their investment priorities, with erasing the most glaring differences between rural and urban life styles; and their penchant for sending urban office workers out to the cane fields for a round of voluntary labor. In each instance there is an explicit and underlying ideological purpose, relating to the ultimate goals that the Cuban leaders have posited for their national society. In the case of voluntary labor, for example, the basic ideological rationale was laid bare by Ché Guevara in a speech delivered to a workers' rally in Havana in mid-1964:

We say that voluntary work ought not to be viewed for the economic importance it has today for the state. Fundamentally, voluntary work is the factor that develops the conscience of the workers more than any other; and still more so when workers carry out their work in places that are not habitual for them. Our administrative workers and technicians know the fields of Cuba and know the factories of our industry by having done voluntary work in them, at times under very difficult conditions. As a result, a new cohesion and comprehension is established between the two sectors, which the capitalist technique of production always keeps separate and in rivalry. . . .

Voluntary work, then, is changed into a vehicle of union and of comprehension between our administrative workers and the manual workers. It is a way of preparing the road toward a new stage of our society, a new stage of society where classes will not exist, and therefore, where there will be no difference between a manual worker and an intellectual worker, between worker and peasant.[21]

In the light of this kind of exposition, it is clear that the Cuban brand of egalitarianism cannot be dismissed simply as an arbitrary and single-minded desire to level material differences among the population. The Cubans seek to erase more subtle lines of social division as well and, on the other side of the coin, to forge a completely integrated and cohesive community in which all members are not only intrinsically equal but actually share a measure of common experience and achieve, through such experience, a common empathy. Thus, it is not sufficient merely to narrow the income gap between manual and nonmanual occupations; nonmanual workers, from the Cabinet on down, must actually engage on occasion in manual work. And even students must combine their formal course work with their time in the field.

Both in the abstract and in its reflection in concrete policy, the Cuban commitment to egalitarianism breaks sharply with the social tradition inherited from the Spanish colonial past, a tradition with a rigid sense of social hierarchy and a hardly concealed disdain for manual labor and, by extension, for those who must engage in it. Some years ago after returning from a trip to Cuba, Juan Gomez Millas, then Minister of Education in the Chilean Cabinet, remarked to me that, whatever else Fidel Castro might have done, the true importance of his accomplishment lay in the fact of his having broken Cuba loose, once and for all, from the retarding influence of Spanish colonial culture. More recently, a North American visitor has neatly summed up this facet of the Cuban Revolution:

> By rubbing his peoples' noses in the countryside, Fidel Castro is smashing the class distinctions and social relations of what was once a very Latin society. In all of Latin America, only in Cuba are boots, rough hands, dirty clothes, first names, and agricultural talk among the marks of honor and status.[22]

Without being facetious, it is difficult at times to avoid the impression that Castro and his fellow fidelistas are determined to do nothing less than turn their country into one vast Israeli kibbutz. It is a phenomenon that should not be lightly dismissed, for it is in keeping—if one can forget for the moment its Marxist overtones—with much of the development theories current in the United States. It signifies, at bottom, an attempt to supplant traditional values toward the community and toward work itself with a value set conducive to modern development.

Interestingly, Cuba's egalitarian version of Marxism, more radical and uncompromising than anything the Soviets or their East European partners have attempted, is in some respects more flexible and tolerant, especially in its treatment of the individual within society. In the early days of the Russian Revolution an individual's class ancestry was in most cases as indelible as the mark of Cain; it was regarded as sufficient reason for closing off access to educational and occupational opportunities and, in the most extreme of cases, to the basic means of survival. It was not simply former aristocrats who were thus stigmatized, but also, in the course of time, such collective groups as the wealthier peasants, or kulaks. A similar screening process, albeit less stringently applied, could be observed in the new Communist states established in Eastern Europe after World War II.

In contrast, within the Cuban Revolution any individual—so long as he is not a bastistiano—is eligible for membership in the new national community. The determining factor is not class origin but the willingness of the individual to accept the revolutionary ideology and the revolutionary modus operandi. Guevara, perhaps the most radical of Castro's entire entourage, explicitly enunciated this position as early as mid-1960 in a speech to a meeting of the Cuban militia:

> But we must not . . . separate all men into either children of the working and peasant classes of counterrevolutionaries, because it is simplistic, because it is not true, and because there is nothing which educates an honorable man more than living in a revolution.[23]

It is a statement that has been reiterated since many times, both in statement and in practice. Its implication, if one may draw the larger inference, is that in the Cuban universe it is an individual's conscious choice, rather than any accident of birth, that should by rights determine his life pattern. In essence, it represents a view of man and society from which all trace of ascription has been removed. It also is symptomatic of the generally voluntaristic, rather than deterministic, cast that has characterized the Cuban Revolution from its inception.

In most of the literature on contemporary Cuba, this voluntaristic dimension has usually been treated only insofar as it is revealed in the Cuban position on guerrilla warfare, that is, in the notion—first advanced by Ché Guevara and later codified by the French theoretician, Régis Debray—that a small group of revolutionaries can, if they are sufficiently committed, make a revolution. They do not have to wait for the inexorable course of history to work itself out. On closer inspection, it is clear that this same voluntarism colors much of the Cuban approach to their problems of development and social change. At its most basic level it conditions their view of man himself: man is not simply a blind object; he has the ability to change and perfect himself.

At the same time, it is not the Cuban view that man can work out his destiny alone. Rugged individualism has no place in Fidel's ideology. Once he has been freed from the alienation and the "wolf instinct" engendered by the capitalist class system, man will be able to reach his highest level of creativity and self-expression, but only within the community of his fellows and only when that community has developed to the point where it can provide equal material abundance to everyone. It is inherently a Marxist vision, but the Cubans—as they have done with much of their Marxism—have set it squarely within the frame of their national society.

Given its sharp break with the dominant social traditions in the rest of Latin America, the Cuban case represents an interesting departure from the general developmental pattern of the region. To dismiss it simply as a standard Communist takeover is to miss much of the richness and variety in the Cuban experience. To chalk it up, alternatively, solely to Fidel Castro's personal makeup and his charismatic brand of leadership is equally simplistic and analytically unrewarding. The Cuban approach to man and society is related both to currents that are at play in much of the Third World today and to the peculiar cast of the Cuban historical experience.

In one form or another, and in guises that range from the pragmatic to the visionary, egalitarianism has been a major ideological current on the world scene for at least two hundred years. In the eighteenth century it came to fullest expression in the United States Constitution and in the much-quoted slogan of the French revolutionaries, "Liberty, Equality, Fraternity." This early version of egalitarianism was, however, set within strictly circumscribed limits. At its root it represented the demand of a rising middle class for equal participation in a society that had been dominated by the remnants of a feudal aristocracy. Although it ascribed to all citizens a certain basic cluster of equal and inalienable rights, it was not inherently antithetical to vast extremes of wealth and poverty or to a fairly elaborate hierarchy of social classes. Indeed, until well into the mid-nineteenth century, the egalitarianism of the French and American revolutions managed to coexist in relative harmony with the practice of human slavery.

In the last several generations a more radical and inclusive brand of egalitarianism has come to loom increasingly larger on the international stage. Coinciding in its genesis with the development of the capitalist system in Western Europe and the United States, this contemporary version of egalitarianism has found its most significant form of expression in opposition to that system. A distinguished social scientist, T. B. Bottomore, depicts the phenomenon as follows:

> The egalitarian movement which came to life in socialist clubs, trade unions, cooperative ventures and utopian communities grew stronger throughout the nineteenth century as capitalism developed. In the course of time this movement has taken many different forms—struggles for women's rights and against racial discrimination, and most recently the efforts to close the gap between rich and poor nations—but its driving force has remained the opposition to the hierarchy of social classes. The class system of the capitalist societies is seen as the very fount of inequality, from which arise the chief impediments to individual achievement and enjoyment, the major conflicts with and between nations, and the political dominance of privileged minorities.[24]

It is an ideological current to which even affluent societies are not immune, as demonstrated by the social credos of the New Left and the Black Panthers in the United States. But it is in the underdeveloped countries of the contemporary world—where traditional class systems hold society within a rigid and static mold and where the boundaries between social classes are more palpable and unyielding than in modern, industrialized nations—that this latter-day egalitarianism becomes a particularly seductive doctrine as it comes into confluence with inchoate strivings toward national identity and modernization. To the new nationalist elites emerging in the Third World, it offers a ready-made and not altogether unsatisfying explanation of their backwardness. It gives them a persuasive rationale, imbued with a certain measure of moral authority, for rearranging the social order and dislodging the traditional upper classes that have heretofore presided—alone or in concert with a colonial power—over their societies. And, finally, in the reality of the Soviet Union, with its massive industrial plants and its lunar rockets, they find an Horatio Alger kind of success story with rapid development that seems to confirm the efficacy of the egalitarian premise. That the social and political cost of the Soviet formula may be high is not of direct relevance; the cost in human suffering of failing to develop will be considerably higher in the countries of the Third World.

The pervasive currents of modern egalitarianism blowing in upon the underdeveloped, or prenational, countries have induced a qualitative change in the process of development and nationbuilding in the present-day world. It is unlikely that any country now engaged in the transition to modernism can ever retrace the precise route traversed by those nations that developed well over a century ago. Both new ideologies and new levels of technology dictate that the measured and essentially serene advance of a nineteenth-century England toward industrial modernity will not be duplicated again. There, first one class, and then another, gained access to the full prerogatives and benefits of British national society in a dilatory process which is no longer possible in much of the developing world. Among other things, the so-called "revolution of rising expectations"—a phenomenon that has received considerable notice in recent years—mitigates against solutions that are either slow or partial. As an American political scientist has cautioned:

> The ideas of the national world are another factor new to history playing on the prenational world; not only the new techniques but the baggage of values and norms they carry with them are unique. When England was going through the process of the slow emergence of a strong and self-conscious middle class there was no hortatory body of doctrine or concrete messianic example urging that no groups should be left outside the social pale, that society should be "classless." Underdeveloped nations now have the economic model of the Western industrialized countries to demonstrate that class differences can effectively be blunted, and the communist ideological teaching that they should be erased in some Utopian future. The modernization process now tempts to total revolution instead of only partial adjustment. . . . The politicians of development must now answer to immediate demands for permitting lower economic groups to be identified with the total society, and provided with more than a mystical hope of climbing upward. The ideological acceptance of anything less in the way of social openness now dooms any developing country to warped and interminably repressive politics and faltering economic advance.[25]

It is against this background that the Cuban case takes on a broader relevance and becomes more than merely an isolated and eccentric Caribbean happening. The imposition of a radical social doctrine on the Cuban body politic, although it may have certain special characteristics of its own, is not unrelated to the general array of problems and pressures playing upon the underdeveloped countries of the contemporary world.

EQUALITY AND MODERNITY

For the student of comparative development, then, the more significant question with respect to the Cuban phenomenon would seem to be not so much its original whys and wherefores—an issue that has already preoccupied battalions of scholars and State Department officials alike—but, rather, the relationship between the radical social ideology of the fidelistas and the process of modernization and nation-building in their country. The question is not simply of abstract or academic interest, for the Cubans themselves have explicitly proclaimed modernization, or "development," to be among the crucial goals of their Revolution. And it is in this guise, as much as in any other, that the Cuban adventure strikes a responsive chord with certain nationalist groups elsewhere in the Latin America region.

All countries commonly classified as "developed" have their own peculiar variations on the basic theme. And different schools of social scientists apply a multitude of varying definitions and measurements to the concept of "development." Nevertheless, while recognizing both the real and the theoretical pitfalls on either side, it is probably moderately safe to suggest that there is a minimum cluster of attributes that is the hallmark of a modern nation-state at this juncture in historical time. Industrialization, urbanization, and a certain level of economic and technological advancement are only the most obvious concomitants of modernism. Although frequently treated as independent variables in the popular imagination, these classical indices of development are intimately bound up with certain necessary conditions of a political and social order. In the social sphere these enclude, at a minimum, secularism; tolerance rather than rejection of change; a general value stance that is rationalistic rather than ritualistic; and a social system that is open, with mobility based on achievement rather than ascription, by merit rather than birth. Politically, modern nationhood necessarily implies that the state is the ultimate claimant of citizen loyalty, superseding all other allegiances. Finally, a modern nation-state depends upon a particular kind of nationalism, or national identity, that goes well beyond the basic juridical definition of the nation and the symbolic trappings of patriotism. It is a sense of loyalty to one's fellow citizens that has been neatly characterized by certain writers by the term "empathy." It signifies, at its root, the ability and willingness of individuals to identify with other members of the national community across expanses of both social and geographical distance.

In those countries of the world that were launched on a developmental trajectory well over a century ago, the journey toward what is now considered modern nationhood was achieved only gradually and piecemeal. The effective national community was extended in leisurely stages, first to the rising middle groups and only later to the lower socioeconomic strata of the nation.

As industrialization proceeded and technology advanced, increasing occupational specialization demanded an increasingly mobile and educated labor force, and this in turn created the pressures that led inexorably to the progressive widening of the effective national community. It was a slow process of interaction between economic and social variables that took several generations before finally culminating in the stage that is now commonly defined as modernism.

Viewed from this perspective, the fidelista strategy vis-à-vis the Cuban social order appears to be an attempt to collapse into the space of a relatively few years a process that in the developed countries of the world took well over a century. If it is generally accepted that in underdeveloped societies the rigid boundaries of class or caste may be an obstacle to national integration and also that as industrialization and modernization proceed class boundaries must necessarily tend to blur, then the fidelista position on social class and social organization would seem to represent nothing less than a conscious effort to leap the massive gap between the underdeveloped and developed worlds by erasing class divisions altogether, while at the same time stressing national symbols that are to be the ultimate claimants of each citizen's loyalty.

In this process, which implies the total reordering of Cuban society, the role of Marxism has a particular importance. First, it stands as a central and unifying national ideology. In the developed countries the function of ideology is often lightly dismissed as irrelevant or forgotten altogether. But in the underdeveloped areas of the world, where traditional values and beliefs are being weakened and shed, ideology plays a crucial role in filling the vacuum both for individuals and for society-at-large. Thus, in Cuba Marxism functions as something of a secular religion welding the citizenry together in a common belief system.

At another level, Marxist ideology justifies many of the more cataclysmic measures of the Cuban revolutionary leadership by imbuing them with both an ethical and a rational significance. Also, by positing an ultimate utopian goal, it gives a sense of national purpose of the citizenry-at-large, rationalizing present sacrifices in terms of a future good in which all will share equally. That Marx's vision was essentially international in scale does not lessen its effectiveness as an integrating and mobilizing concept when set, as in Cuba, within a national framework; on the contrary, one can speculate that the added dimension of nationalism may well give to Marxism a meaning and cogency that, when couched solely in universal terms, it would otherwise lack.

In terms of the Cuban social order, Castro and his colleagues have essentially used Marxixm and the Marxist stance on social class as a device for redrawing the boundaries of the Cuban national community, extending the frontiers to include the great mass of Cuban citizens. That they have done so without the massive strife and lethal conflict that accompanied the Russian Revolution is in part a reflection of the class order they inherited from prerevolutionary Cuba. The class structure of pre-Castro Cuba has already been treated in basic detail in the first chapter. The upper class, lacking any profound moral legitimacy within Cuban society and identified, moreover, with foreign economic interests, could be dislodged by the fidelistas with relative ease. The middle class likewise posed no intrinsic threat. Basically fragmented, it contributed to the revolutionary ranks as well as to the swelling tide of exiles. Finally, the Cuban lower classes were, in their bulk, at least partially "modern." Unlike the lower classes in more traditional underdeveloped societies, the Cuban lower groups had generally achieved a level of awareness and identification to the point where they could be readily mobilized on a national scale and, more importantly, could provide a reliable base of mass support for a national leader. They were, in short, widely and immediately available for recruitment into the national mainstream and to the revolutionary cause. The net result was that the rearrangement of the Cuban social order along Marxist lines could be accomplished with relatively little difficulty.

By the very alienation of certain categories of citizens and by the consequent exodus of persons who had hitherto occupied important technical, managerial, and professional positions, the tangible effect of the fidelista class strategy—whether intentional or not—has been to produce what might best be called "instant social mobility." The exodus has created an occupational vacuum that can only be filled by co-opting persons from the lower socioeconomic strata. While creating something of a temporary manpower crisis, it has also meant the opening up of mobility channels that in the past were rigidly narrow, if not totally closed. That the social cost, in human terms, has been high is undeniable; the price in lost expertise and efficiency has also been considerable. But the social effect, in terms of increased mobility and participation, is also unquestionable. In this important respect Castro's use of Marxism has indeed introduced into the Cuban social order one of the standard features of modern nationhood.

If Fidel Castro has used Marxism to erase the more manifest aspects of class cleavage and to create social openness, he is also using Marxist ideology to forge a new sense of national identification and national empathy in Cuba. Speaking to the Cuban populace on July 26, 1968, Fidel described his vision of the ultimate communist society as follows:

> No human society has yet reached communism. The ways along which a superior form of society is reached are very difficult. A communist society means that man will have reached the highest degree of social awareness ever achieved; a communist society means that the human being will have been able to achieve the degree of understanding and brotherhood which man has sometimes achieved within the close circle of his family. To live in a communist society is to live without selfishness, to live among the people and with the people; as if every one of our fellow citizens were really our brother.[26]

Putting aside the Marxian and utopian verbiage, what Castro is essentially talking about is nationalism as social value, as the norm that decrees empathy and common cause among all citizens of a national polity. It is an ideological construction that lies at the heart of what the Cuban Revolution is about. Whatever its practical merits, it falls within the basic set of values that together comprise the hallmark of a modern nation-state.

In essence, then, the Cuban position on social class and national community, whatever may be its defects, is modern rather than traditional in orientation. It represents, moreover, one of the key aspects of the Cuban Revolution, conditioning much of the regime's explicit policy in the major institutional areas of Cuban life.

Egalitarianism and the sense of total national community can be seen, on reflection, to underlie many of the fundamental decisions of the Cuban leadership in the economy, in the educational establishment, and in political matters overall. In this respect the Cuban phenomenon is an interesting departure both from standard Marxism and from the general pattern of Latin American development policy. The ideological definition of national community—which is basically political in nature—affects decision-making in all other institutional spheres. Thus it is politics, rather than economics, that is the fulcrum of Cuba's developmental strategy. Marx turned Hegel on his head; Castro has done the same to Marx.

NOTES

1. Castro's Revolution: Myths and Realities (New York: Frederick A. Praeger, 1962), p. 10.

2. Cuba: Anatomy of a Revolution (New York: Monthly Review Press, 1960), p. 78.

3. Cuba and Marxism, Joint Publications Research Service, U. S. Department of Commerce (Washington, D.C.: 1962), p. 27.

4. "The Cuban Revolution: An Analysis," Problems of Communism XII, no. 5 (September-October 1963): 3.

5. "The Revolution Next Door: Cuba," The Annals of the American Academy of Political and Social Science 334 (March 1961): 114.

6. History Will Absolve Me, (London: Jonathan Cape, 1968), pp. 41-42.

7. Rolando E. Banachea and Nelson P. Valdés, eds., Ché: Selected Works of Ernesto Guevara (Cambridge: The MIT Press, 1969), p. 374.

8. Ibid., p. 382.

9. Reminiscences of the Cuban Revolutionary War (New York: Monthly Review Press, 1968), p. 102.

10. Bonachea and Valdés, op. cit., p. 211.

11. La Calle, March 30, 1960, as quoted by Theodore Draper, Castroism: Theory and Practice (New York: Frederick A. Praeger, 1965), p. 125.

12. Thus, Castro, in his speech of February 11, 1961, attempted to assure Cuba's smaller businessmen that there was indeed a place for them in the island's life "in perfect harmony with the Revolution." But he made the explicit assumption that eventually they would find it to their interest to join the wage-earning labor force. "When our country becomes more developed and there is a great demand for labor, this army of small businesses will start to disappear completely. Why is that? Because men will prefer better paying work, because families will prefer a kind of work and income which is more secure than eking out one's living with a hot dog stand or some small business where you have to wear yourself out just to make ends meet." (Fidel Castro Speaks on Unemployment, Young Socialist Forum, n.d., p. 8.)

13. The conclusions of the PSP plenum were carried in Hoy, June 7, 1959.

14. See Partido Socialista Popular, VIII Asamblea Nacional: Informes, Resoluciones, Programa Estatutos, (Havana: Ediciones Populares, 1960).

15. Revolution in the Revolution? (New York: Monthly Review Press, 1967), p. 87.

16. Martin Kenner and James Petras, eds., Fidel Castro Speaks (New York: Grove Press, 1969), pp. 72-73.

17. "Castroism—Challenge to the Latin American Communists," Problems of Communism, op. cit., p. 9.

18. *Those Who Are Not Revolutionary Fighters Cannot be Called Communists* (New York: Merit Publishers, 1968), p. 62.

19. Speech of July 26, 1968, Kenner and Petras, op. cit., p. 291.

20. Ibid., pp. 294-295.

21. Speech of August 15, 1964, in John Gerassi, ed., *Venceramos: The Speeches and Writings of Ernesto Guevara* (New York: Simon and Schuster, 1969), p. 179.

22. Richard R. Fagen, *The Transformation of Political Culture in Cuba* (Stanford: Stanford University Press, 1969), p. 179.

23. Speech of August 19, 1960, Gerassi, op. cit., p. 116.

24. *Classes in Modern Society* (New York: Pantheon Books, 1966), pp. 76-77.

25. Kalman H. Silvert, *Expectant Peoples: Nationalism and Development* (New York: Vintage Books, 1967), pp. 5-6.

26. Kenner and Petras, op. cit., pp. 286-287.

CUBAN AGRICULTURE: A STRATEGY OF ECONOMIC DEVELOPMENT

David Barkin
Herbert H. Lehman College
City University of New York

The Cubans' disillusionment with their economic structure and their aspiration to be numbered among the modern industrialized countries was best summed up by Fidel Castro (1953: 70-1) in a famous speech:

With the exception of a few food, lumber, and textile industries, Cuba continues to be a producer of raw materials. We export sugar to import candy, we export hides to import shoes, we export iron to import plows. Everybody agrees that the need to industrialize the country is urgent, that we need steel industries, paper and chemical industries, that we must improve cattle and grain production, the techniques and the processing in our food industry, in order to balance the ruinous competition of the Europeans in cheese products, condensed milk, liquors and oil, and that of the United States in canned goods; that we need merchant ships; that tourism should be an enormous source of revenue. But the capitalists insist that the workers remain under a Claudian yoke; the State folds its arms, and industrialization can wait for the Greek calends.

Few examples of Latin American rhetoric match Castro's, but the dissatisfaction to which he gives vent is widespread throughout the region. Though Cuba's was an extreme case of dependent development, many nations are similarly subjected to the vagaries of international commodity markets and to the economic self-interest of the developed nations. All emerging countries desire industrialization, and industrial nirvanas are forever being promised by ruling elites. Few, however, are able to reconcile their existing economic and political structures with the insistent nationalistic demands of the impoverished masses.

During the first years of the Revolution, little thought was given to long-range planning and to the elaboration of a consistent program which would encompass various sectors of the economy. Instead, individual administrators were allowed to make decisions about the expansion of their own activities without regard to the effects. At the same time, policies were implemented to increase the purchasing power of large segments of the population: rents were lowered dramatically, public utility charges were slashed, social services were expanded, and people's stores were established throughout the rural areas to eliminate the usurious interest rates and monopolistic prices of the previous epoch. Programs were undertaken to build new housing and tourist resorts throughout the country for people who never dreamed of having such opportunities.

These programs were financed by the reserves of productive capacity, men and equipment, and by the dollar resources which Cuba could count on as a result of her substantial exports of sugar. They were all mobilized to increase production

---

Work on this paper was conducted while the author was a Research Associate at El Colegio de México and was on a grant from the Joint Committee of Latin American Studies of the Social Science Research Council and the American Council of Learned Societies. Financial assistance from the University Institutional Grants Committee of New York University is gratefully acknowledged. Helpful comments were received from the members of the Union for Radical Political Economics, but, of course, the author bears all responsibility for the article in its present form.

and, in spite of the depressing effects of the nationalizations, industrial production in 1960 was somewhat higher than in 1959 and about 30 percent higher than in 1958 (Boorstein, 1968:60). By 1961, however, preexisting inventories were exhausted and the American embargo was beginning to make its effects felt. As a result, total industrial production declined; similar problems arose in agriculture a year later. The ambitious plans to expand the area under cultivation and to diversify new crops were scaled down because of a large balance of payments deficit. Money was not available for new machinery or fertilizer. The initial impact of the U. S. embargo was particularly severe, because a large proportion of total food consumption and spare parts for most machinery had been imported from the United States.

Insufficient foreign exchange and inadequate coordination plague most economic development programs, but in the euphoric atmosphere of the first years of the Revolution they were pushed to the backs of the leaders' minds and optimism reigned. (In the Central Planning Board the pessimists were projecting a 10 percent rate of growth for the following years!) The hard realities of economic development, however, did impose themselves on the planners. Throughout the economy, shortages and production imbalances forced a reexamination of the industrialization strategy.

In 1963, the leadership decided that agriculture should be the "pivot on the road to development" (International Symposium . . ., 1967:68). This was an important shift from the ad hoc decision-making of previous years. It represented a realization that long-range planning was required to develop the Cuban economy. The new regime was thus enabled and impelled to take advantage of the productive potential which was most easily mobilized in order to finance the future diversification of the economy. The touchstone of this new economic policy was the goal of 10 million tons for the 1970 sugar harvest. This turnabout called for substantial future investments in agriculture to improve productivity and to diversify and increase total production. Domestic production had to substitute for food and raw material imports and provide a surplus for increased exports (Third Interregional Seminar . . ., 1968).

Unbalanced Economic Growth: Impatience and Ideology

The Cubans explicitly reject an autarkic approach to economic self-sufficiency. Impatience and ideology has led them towards an unbalanced developmental strategy—one which relies on the expansion of sugar and other agricultural products to provide the capital necessary for subsequent growth more rapidly.

For their ideological direction, the Cubans looked to Marx. Although Marx envisaged communism as a social structure best suited to a highly developed society, many people in the developing countries today find his prescriptions an attractive way of bridging the chasm between a traditional and a modern society. Communism can function best in a technologically advanced and affluent society. For a developing country it can provide a model for development; a motor for pulling up a developing country into a technologically advanced world.

Castro's version of communism is designed to guide Cuba in its quest for rapid growth and social justice. The Marxian model provided the underpinning for an efficient development effort. Not only did it make acceptable an extreme form of government centralization, but it also provided a basis for redistributing consumer goods. Strict control enabled the masses to enjoy a rising standard of living without diverting increasing resources to consumption. Economic development, otherwise limited by the amount freed for investment, was not hindered. Thus, broad support was gained for the new strategy.

The decisions made since 1963 reflect the leadership's sense of urgency. An examination of their statements and policies suggests that the Cubans intuitively seized upon the route which economists consider optimal for economic growth. Known as the "turnpike" (because of its similarity to the high-speed circumferential roads being built around many cities), it follows the logic that the most direct route between two points is not always the fastest. The greater the distance that separates them, the more expedient it is to take a detour onto the expressway. Analogously, economists have shown that when the planning period for development is long enough and the final objectives are specified, it may be worthwhile to set these ultimate goals aside and concentrate on increasing production in the most efficient manner. Once a larger productive base is achieved, the planners can transform the economic structure by means of investment in new industries. In this way a society can reap the benefits of economic efficiency while not committing itself eternally to the production of capital goods that this implies.[1,2]

The Marxist-Leninist climate of central control and egalitarianism facilitated the evolution of a concerted development program. Castro and other leaders have always displayed a fiercely pragmatic approach to the problems of modernization. Although numerous errors in investment decisions have been made (sometimes as a direct result of the personal intervention of the Prime Minister), a basic commitment to rationality governs Cuban policy-making. The unbalanced strategy, for example, emphasizes development in the most efficient industries.

Socialist organization empowers planners to use the proceeds from profitable enterprises for the creation of new industries or for the expansion of old ones. In a capitalist setting where decision-making is decentralized and to a large extent concentrated in the private sector, a smaller proportion of the proceeds is available for further investment because it is more difficult to contain consumption levels. Moreover, without central planning more resources might be invested in the expansion of relatively inefficient production facilities or in new lines of the same firm. With a centrally directed socialist economy, the planners may have greater freedom to shift profits and investment from one industry to another in line with their decisions about the relative importance and efficiency of different products. These conditions have materially assisted Cuba to mobilize a larger part of its economic surplus for economic growth.

The early decision to redistribute consumption to the poor and to increase the importance of publicly provided social services is a part of the Marxist ideology permeating the Cuban Revolution. Ambitious plans were drawn up for investing almost all of the increasing production in a further expansion of productive capacity in the initial phases of development. The rationing system allowed a rapid rise in consumption for the poor, especially in rural areas, without increasing aggregate consumption by shifting goods from urban and wealthy groups. With the success

---

1. Discussions of the turnpike growth models are generally of a very technical nature. Among the first Western economists to develop such models were Ramsey (1928) and Von Neumann (1945-6). Similar models of optimum economic growth were also developed early in this century by some Soviet economists; see, e.g., Strumlin (1951). Recently, the literature has grown explosively following the presentation of an optimum growth model by Dorfman et al. (1958). Vanek (1968) attempted to make the model more accessible by outlining a geometric approach and Lancaster (1968) includes a short discussion of the theory in his textbook. Findlay comes closest to examining a situation similar to the Cuban case by showing some of the relationships between the turnpike models of efficient capital accumulation and international trade (1968). Dobb (1960) also has examined problems of optimal investment planning in many of his works.

2. The policies resulting from the turnpike theory are similar to those that would emerge from the combination of a dynamic theory of comparative advantage and theories emphasizing the importance of higher investment coefficients. The value of the modified approach is that it combines these in a single analytical approach to optimal economic growth. See Johnson (1969) for a discussion of the development and application of a theory of dynamic comparative advantage.

of individual production programs for consumption goods, a gradual easing of rationing restrictions is foreseen. In the meantime, greater emphasis is being placed on the provision of collective public services to ensure equal participation in the development effort by all groups. This includes education which not only enables people to participate more fully in the development effort but also is an essential element in the modernization process.

In practice, the Cubans modified the so-called theoretical "turnpike" model to take account of a growing population and their inability to produce a broad range of machinery and consumer goods. They decided to concentrate on agricultural products and to develop trade relationships with other nations, so that needed capital equipment could be purchased from the proceeds of agricultural sales. From their perspective, agriculture was the least expensive sector to develop and represented the most expedient way of increasing their limited export base. They explained that it not only offered the possibility of exporting a large proportion of the expanded production and reducing present imports of foodstuffs, but it also could make use of unexploited reserves of fertile land. Both land and labor productivity could be raised without demanding the numbers of trained personnel and imports of capital goods which other sectors would require.[3]

The first step taken to implement this strategy was the 1963 declaration of the 10-million-ton goal for the 1970 sugar harvest. Some people in Cuba doubted the wisdom of this campaign since the nation's past dependence on sugar was blamed for the deplorable social and economic situation which existed on the eve of the Revolution. But the choice of this sector, after the initial flirtation with the more orthodox socialist route of rapid industrialization, was not an accident; Cuba has an overwhelming comparative advantage in the production of sugar.

Sugar is only part of the present development effort. Cattle-raising is second in priority. The aim is to increase the herd of cattle and raise its productivity to permit a rapid increase in milk and meat production. Simultaneously, other agricultural products are being developed as part of the first phase of the new development strategy; these include citrus fruits, rice, coffee and tubers. They are important because they will reduce the amount of foreign exchange needed for the purchase of consumption goods and also permit an increase in and a diversification of exports.

The Cubans are fully aware of the inherent limitations of agricultural development. Not only do they point out that the market for a sugar harvest in excess of 10 million tons is limited, but they also acknowledge that export receipts from other agricultural and livestock products cannot continue to expand indefinitely and that the quantity of arable land is severely limited. Even with improvements in organization and technical efficiency, the agricultural sector cannot finance large increases in investment expenditures for very long (Gutelman, 1967, Ch. 7).

Consequently, the next stage of development will concentrate on exploiting Cuba's ample mineral resources. Although more costly than agriculture, the import content of new investment for this sector is lower and the production of exportable surpluses is higher than alternative industries. Present plans call for the development of metallurgical industries to tap the vast laterite reserves in Oriente province for the production of nickel, cobalt, alumina, chromium, iron, steel and subproducts. Other industries planned for this period are to be based on sugar products and Cuba's as yet undeveloped forest potential.

Agriculture and metallurgy are to pro-

---

3. The description of Cuban economic policy since 1963 is based on official documents and speeches by various ministers. One of the most informative documents (Third Interregional Seminar..., 1968) formed the basis for this section. In the last part of this article we shall analyze the production data to see if and to what degree this strategy was actually followed.

vide the basis for the development of an export base and the financing of industrial capacity for the further diversification of the economy aiming ultimately towards the goal of balanced production in accordance with the planners' and/or the consumers' demands. The present strategy, which increases the economy's dependence on sugar and other agricultural products, is eventually expected to lead to a more diversified economic structure in which agricultural and mineral products will play a much less important role.

Among the many difficulties which the turnpike approach may present is the danger that vested interests created during the development process will resist changes to achieve the final goal. If, for example, the ultimate goal is the realization of maximum sustainable consumption levels 20 years from now, and if, as the date for switching from the accumulation of additional capital goods nears, the pressure for continued emphasis on accumulation of additional productive capacity increases, the (new) planners may yield and continue to emphasize the production of basic and intermediate goods. Thus, the attractiveness of high growth rates may force a further postponement of the planned transformation to consumer goods production.

Deciding how large a proportion of income will be devoted to investment rather than to consumption may create a similar conflict. In most situations and with most strategies, it is possible to achieve faster rates of growth with more investment. The temptation to divert resources to investment goods may be greater with the turnpike strategy than in other cases because it is necessary to channel a substantial proportion of a nation's investment budget explicitly into activities which will not satisfy the immediate consumption demands of the population. Those who are interested in maximizing the rate of growth by keeping investments high will have to challenge those who want to increase existing consumption levels.

A further difficulty arises when selecting production techniques. Choices often have to be made between highly mechanized and labor intensive production processes. The selection of the appropriate technology may be difficult because of the conflicting goals of absorbing people into productive activities in which they make a social contribution and the need to increase labor productivity as rapidly as possible in order to raise income. With the modernization of production it often becomes increasingly expensive to create employment for additional workers. Mechanized production requires more investment and is often more efficient than human beings. Thus, if labor absorption is a problem, a conflict between economic and social goals may arise.

The most difficult decision is the actual selection of the industries on which to build the development effort. The turnpike strategy is a supply-oriented approach. It assumes that new production can be used either directly or after trade for further growth and the eventual transformation of the economy. Many less developed countries find it difficult to finance capital equipment with which to continue the growth process. Domestically, the market is restricted by the concentration of personal incomes in the hands of a small group of people. Internationally, it is unlikely that it will be easy to obtain all of the necessary capital equipment through trade because export markets for many products are growing slowly and open to competition from many other countries with similar problems and capabilities. Foreign investment might provide some of the needed resources. But the drain on domestic resources for the payment of interest and amortization of foreign capital and the profits remitted to foreign investors is a substantial barrier to further accumulation and therefore not acceptable to the Cubans as a long-term source of financing for the investment process.

The turnpike strategy is by no means free of tolls. Eventually the Cubans will have to face the problem of "getting off."

The Social and Political Framework

The Cubans are chary about sacrificing social goals of the Revolution to rapid economic growth. From the very beginning, it was clear that Castro had undertaken an ideological commitment to eliminate unemployment—the bane of the peasant in prerevolutionary Cuba. Castro (1953:61) pointed out that there were "... 600,000 Cubans without work, who desire to earn their daily bread honestly without having to emigrate in search of a livelihood." A survey conducted in 1958 spelled out the situation in greater detail. The average unemployment rate was about 16.4 percent; the underemployed were estimated to comprise as much as 30.2 percent of the population. The situation was much worse during the "dead" season from August to October, when 20.5 percent of the labor force was fully unemployed. During the height of the sugar harvest the figure fell to 9.1 percent (Consejo Nacional de Economía, 1958). Guevara expressed the leadership's concern with the adverse effects of unemployment in a speech to an assembly of workers:

Now, the duty of our revolutionary government is, above all, in economic terms, to take care of the unemployed, in the first place; to take care of the underemployed in the second place. That is why we have fought hard against wage increases because wage increases also mean one less man working. The nation's capital is a hard fact. We cannot create it with a little printing press. The more money we create, the less that money is worth. So that capital is a single entity, and with that capital we have got to develop our country. We have to plan carefully so that each industry, each field worked, is the one that gives the most employment, because our duty ... first of all, before anything else, to see to it that no one goes without food in Cuba; then, to see that everyone eats daily; after that, in addition to that, to see that everyone in Cuba dresses and lives decently; later, to see to it that everyone has the right to free medical attention and a free education [Gerassi, 1968: 99].

He went on to say that "by the end of 1962... we want to eradicate unemployment in Cuba" (Gerassi, 1968:107). Although Guevara later pointed out that: "In a regime of social justice the contradictions between technical advance and full employment must be resolved through unproductive expenditures" (Gerassi, 1968:199-200). Cuba did not, however, have to take this route. Rather it made a frontal attack on the problems of insufficient infrastructure and educational, medical, and other social services during the first years of the Revolution which required many workers. Efforts to fully utilize existing productive capacity and create new industries abosrbed still more people. Finally, the belligerent attitude of the United States made it necessary to maintain many thousands of potential workers under wraps in an economy that was straining to increase physical production. Thus, workers were absorbed productively in constructing homes, roads, dams, etc.; expanding agricultural land and farming it more intensively; introducing new crops and technology; producing agricultural inputs and processing agricultural products; education and other social services; and defense.

By the time the change in economic strategy was decided upon, Cuba's problem was how to allocate its relatively limited manpower in the most efficient possible manner given the low levels of education and training which were substantially reducing productivity. The sizeable exodus of trained workers and professionals in all fields as the Revolution proceeded contributed to the decline in productivity and emphasized the need to invest a large proportion of all resources in educating the population.

Since there was work for everyone, it was easier to implement the egalitarian distribution policies. One of the first effects of the Revolution was the redistribution of real income from the urban centers to the rural peasantry. Almost from the beginning, people's stores, guaranteed prices, improved social services, higher rural wages and construction programs were established for the beneift of the peasant. As Ania Francos (1962:56) said, "one thing is certain: nothing is too good for the peasants."[4]

The egalitarian ideas so glibly mouthed in other revolutionary settings became an important precept guiding policy-making; they probably lost the present regime many of its middle-class supporters, but they created the ideological basis for an important mobilization of labor in present-day Cuba. These ideas had an important influence on the final decision to abandon material incentives as a reward for work which was announced in 1966. Castro's decision climaxed a long debate among many of the members of Cuba's Council of Economic Ministers and several prominent European Marxists about the appropriate way of motivating people to work at their fullest capacity and contribute to national goals. The "Great Debate" about these issues between 1963 and 1965 reflected an encounter with the economic problems that forced the initial shift in development strategy. The advocates of revolutionary ethics, led by Guevara with support from Ernest Mandel and others, confronted the supporters of economic rationality, spearheaded by Carlos Rafael Rodríguez with backing from Charles Bettleheim, René Dumont and others.

These groups also reflected the competing forms of economic organization then prevalent in Cuba; under Guevara's tutelage, the industrial sector moved rapidly towards central control and direction while in agriculture, Carlos Rafael Rodríguez had created a decentralized system of self-finance within a general framework of central planning and with the retention of material incentives.[5]

One factor that contributed to the move to moral incentives was the scarcity of goods and the inability to provide large wage differentials. Furthermore, in order to fulfill the short-run planting and harvesting goals in agriculture, substantial numbers of workers were needed for menial and unskilled tasks. Large wage differentials would have been needed to induce workers to leave jobs which often required more skills and were more productive. Unpaid voluntary labor was a logical solution and when combined with increasing real incomes of the peasantry and a growing labor force, the pressure on food and other goods forced the government to impose rationing regulations. From the government's point of view, this move was essential if the ambitious investment plans for the following years were to be implemented without causing inflationary pressures which "would have been nothing short of a ruthless sacrifice of those sectors of the population with the least income" (Castro, 1970).

The ration program began with meat and has progressively expanded to include almost all food items, clothing and consumer durables. Now there are few things not subject to rationing, and they are all in great demand. It is not uncommon to see long lines waiting to purchase unrationed goods such as restaurant meals, transportation, hotel reservations, ice cream and even pencils when they are available. Books and magazines are sold out almost as soon as they are published.

Although there are still large differences in the money wages of different groups of people, variations in real wages are considerably narrower because of the high prices of nonrationed goods. Since the prices of rationed goods are controlled, most people in Cuba have the financial resources to purchase their full quota. The amount of nonrationed goods which a person can obtain depends upon his money income and the time he has to search for products to buy. There has been concerted effort to divorce money earnings from productivity by reducing wage differentials and by asking workers not to request pay for overtime. Equalization is further reinforced by the elimina-

---

4. Dumont (1964) strongly criticized the early policies of the Cuban government to redistribute income to the peasants; see his section on "The dangerous generosity of the Cuban revolutionaries."

5. For a fuller description of the evolution of this debate, including a complete presentation of all the important contributions, see Silverman (1971). He also wrote an important article (1969) evaluating the role of moral incentives in Cuban development from which most of the above material is taken.

tion of most property income and the provision of an increasing range of social services like education, medical care, day-care centers, cultural activities and tourist facilities.

The egalitarian orientation was reflected in the heavy emphasis on education in the early years and the continued efforts to upgrade technical preparation of the people. In prerevolutionary Cuba, more than one-quarter of the population was illiterate in contrast to the 3 percent of the population in similar straits today. The spectacular campaign to eradicate illiteracy was superseded by an ambitious educational program; the proportion of the population attending school was doubled. Immediately prior to the Revolution, 835,000 students, or 12.8 percent of the population attended some kind of school in Cuba; in 1967, the number was 2.2 million people or 26.6 percent. Of these, about 425,000 were in adult education programs (JUCEPLAN 1967:35).[6]

The usual social dislocations accompanying mechanization are of less concern to the Cubans because of the many new jobs which remain unfilled. The objective of liberating men from alienating work reinforced the decision to mechanize, and when combined with egalitarian principles led the planners to search for ways to eliminate unpleasant tasks. Careful cost analyses are made of the relative efficiency of alternative methods of mechanizing production, but social (nonmarket) considerations play an important role in influencing decisions about the allocation of labor. The dislike for and the difficulty of cutting cane combined with the need for additional labor in other activities tend to place a high premium on designing a mechanized cane-cutter. Other tasks being mechanized for a combination of reasons based on economic and humanistic criteria are the transfer of cane to carts which take it to the mills and the transportation of cement, sugar and other bulk commodities. These innovations are understandable and rational only when distasteful tasks themselves are considered to be a costly use of manpower.

Economic Effects of the Social and Political Context

Since the Cuban development program transformed a labor surplus economy into one with a labor shortage, it is not surprising that heavy emphasis was placed on raising the technological level of the economy. Castro and other leaders repeatedly stressed the importance to a developing country of being in the vanguard of technological development and of constantly applying the knowledge developed elsewhere.

Technology was but one element in the effort to raise labor productivity. The massive educational effort also contributed by preparing thousands of trained technicians and other personnel. In the first years of the Revolution, the many skilled people who had emigrated had to be replaced. Subsequently, manpower programs were drawn up, and educational programs were developed to supply needed skilled personnel at both intermediate and advanced levels.

As increasing numbers of trained operators become available, labor productivity can also be raised by mechanizing production. The principal thrust of this effort is presently in agriculture where traditional production methods are being used side by side with the most modern ones. One of the most striking achievements is the almost complete mechanization of rice cultivation.

The manpower needs of the development effort also make it imperative to raise the labor participation rate and increase the length of the working day. Women are being encouraged to assume jobs formerly performed by men and to participate actively in new productive enterprises. School children are spending a part of their time in productive work. All workers are being asked to contribute extra hours of voluntary labor to help meet production goals. The use of voluntary labor is an attempt to deal with an

---

6. For a more complete description of Cuba's educational achievements, including a discussion of recent innovations, see Liner (1970).

important short-run problem of labor scarcity. As the mechanization program expands during the coming years fewer workers will be needed in agriculture and the mobilization for the harvest will be less disruptive. Although these efforts have been successful in increasing the number of man-hours worked, declining labor productivity and inefficient organization have vitiated part of their value.

Although new investments and education offer the promise of rising productivity in traditional occupations and of ience suggests that the Cubans will face a continuing problem of declining productivity in traditional occupations and of increasing absenteeism. Both of these problems are, in part, a reflection of the success of the rationing program and the redistribution efforts to improve, at the expense of the urban dweller, the material welfare of the rural peasant. However, the organizational inefficiency of these policies has contributed to disturbing declines in crop yields and the inefficient use of capital equipment.

Mechanization is one of the ways in which declining labor productivity can be counteracted. Not only does the addition of capital equipment make it possible for men to be more productive, it often spurs productivity further by pacing workers at a rate determined by a machine's capacity. If this can be achieved, then perhaps some of the built-in tendencies for labor productivity to decline with the elimination of material incentives will be counteracted. For some time to come, however, it seems likely that there will continue to be some sacrifice in production as a result of both the improvement in human welfare and the implementation of a program of moral incentives. At the end of the initial development stage, when some judgment can be made about the overall productive capacity of the agricultural sector, the cost of this sacrifice may be measurable.

The revised development strategy adopted by the Cubans is a response to the severe limitations of their present export capacity and a reflection of their immediate agricultural potential. An increasingly well-educated population is being asked to exert itself more than ever before in spite of the fact that all are guaranteed a minimum standard of living. The Cubans were promised that, after a few years of material sacrifice required by the turnpike strategy, production would increase rapidly enabling them to enjoy a higher standard of living in a more egalitarian society. Cuba would be a showcase of socialist development, vindicating the challenge to United States imperialism. After the erosion of the initial optimism, however, it has become clear that the new society will require more than a few years to construct.

Economic Data

What does economic development mean to the Cuban worker? Although the data are incomplete,[7] they do clearly suggest that the vast majority, who were poor before the Revolution, are materially better off in spite of the fact that aggregate production has grown slowly. Milk, meat, eggs, clothing and many other commodities, though rationed, are still more accessible to the poor than they were previously.[8] Some goods are not rationed and, like ice cream, can be obtained by queueing. Public education and medical care are also more readily available, especially outside of Havana.

The test imposed by the turnpike strategy, however, lies in the volume of resources withheld from consumption. Investment funds have to be used for the development of efficient industries and for the steady expansion of productive capacity. Foreign exchange is also required for these tasks. In this section we shall evaluate the ways in which the

---

7. It is difficult to judge how reliable these data are. For an evaluation of statistical material in Cuba see Mesa-Lago (1969). The data, at a minimum, provide a general picture of economic progress and problems in Cuba.

8. Some indication of the changes can be gleaned from a comparison of a survey made by the Agrupación Católica Universitaria in 1957 and the present level of rations published in Dumont (1970).

COMPARATIVE INTERNATIONAL DEVELOPMENT

Table 1 Cuba, Principal Economic Indicators 1959-68[1]

	1959	1960	1961	1962	1963	1964	1965	1966	1968
Population[d,5]	6693	6826	6939	7068	7236	7434	7631	7800	8074
Labor Force[d]				1822	1851	1883	1960	1992	
National Income[b]				3510	3544	3857	3888	3727	
per capita[a]				497	490	519	510	478	
State Investments[b]				608	717	795	827	910	
Total Consumption[b,e]				2908	3050	3269	3362	3246	
per capita consumption[a]				352	367	324	378	355	
Net Trade Balance[b]				-95	-293	-433	172	-308	
Government budget[c]	390[2]	756[2]	1330[2]	1854	2087	2419	2639	2718	
Investment as a Proportion of GNP:			17.9	16.5	19.1	19.5	20.0	24.0	31.0[3]
Sectoral Distribution of Investment:									
Directly Productive Investment			100.0	100.0	100.0	100.0			
Agriculture			51.5[2]	68.3[4]	72.2[4]	79.0[4]			
Industry			16.8[2]	27.8[4]	21.6[4]	33.3[4]			
Social Services			15.7[2]	21.7[4]	30.4[4]	27.4[4]			
			48.5[2]	31.7[4]	27.8[4]	21.0[4]			
Structure of Investment									
Machinery and Equipment			100.0	100.0	100.0	100.0	100.0	100.0	
Construction			23.7[2]	29.2	41.8	38.8	34.3	37.8	
Other			66.9[2]	60.1	37.4	43.4	53.0	48.2	
			9.4[2]	10.7	10.8	17.8	12.7	14.0	

Sources and Notes:
1. Unless otherwise noted all figures are from UCLA (1970).
2. UN (1963).
3. Mesa-Lago (1969b), planned levels.
4. JUCEPLAN (1964).
5. JUCEPLAN (1967).

a) 1965 prices.
b) millions of 1965 pesos.
c) millions of current pesos.
d) thousands.
e) includes government consumption expenditures.

leadership has translated aspirations for rapid development into concrete plans for allocating resources towards the appropriate sectors of the economy.

Aggregate Production

Since the Revolution, the population of Cuba has been growing at slightly more than 2.5 percent per year. This has been counterbalanced by a 0.5 percent rate of emigration since 1961 (JUCEPLAN, 1967:14). In 1970 there were approximately 8.3 million people living on the island. The labor force has been growing somewhat more slowly as people have emigrated. The significant upswing in the participation of women in the workforce has raised the proportion of people in the labor force to about 30 percent. The number of people working in agriculture, industry and commerce has remained relatively stable, except for the seasonal demands of the sugar harvest. Production increases in these three sectors are being achieved by increasing machinery and labor. Additional workers are being used in public services, like education, medicine and construction.

Real national income has gone up. It rose about 11 percent between 1962 and 1965, but then fell back to 6 percent (when measured in constant 1965 pesos) with the drop in sugar production in 1966. This means that per capita income has hovered about its 1962 level of $500. Per capita consumption rose 7.4 percent between 1962 and 1965, but some belt tightening was called for when the drop in national income led the Cubans to restrict individual consumption to its 1962 level. These figures are all expressed in aggregate per capita terms which means that the total consumption fund has increased enough to provide similar amounts of consumption for the increase in population.[9]

While consumption levels have been held constant, governmental expenditures have been rising rapidly to help finance large increases in both social services and productive activities. State investment rose by about 50 percent between 1962 and 1966; by 1966 it was almost one-quarter of GNP. Although spectacular increases in spending occurred in science and technology (122 percent), and for sports and recreational purposes (136 percent), the bulk of these expenditures was allocated to industrial and agricultural activities (UCLA, 1970).

These aggregate data reflect a policy of freezing or even lowering personal consumption levels in order to divert resources to investment and to the provision of collective consumption services. This confirms the visitor's impression that consumption levels for rationed goods, which now encompass almost the entire range of consumer goods, were further restricted during 1969 and 1970 as part of the effort to make more resources available for the sugar harvest. At the same time there has been a steady improvement in the quantity and quality of governmental services like education, medical care, child-care centers and other collective consumption goods. This reflects the changing orientation of the Cuban economy towards the improvement of living standards through collective rather than individual means.

Material resources, meanwhile, are being withheld from individual consumption to permit dramatic increases in investment to raise the productive capacity of the country. The proportion of GNP

---

9. Interviews with peasants and an examination of some of the findings of a 1957 expenditure survey (Agrupación Católica Universitaria, 1957) indicate that consumption levels are still higher than they were for the lower strata of the population before the Revolution. The per capita figures must be used with extreme caution as the distribution of consumption has changed dramatically and a large number of former upper-class members have emigrated. In addition, as pointed out below, large increases in collective consumption raised living standards without raising personal income figures.

10. Thus, in contrast to 1962, shortages of consumer goods in recent years were planned to permit an increase in the rate of investment. It seems, however, that some of the shortages which appeared during the 1970 harvest were unexpected (Castro, 1970).

Table 2 Cuba, Principal Agricultural Products 1948-69[1,2]

	1948/52	1952/56	1959	1960	1961	1962	1963
Agricultural Products							
Sugar	5786	5002	5964	5862[5]	6767[5]	4815[5]	3821[5]
Goal						6141	
Coffee	31.2	38.4	48.0	42.0	37.0	52.2[7]	34.7[7]
Tobacco	32.4	36.9	41.1	52.2	47.2	51.5	47.9
Rice - husk	164	206	282	307	213	230	237
Corn	275	174	193	214	160	152	140
Citrus Fruits	55	75	70[6]	73[6]	91[6]	117[6]	86
Livestock, Meat and Poultry							
Cattle - million head	4.2	4.1			5.8[6]	5.8[6]	6.2
Meat: beef	179	171				196[3,8]	227[3,8]
pork	36	37					39
Milk	460	723	979	1130	1281	1185	1827[3,7]
Eggs	312	316	400	490	580	660	750
Fish		22.0[4,6]		30.1[6]	30.4[10]	35.5[10]	35.5[10]
Value of All Agricultural Products (million pesos)							840.5

Sources and Notes:
1. All data are from FAO (1968) unless otherwise noted.
2. All quantities are in thousand metric tons unless otherwise noted.
3. Government procurements only.
4. 1957.
5. International Sugar Council.
6. UN (1963) based on data from JUCEPLAN.

invested rose from 18 percent in 1961 to 24 percent in 1966. The planned rise for 1968 was to 31 percent.[10] This is a very revealing indicator of the sacrifices being asked of the Cuban people.

New priorities were evident as the large increase in investment funds was channeled towards new activities. With the maturation of the development programs, a steadily rising share of all investment has been shifted into production rather than social services which, in the early years of the Revolution, had received almost one-half of the new investment. While the percentage of social welfare investments declined by almost 45 percent in 1961-1964, industrial and agricultural investments doubled their proportion of the steadily increasing investment fund. In 1964, these two strategic sectors received 60 percent of the investment budget. The switch to agricultural production resulted in a 50 percent increase in its share of total investment, while industrial investment remained almost constant (in 1965 pesos) and declined slightly in relative terms.

The decision to aim for a sugar harvest of 10 million tons in 1970 is also reflected in the investment figures. In 1964, the first year after the introduction of the turnpike strategy, total investments in the sugar industry in both the agricultural and industrial sectors accounted for as much as 15 percent of the total budget; 8.7 percent of the industrial investments was programmed for the sugar industry (UN, 1963:287), while one-third of all investments in agriculture were for sugar production and related facilities (Aranda, 1968:76). These improvements clearly became even heavier in later years as

CUBAN AGRICULTURE

Table 2 Continued

1964	1965	1966	1967	1968	1970	Agricultural Products
4398	6015	4455	6129	5100	8535	Sugar
6500	7000	6500	7500	8000	10000	Goal
	32.0[7]	23.9[7]	33.4[7]			Coffee
	43.8[7]	43.7	51.2	51.2		Tobacco
123[11]	50[11]	68[11]	93	50[9]		Rice - husk
129	117	127	120			Corn
112	111	160	167			Citrus Fruits
						Livestock, Meat and Poultry
6.4	6.6	6.7	6.8			Cattle - million head
269[3,8]	310[3,8]	326[3,8]				Meat: beef
44	48	50	50			pork
2906[3,7]	2606[3,7]	3092[3,7]				Milk
830	911[8]	1011[8]	1185[8]	1191[9]		Eggs
36.4[10]	40.3[10]	43.2[10]	62.9[10]			Fish
889.6	973.6	969.5				Value of All Agricultural Products (million pesos)

7. UCLA (1970).
8. FAO (1967).
9. Bohemia (1970).
10. JUCEPLAN (1964).
11. Gutelman (1967).

production was stepped up in the agricultural machinery industry and as new plantings increased in sugar cane areas. Expenditures were also needed for collection centers where cane is prepared for shipment to the mills. These centers are an important Cuban innovation. Located in the fields, they save on transport costs and manpower; the cane cutter now makes one cut instead of the three or more previously customary for the longer hauls.

Production Data

According to the production data for individual crops (Table 2) the hopes for rapid increase in output have not yet been realized for some of the most important products. The most publicized failure is the sugar harvest, which has had a bumpy career since the spectacular success in 1961. At that time, large areas of cane were uprooted in an effort to diversify the agricultural economy and lessen Cuba's dependence on sugar. Subsequent efforts to increase production and stabilize the harvest at a new higher level of output have not yet met with success. Seven years was simply not enough time for the ambitious sugar program. In spite of these disappointments and the sharp fluctuations in output, the average production, 5.6 million tons, during the first 11 years of the Revolutionary government (1959-69) is slightly more than the 5.3 million ton average of the previous decade.

Needless to say, the frustration was hard to bear after the long years of sacrifice and great expectations. Now, however, the new investments in cane

Table 3 Cuba, Selected Industrial Products[1,2]

	1958	1959	1960	1961	1962	1963	1964	1965	1966	1967	1968
Fertilizers											
Production:											
Nitrogenous	13.8(52/56)									5.0	10.0
Phosphate									15.0	15.0	10.0
Consumption:											
Nitrogen	15.2			36.0	40.0	48.8	63.6	76.0	100.0	105.0	120.0
Phosphate	11.4			33.0	35.0	43.9	63.6	75.0	80.0	50.0	100.0
Potash				25.0	30.0	40.1	45.1	50.0	60.0	75.0	85.0
Cement 405(53)	750	663	813	871	779	812	806	801	800	800	
Electricity[3]											
Millions kwh	1795	1993	2145	2237	2258	2344	2494	2592	2813	3019	
Installed capacity 000kw	464	939	944	956	966	976	976	976	1100		
Nickel[3] million tons	18.0	17.9	14.5	18.1	24.9	21.6	24.1	29.1	27.9	34.9	
Textiles million m²											
Cotton cloth	60 (57)					60.4	105	96	92.0		
Wool					94	90			108		
Shoes million pairs						11.8			12.6		
Beer million liters	118.8(53)155.7		88	139.4	92.7	89.1	103.6	99.3	108.8		
Index of Industrial Production		78			95	100	107	116	119[a]		

Sources and Notes:
1. Unless otherwise noted all quantities are in 1,000 metric tons.
2. All data are from UN (1968) unless otherwise noted.
3. Fidel Castro, 2 January 1968, quoted in Huberman and Sweezy (1969).
a) Estimate based on data from UCLA (1970).

fields, cutting and transportation machinery and milling capacity may begin to pay off, as mechanical and administrative problems are ironed out. A pressing task of the current decade will be to correct some of the imbalances arising from the great national effort to achieve the 10 million tons of sugar in 1970. After an extended harvest and a massive mobilization of human and material resources Cuba was able to produce a record 8.5 million tons of refined sugar.

The organizational problems and technical imbalances that emerged during the 1970 harvest are symptomatic of the disjuncture between the physical availability of productive capacity and the inability to use it effectively. Although more than enough cane was available to produce 10 million tons of sugar, only 8.5 million were produced because of mechanical failures in the mills, transportation bottlenecks, and inadequate coordination mechanisms. The 1970 experience suggests, furthermore, that if production goals for other products are to be given priority in the coming years, it may be necessary to continue to restrict sugar harvest to less than the 10 million ton level.

Following sugar, livestock is the next most important product in the first stage of the development program. The present goal is a herd of about 12.5 million head by 1975, about three times its size in the early fifties. According to Cuban estimates, this will permit an adequate supply of milk and meat for domestic consumption, in addition to between $10 and $15 million of exports annually. Recent increases in milk and meat production have been substantial. They are still insufficient, however, to meet higher domestic consumption demands. Both products are imported and rationed.

Citrus fruit, tobacco and coffee production are all being expanded for export. The rapid expansion of the first two reflects recent increased plantings. Fruit production will continue to grow rapidly as new plantings mature; a quadrupling of the area planted with citrus trees is planned. Coffee output declined in the private sector where it is traditionally grown; recent plantings on state farms are not yet reflected in production figures.

With the adoption of new technology, egg and fish production have expanded rapidly, and both are being exported in small quantities. Industrialized techniques are used for egg production, and a modern fleet of fishing vessels has been acquired. Rice production declined precipitously after the signing of a trade agreement with the Chinese. When political difficulties arose, Cuba initiated a crash program to increase plantings which should be reflected in this year's figures. Cuba expects to be self-sufficient in rice by 1971.

Large investments have been made in industries which are directly related to agriculture. Two notable efforts are the expansion of milling capacity in the sugar industry and the construction of two large fertilizer manufacturing units. Additional capacity for the production of cement and electricity is being installed. Some indicators of this progress are provided in Table 3. In 1967, the promises of substantial increases in electricity production were just beginning to be fulfilled. Additional cement capacity had clearly not yet been completed. On the other hand, some fertilizer plants have been built, and more have been put "on stream" since 1967. The figures also suggest that it may be easier for Cuba to increase its production indices in the early seventies as current construction projects are completed.

All of these programs, in both the agricultural and industrial sectors, were affected by the effort to harvest 10 million tons of sugar in 1970. This effort, which began slowly and steadily grew to a crescendo in 1970, required the diversion of rapidly increasing quantities of resources, both human and material, from other activities to the sugar sector. Unfulfilled production goals were apparent in all sectors of the economy long before the well-publicized failures analyzed by Castro in his now famous speech of 26 July 1970.

These shortfalls in production, how-

Table 4 Cuba, Foreign Trade 1954-67

	1954		1958		1960		1962		1964		1966		1967	
	X	M	X	M	X	M	X	M	X	M	X	M	X	M
Total Trade														
millions of pesos	539.0	487.9	733.5	777.0	618.2	637.9	520.7	759.3	713.8	1018.8	592.5	925.5		
(merchandise) balance	+52.1		−43.5		−19.7		−238.6		−305.0		−333.0			
By Area (%)														
Capitalist	99.9	99.8	81.1	99.7	75.8	81.3	18.0	17.2	40.8	32.5	18.6	20.2	18.6	20.9
United States	68.5	75.5	67.1	69.6	52.8	48.5	0.8	0.8	0.0	4.1	0.0	0.0	0.0	0.0
Japan	4.2	0.6	6.4	0.6	2.4	1.6	4.9	1.4	7.0	4.0	2.4	0.5	2.6	0.9
Spain	2.1	2.0	2.4	1.7	1.2	2.1	1.7	0.2	9.5	3.8	5.5	8.1	4.6	2.9
France	0.8	0.8	1.1	0.9	1.4	2.0	0.3	0.2	0.4	1.8	1.7	1.4	2.2	4.1
Socialist	0.1	0.2	18.9	0.3	24.3	18.7	82.0	82.8	59.2	67.5	81.4	79.8	81.4	79.1
U.S.S.R.	0.1	—	14.1	—	16.7	13.8	42.3	54.2	38.5	40.2	46.2	56.3	52.1	58.3
China	—	—	3.6	—	5.2	1.7	17.1	11.8	11.4	10.7	14.7	9.3	11.1	7.3
East Germany	—	—	—	—	0.1	0.7	4.7	3.5	2.2	3.7	5.2	3.9	5.1	5.0
Czechoslovakia	—	0.2	—	0.3	0.2	1.2	7.1	4.9	2.1	6.3	7.8	3.9	5.8	3.6
By Commodity (%)														
Sugar and by-products	80.5		80.1		79.4		83.0		87.4		85.0		90.0[4]	
Tobacco	7.5		6.8		10.2		4.8		4.1		2.5		n.a.	
Ores	5.6		3.8		3.8		7.2		5.8		8.0		7.5[3]	
Coffee	n.a.		1.0		0.7		1.3		0.0		0.0		n.a.	
Food		30.6[1]		22.2[1]		13.5[2]		20.5		22.5		20.7[3]		21.3[3]
Fuels		8.0		10.5[2]				10.8		8.7		9.9[3]		9.4[3]
Raw Materials and Internal goods		n.a.		25.2[2]		30.6[2]		30.8[2]		23.1[1]		n.a.		n.a.
Fixed capital goods		n.a.		22.6[2]		23.6[2]		34.2[2]		31.1[1]		n.a.		n.a.

Sources and notes:
Unless otherwise noted all data are from UN Yearbooks of International Trade Statistics.
Area Trade: 1960-67: JUCEPLAN (1967).
Commodity Trade: these figures are approximate as definitions change among sources.
1. University of Miami (1965)
2. UN (1963)
3. JUCEPLAN (1967)
4. JUCEPLAN (1967). Includes all food, drink and tobacco.

ever, need not mask the basic outlines of the Cuban development strategy. The failure to achieve specific production goals at their appointed times corresponds to a series of organizational problems and an excess of optimism by the leadership about the possibilities of overcoming the heritage of underdevelopment. Had the 1970 sugar harvest goal been set at 8.5 million tons instead of 10 million tons (as suggested by Gutelman [1967] in 1966), the sacrifices in the rest of the economy might have been less: fewer resources need have been diverted from other areas and a more rational coordination of scarce transportation facilities and human resources might have been possible.

Nevertheless, current production programs indicate that the basic determination to continue with the development strategy described above has not waned in spite of the disappointing results of the 1970 harvest. Carlos Rafael Rodríguez (1970) was quite clear about this in his recent speech to the XI Regional Conference of the FAO. With a fuller appreciation of the interrelationship between sugar and other sectors of the economy, it is likely that less emphasis will be placed on sugar in the coming years; livestock breeding programs continue according to schedule even as transportation bottlenecks caused disturbing declines in milk and meat deliveries to the consumers. Some of the planting goals for fruit and coffee were affected by the massive mobilizations of 1970 but there is no indication that less emphasis will be placed on ensuring rapidly growing fruit exports in the coming years. The construction of basic elements of the agro-industrial branches, like the fertilizer complex in Cienfuegos, were also affected only marginally by the events prior to and during the 1970 harvest.

The Role of Foreign Trade

Cuba's dependence on sugar in international trade continues and became even more intense as production increased. Exports are not yet growing while the need for imports is rising (Table 4). As a result, Cuba has faced a steadily growing negative balance of trade. This deficit is now financed primarily by the socialist countries. Eighty percent of Cuba's trade has been redirected from the capitalist countries (most notably the United States prior to 1961) to the socialist countries with the Soviet Union dominating. Whereas the United States in the fifties accounted for more than two-thirds of both imports and exports, the Soviet Union now takes up about one-half of all trade.

The historical reliance on food imports is not easily overcome, as recent Cuban experience demonstrates. However, industrialization and the restrictive consumption policies have forced a trade-off between food imports and capital equipment. Prior to the Revolution, food imports declined from their 1952 high of 30 percent of all imports to a low of 22.2 percent in 1958, but this was compensated by an increase in the imports of consumer durables. During the past ten years, food imports have comprised more than one-fifth of the total, but the importation of fixed capital equipment has increased by about 40 percent from the 1958 level of 22.6 percent.

Conclusion

The striking contrast between the hopes to rapidly raise income levels and the frustrations encountered in implementing the Cuban development strategy requires some discussion. For almost eight years the Cubans have been investing steadily increasing proportions of total resources and, consequently, restraining the volume of resources available for consumption. A natural question, given the persistence of tightly restricted consumption, is whether these investments have been fruitless or when will they begin to raise national production.

The heavy investments of recent years were for productive capacity for sugar, livestock, and citrus fruit production. In addition to the large deficit in economic infrastructure (roads, reservoirs, electricity, etc.) which had to be provided to permit an expansion in agricultural production, other investments in the agro-industrial complex (fertilizers, machinery, cement, etc.) accounted for a large proportion of total investment.

These investments were principally in intermediate goods production which were not designed to directly affect the volume of final goods available for consumption or export. Instead, they were designed to facilitate the success of other production plans. This is the meaning of long-term planning in the way it is used in this paper—the immediate implementation of programs which will permit a more rapid rise in production in the future; increased fertilizer capacity and reservoirs are the clearest examples of this approach. It is expected that after a suitable gestation period, there will be a rapid rise in the production of products using these inputs.

This is the strategy followed by the Cubans but they overlooked the difficulties that they would confront in implementing it. Most of the problems that have arisen are the result of a series of assumptions about the ability of the people to perform at productive levels near those obtained under experimental or laboratory conditions; little allowance was provided for human or material fallibility—and without productive reserves to cushion individual failures the shocks were transmitted throughout the system.

This was further compounded by a problem which many have criticized—Castro's unbending desire to set and maintain unrealistic production goals. It is not a question of their being unachievable or not but rather the consequences for the rest of the economy while trying to reach them. Thus, the unchallenged priority accorded to sugar in recent years required the abandonment of many other sectors of the economy. The sacrifices in the other sectors would have been just as great had the 10-million-ton goal been achieved; its underachievement was the result of problems in the utilization of milling capacity and in human errors of coordination—not a lack of physical capacity.

Throughout the past decade the one lesson which has been repeatedly demonstrated is the very heavy burden of the heritage which underdevelopment left in Cuba. The lack of skills, industrial discipline, economic and social infrastructure, and myriad other factors are having their impact on the fulfillment of productive goals. At every juncture problems arise because of insufficient information, inadequate experience and skills, missing physical or human inputs and many other lacunae; they are not felt as strongly in other underdeveloped countries because the concentration of effort in trying to overcome these defects is much less—as are the achievements. Perhaps one of the most unfortunate aspects of this problem is the difficulty of learning this lesson; on several occasions when analyzing past failures, there has been an explicit recognition of the importance of these problems—just recently, Carlos Rafael Rodríguez (1970) said: "We have been unable to develop evenly the subjective factors and the administrative methods to employ resources with maximum efficiency."

The 1970 experience is an excellent example of some of the problems of implementing any development strategy. The Cubans purposefully abandoned the market mechanism because of the social costs that they thought that its retention would impose. They substituted central administration and direction to mobilize people and coordinate production efforts in an economy without reserves. They did this, moreover, in an underdeveloped country without the information, skills and experience on which other socialist countries depend; the inevitable result was a series of planning and allocation errors—many of which were forseeable and predicted by such foreign advisors as Gutelman (1967) and Dumont (1970).

The Cubans continue, however, to follow the outlines of their original investment guidelines. Unlike the failures of the early sixties, the production shortcomings of 1970 have not been interpreted as revelations of fundamental contradictions in their present approach. There is little reason to doubt their ability to increase personal consumption and reduce imports of those goods which can be produced domestically as their new investments mature—although it may take more time than they planned. At the same time the Cubans anticipate the maintenance of high levels of sugar exports, while increasing those of citrus fruits, coffee and other products for which there are markets in either the capitalist or socialist countries. The first sign of the easing of domestic food pressures was the rise in the rice ration from three to six pounds during 1969; this advance was counterbalanced, however, by serious restrictions in other food products during 1970 as a result of the problems caused by the harvest. Similar increases in rations can be expected in meat, milk, tubers and sugar in the coming years in spite of the substantial underachievement with regard to planned levels in 1970. With the completion of new cement production and the labor that will gradually be liberated by agricultural mechanization during the coming decade, it should also be possible to increase home construction while maintaining the present rhythm of industrial and public works construction.

The turnpike model of development facilitates our understanding of these data. Instead of concentrating on the direct benefits which the ten years of central direction have afforded the people, we turn our attention to the productive structure of the economy which has begun to emerge with the new emphasis on investments in agriculture and industries tied to agriculture. The promise of rapidly rising output for a number of important export products and consumer goods in the coming years is exactly what one would expect from this approach. These achievements would probably have been much more difficult to realize and even slower in coming, however, were it not for the centrally directed economy and egalitarian outlook which emerged from the prevailing Marxist ideology.

The turnpike strategy imposes many difficult decisions on a government. A fine line must be drawn between increasing demands for consumption and the requirements of ambitious investment programs. Central control helps not only to implement the strategy but also to resolve many of the problems which might arise. In order to achieve the objectives rapidly, the government must be able to mobilize its people. Both effort and sacrifice are required for rapid growth. Because of the political and economic problems which might arise, it is probably impossible for a country to choose such a course unless it is able to count on a complete coincidence of a number of social, political and economic circumstances. Similarly, it is necessary to examine Cuban economic development within a broader ideological and social context to understand it more fully.

REFERENCES

Agrupación Católica Universitaria
  1957 ¿Por qué reforma agraria? Havana.
ARANDA, SERGIO
  1968 La revolución agraria en Cuba. Mexico: Siglo XXI.
Bohemia
  1970 October 16. Havana.
BOORSTEIN, EDWARD
  1968 The Economic Transformation of Cuba. New York: MR Press.
CASTRO, FIDEL
  1953 October 16. "History Will Absolve Me." Havana.
  1970 July 26 (Speech reprinted in New York Review of Books, September).
Consejo Nacional de Economía
  1958 El empleo, el subempleo y el desempleo. Havana.
DOBB, MAURICE
  1960 An Essay on Economic Growth and Planning. New York: MR Press.
DORFMAN, R., et al.
  1958 Linear Programming and Economic Analysis. New York: McGraw-Hill.
DUMONT, RENE
  1964 Cuba, socialisme et développement. Paris: Le Seuil (English language edition from Grove Press, 1970).
  1970 Cuba, est-il socialiste? Paris: Le Seuil.
FAO (Federation of Agricultural Organizations)
  1967 Agricultural and Livestock Production in Cuba. Rome: Cuban delegation to XIV session of FAO.
  1968 Production Yearbook, 1968. Rome.

FINDLAY, RONALD
  1968 "Efficient Accumulation, International Trade and the Optimum Tariff." Oxford Economic Papers 20: 208-17.
FRANCOS, ANIA
  1962 La fête cubaine. Paris: Julliard.
GERASSI, JOHN (ed.)
  1968 Venceremos! The Speeches and Writings of Che Guevara. New York: Simon & Schuster.
GUTELMAN, MICHEL
  1967 L'agriculture socialisée à Cuba. Paris: François Maspero (Spanish language edition from Era, Mexico City, 1970).
HUBERMAN, LEO, and PAUL SWEEZY
  1969 Socialism in Cuba. New York: MR Press.
International Symposium in Industrial Development
  1967 Industrial Development in Cuba. Havana: Cuban delegation to Symposium.
JOHNSON, HARRY
  1969 "A Dynamic Theory of International Economic Relations." Part II, Wicksell Lectures (reprinted in Pakistan Development Review 9, No. 1).
JUCEPLAN
  1964 Boletín Estadístico de Cuba. Havana.
  1967 Compendio Estadístico, 1967. Havana.
  1968 Compendio Estadístico, 1968. Havana.
LANCASTER, KEVIN A.
  1968 Mathematical Economics. New York: Macmillan.
LINER, MARVIN
  1970 "Cuba's Schools, Ten Years Later." Saturday Review (October 17).
MESA-LAGO, CARMELO
  1969a "Availability and Reliability of Statistics in Socialist Cuba." Latin American Research Review 4 (Spring and Summer).
  1969b "The Revolutionary Offensive." trans-action (April): 22-9, 62.
RAMSEY, FRANK
  1929 "A Mathematical Model of Savings." Economic Journal 38: 543-59.
RODRÍGUEZ, CARLOS R.
  1970 Report to the XI Regional Conference of FAO (Reprinted in Granma, October 25). Havana.
SILVERMAN, BERTRAM
  1969 "Moral Incentives: The Cuban Road to Socialism." Mimeo.
  1971 Man and Socialism in Cuba: The Great Debate. New York: Atheneum.
STRUMLIN, O.S.
  1951 "The Time Factor in Capital Investment Projects." International Economic Papers 1.
Third Interregional Seminar on Development Planning
  1968 La estrategia del desarrollo económico. Santiago de Chile: Cuban delegation to Seminar.
UN (United Nations)
  1963 "The Cuban Economy in the Period 1959-1963." Pp. 259-89 in Economic Survey for Latin America, 1963.
  1968 Statistical Yearbook, 1968. New York.
UCLA (University of California at Los Angeles)
  1968 Statistical Abstract for Latin America, 1968. Los Angeles: Latin American Center.
  1970 Cuba, 1968. Los Angeles: Latin American Center.
University of Miami
  1965 A Study on Cuba. Coral Gables: University of Miami Press for the Cuban Economic Research Project.
WANEK, JAROSLAV
  1968 Maximal Economic Growth. Ithaca: Cornell University Press.
VON NEUMANN, JOHN
  1945-46 "A Model of General Economic Equilibrium." Review of Economic Studies 13: 1-9.

APPENDIX

> Comments on the preceding article written by Instituto de Economía, Universidad de la Habana, and published in ECONOMÍA Y DESARROLLO, Vol. I, No. 3, July-September 1970. (Institute of Economics, University of Havana)

Dr. Barkin's article is a serious effort to explain the Cuban economic development strategy. It is clear that its validity for other countries and other conditions is questionable, as the author indicates, since the bases of the Cuban political, economic and social structure are not present elsewhere. But, in addition, a <u>sine qua non</u> mentioned by the author—but not sufficiently stressed—is, in the first place, the assurance—in both the short and long run—of a foreign market for the surplus of exportable production of the sector under analysis and prices which permit the generation of sufficient capital to accelerate the development process. On the other hand, —and no less important—a certain measure of confidence in the supply is required in order to establish a broad credit policy that facilitates development without requiring that the sacrifices in consumption are either extreme or prolonged.

Finally, we believe that the effect of the blockade should not be underestimated in describing the Cuban strategy of economic development in either its negative or positive aspects. In the force case it impeded the operation of the existing industry and the acquisition of raw materials as well as raising both direct and indirect costs. On the positive side, it forced us to obtain replacement factories with great urgency on a large scale, with more modern technologies and with raw materials and spare parts guaranteed.

Although, we repeat, the article is profound and exhaustive, it might have been convenient to expand the discussion of the political and social structure which facilitated the implementation of a key sector (Turnpike) strategy for the development of our country.

ECONOMIC ORGANIZATION AND SOCIAL CONSCIENCE: SOME DILEMMAS OF CUBAN SOCIALISM

Bertram Silverman*

Introduction

The confrontation between the past and the future is never more visible than in periods of revolutionary transition. During the revolutionary phase what is possible seems unlimited as the weight of oppression and tradition is lifted, and in the euphoria of newly-discovered power the present appears as an unbounded future. But the morning after is not too long in coming. As Marx so aptly wrote, "the tradition of all the dead generations weighs like a nightmare on the brain of the living. And just when they seem engaged in revolutionizing themselves and things, in creating something that has never yet existed, precisely in such periods of revolutionary crisis they anxiously conjure up the spirits of the past.."[1]

This tension between revolutionary will and historical constraint has been an on-going dialectic of the Cuban revolution. In response to the economic difficulties through which Cuba is now passing, the advocates of greater conformity to tradition are again raising their voices inside and outside Cuba. Declining worker productivity[2] is seen as a product of romantic attempts to radically alter social consciousness and to develop new systems of motivation based on social (socialistic) rather than material (capitalistic) incentives. Recently Professor Leontief argued that:

"In Cuba as in other socialist countries such moral incentives failed in their effectiveness to measure up to more conventional individualistic self-

---

* Hofstra University New York

[1] Karl Marx, *The Eighteenth Brumaire of Louis Bonaparte*, New World paperback, p. 15. The same tension between revolutionary will (voluntarism) and recognition of historic constraints are exhibited in the Eighteenth Brumaire. A few pages after this citation Marx writes: "The social revolution of the nineteenth century cannot draw its poetry from the past, but only from the future. It cannot begin with itself before it has stripped off all supersitition in regard to the past. Earlier revolutions required recollections of past world history in order to drug themselves concerning their own content. In order to arrive at its own content the revolution of the nineteenth century must let the dead bury their dead. There the phrase went beyond the content; here the content goes beyond the phrase."

[2] Cuba named 1971 the 'Year of Productivity'.

Reprinted with permission from J. Ann Zammit (ed.), THE CHILEAN ROAD TO SOCIALISM, published in 1973 by the Institute of Development Studies at the University of Sussex, England. All rights reserved.

interest...[3] In prompting an average labourer, sales clerk, manager or technician to exert himself day in and day out in steady purposeful, i.e. productive, work nothing seems as effective as a steady flow of material benefits closely commensurate with the results of his individual effort... this is not to imply however that human nature cannot change in the long run."[4]

Yet, there is no evidence presented to show the correlation between moral incentives, *per se*, and declining worker productivity. Indeed, material incentives were used extensively through 1965 and worker productivity declined during this period. Certainly one would not conclude from this evidence that material incentives are ineffective. The relationship between moral incentives and worker productivity is more complex, and cannot be disassociated from the economic organization of which it is a part.[5] This paper is primarily concerned with examining how pragmatic responses to the problems of the Cuban transition to socialism influenced economic organization and the ideological commitment to moral incentives.[6]

Marxian analysis suggests two fundamental criteria in the transformation of economic organization within a socialist society. On the one hand economic organization must be consistent with the stage of development of the social forces of production, that is, technology, skills, education, work habits, etc. On the other hand economic organization must also be consistent with the formation of socialist values and behaviour. Since all socialist revolutions have occurred in relatively backward economies, an inevitable contradiction exists between the organizational forms held to be most consistent with communist goals and the capacity to establish such an economic organization. Generally, traditional economic analysis has tended to obscure the relationship between economic organization and social character. The rationality of economic organization has been defined primarily in terms of an efficiency criterion (e.g., the rational allocation of scarce resources among competing ends). And the market and

---

[3] Leontief, W., 'The Trouble with Cuban Socialism', *The New York Review of Books*. January 7, 1971, p. 22.

[4] *Ibid.* For a similar view see the writings of Carmelo Mesa-Lago. Inside Cuba the view is expressed by those who were supporters of the system of self-management.

[5] See Benjamin Ward, *The Socialist Economy*, Random House, 1967, pp. 36-37, who argues that questions of incentives within the socialist context have hardly been explored.

[6] In this paper I have not considered the many important political factors influencing policy (e.g. U.S. imperialism) nor have I attempted to describe in any detail the changes in the structure of economic organization and planning. For the latter see Juceplan, *La planificación económica en Cuba*, Santiago de Chile, 1968.

mercantile relations were the most effective means of achieving those ends.[7]

Cuba's rejection, after 1966, of an economic organization based on the money motive reflects strong commitment to revolutionary principles and socialist ethics. Further, Cuba's revolutionary ethics do not mean an end to ideology in the Marxian sense. Cuban economic organization and developmental strategy have been closely tied to Cuban praxis, and ideology has frequently served to rationalize practice and economic policy goals. While ideology has played an important role in mobilizing mass commitment to social and economic goals, it has also had the effect of obscuring real underlying forces. Unravelling the *actual* social and economic relationships that have governed the development of economic organization may help to 'demystify' Cuban ideology: to bring theory and practice into a more conscious harmonious correspondence, i.e. to comprehend socialism in the way that Marx comprehended capitalism.[8]

From Praxis to Principle:
The Development of Cuban Economic Organization

The evolution of socialist economic organization, in this period of the transition to socialism, has historically been the dynamic result of a previously adopted socialist ideology and a pragmatic

---

[7] This is particularly evident in the discussion about the economic rationality of socialist economy. In dealing with the Mises-Lange *et al.* controversy Professor Dobb argued that "most of the socialist critics of Professor Mises have argued, in one key or another, that a socialist economy can escape the irrationality which is predicted of it if, but only if, it closely imitates the mechanism of the competitive market and consents to be ruled by the *values which this market affirms."* (my emphasis). Maurice Dobb, *Political Economy and Capitalism,* International Publishers, 1945, p. 273. Of course, there have been outstanding social scientists who have seen this relationship, e.g., Marx, Weber, Polanyi, Fromm, Riesman to name just a few.

[8] Marx's analysis of ideology is illustrated in the following passage: "In considering such transformations (social revolutions) the distinction should always be made between the material transformation of the economic conditions of production, which can be determined with the precision of natural science, and the legal, political, religious, aesthetic or philosophic — in short, ideological forms in which men become conscious of this conflict and fight it out. Just as our opinion of an individual is not based on what he thinks of himself, so can we not judge such a period of transformation by its own consciousness; on the contrary, this consciousness must rather be explained from the contradictions of material life, from the existing conflict between the social forces of production and the relations of production."
Karl Marx, *A Contribution to the Critique of Political Economy,* in Feuer (ed.) *Marx & Engels,* Anchor, p. 44. Marx's approach was evident in his earlier writing, thus: "The immediate task of philosophy, which is at the service of history, once the saintly form (religion) of human self-alienation has been unmasked, is to unmask self-alienation in its unholy forms (ideology)."
Karl Marx, Toward the Critique of Hegel's Philosophy of Right, in *ibid.,* p. 263.

response to experience. Consequently, the theory of a particular experience has frequently served as the ideological veil to justify or rationalize that experience. Ideology has been an *ex post* response to experience as well as an *ex ante* guide to practice.

Cuba's pragmatic style has been a recognized characteristic.[9] "But an absence of theory 'lends an air of crisis' to the present situation in socialist countries. The apologetic nature of the pragmatic theory of economic practice obscured many fundamental problems that today have become paramount."[10] No doubt Alberto Mora, the former Minister of Foreign Trade, had Cuba in mind when he wrote this comment in 1965. Cuba began her economic experiment without a well-developed theory of economic organization.

During this first phase (1959-1961), the rapid nationalization of the strategic sectors of the Cuban economy presented the Government with serious problems of economic control and planning. The rapid nationalization[11] began with the first Agrarian Reform that led to confiscation of the *latifundia* and sugar *centrales*. This was followed by a confrontation with the United States that resulted in the confiscation of United States holdings. Simultaneously, the nationalization process was accelerated by the confiscation of domestic enterprises that had openly collaborated with Batista or who were resisting the economic programmes of the regime. At this time many owners simply abandoned their businesses. Spontaneous action by workers, led by an aggressive trade union leadership demanding immediate changes in the distribution of income and privilege, resulted in increased labour conflict. These early struggles frequently led to government intervention. According to Luis Alvarez Rom, the former Treasury Minister:[12]

> Toward the end of 1960, the revolutionary government had to confront its first practical economic and financial problem. The problem had to do with the need to take charge of the administration and conrol of nationalized enterprises that had been recuperated or intervened.

---

[9] C. Richard Fagen, "Continuities in the Style and Strategies of Cuban Revolutionary Politics" (mimeographed) 1970.

[10] Alberto Mora, "On Certain Problems of Building Socialism", in Betram Silverman (ed.), *Man and Socialism in Cuba*, Atheneum, 1971, p. 329.

[11] For a description of the nationalization process see: Dudley Seers (ed.), *Cuba: The Economic and Social Revolution*, The University of North Carolina Press, 1964. James O'Connor, *The Origin of Socialism in Cuba*, Cornell, 1970, chs. 5 and 6.

[12] Luis Alvarez Rom, "Finance and Political Development", in Silverman (ed.) *op. cit.*, p. 271.

Some Dilemmas of Cuban Socialism   395

The Industrial Administration Department of INRA (National Agrarian Reform Institute), headed by Che Guevara, had to deal immediately with problems of financing the production of economic units as complex as petroleum refining or as simple as shoe workshops. The centralization of financial control, the keystone of Cuba's organizational model, emerged from a number of related experiences and problems.[13] First, during the initial phase of nationalization the banking system was still in private hands. Credit restrictions were frequently used as a method of opposing government policies. Moreover, the state sector still had to pay interest on loans to finance a growing government deficit. Second, there existed in Cuba highly advanced forms of cost accounting which gradually emerged as a model for the Ministry of Industry (that was subsequently established in 1962). There was (and still is) a strong bias toward adopting the latest administrative techniques.[14] Third, central control provided a method of integrating and controlling small and medium sized workshops, gradually eliminating inefficient shops and relocating labour to other sectors. Fourth, centralization of financing permitted the State to confront the enormous demands for funds associated with the sugar harvest without total dependence on a private banking system. Fifth, the centralization of finance permitted production units to focus their attention on physical output rather than on financial matters.[15]

Finally, the revolution had unleashed dramatic shifts in the administrative structure. The old managerial and staff personnel began leaving as the revolutionary process accelerated. Accountants and financial experts who were trained in the latest United States techniques left the country with transferable skill. Consequently those with the most specialized skills, *and who were committed to*

[13] Many of these observations are based on conversations with Cuban economists during the period 1968-1969 in Cuba and on JUCEPLAN, *Notas sobre el nuevo sistema de dirección* (mimeographed) 1968, hereafter, noted as *Junta Report*. For additional evidence that the initial development of central finance did not arise out of the need to develop the worker's conscience see Alexis Codina, "Experiences of Control under the Budgetary System", in Silverman (ed.), *op. cit.*, pp. 204-206.

[14] Ernesto Che Guevara, "On the Budgetary Finance System", in Silverman (ed.), *op. cit.*, p. 130. "From a technological standpoint, we should borrow the most advanced forms of economic administration available, from whatever source, so long as they can be adopted for use in the new society... the same rule applies with regard to technical standards in production control and administration... We might say, then, that as a technique the predecessor of the budgetary finance system was imperialist monopoly as it existed in Cuba...".

[15] Interestingly Cuban planners cite ECLA advisors for influencing their bias toward physical and structural rather than financial analysis.— see *Junta Report*.

396   *The Chilean Road to Socialism*

the revolution, assumed staff positions at higher administrative levels. Therefore, managerial functions, particularly at the production level, were increasingly left in the hands of more reliable political cadres. Initially, the actual transfer of power to workers and peasants with relatively little formal training symbolized the dramatic transformation of the social structure. This process of permitting the free emigration of old civil servants, and the managerial and administrative strata, is a distinctive feature of the Cuban revolution. It permitted a relatively peaceful transformation of the social structure and at the same time avoided the dominance of the State by the old bureaucracy.[16] But despite their political reliability, the cadres did not fully understand economic problems and the need for a rational distribution of scarce resources that required economic controls and measurement. Thus, central finance and accounting also provided a method of economic control over 'over-enthusiastic' cadres. There were also innumerable problems due to the inconsistency of the budget programme and poor record keeping. Initially many concrete operational problems made it difficult for enterprises to follow the budget programme and as a consequence many enterprises accumulated large unplanned deficits.[17] The standardization of the system of central budgeting did not take place until 1961.

During this initial period specific events and problems transformed conflicts about the development of organizational forms into central issues of principle. This occurred after 1961 when Cuba entered its socialist phase.

The 'Great Economic Debate' over Economic Organization. Phase II

The ideological and theoretical controversy over market socialism versus centralized planning began in Cuba with the formulation of the first economic plan in 1962. Economists from socialist countries, particularly Czechoslovakia, were invited to aid Cuban planners. Many advisors placed considerable importance on financial planning and particularly on 'profitability' as a measure of economic efficiency.[18] But these suggestions were in conflict with the methods

---

[16] See Moche Lewin, *Lenin's Last Struggle.* Vintage, 1970, for discussion of these problems in the Soviet Union.

[17] Codina, *op. cit.*, pp. 206-208.

[18] Junta Report, *op. cit.*, p. 2. See also comments by outside observers such as René Dumont, *Cuba: Socialism and Development,* Grove, 1970.

that were developing in Che's Ministry of Industry.

The economic crisis in that year also raised questions about Cuba's organizational methods and economic development. In August 1961, the Minister of Economy, Regino Boti, predicted that in ten years Cuban living standards would be comparable to those of any European country.[19] But, instead of increasing, Cuban national output may have declined by 10 per cent between 1962 and 1963.[20] It is likely that, initially, declining productivity may be an inevitable phase of socialist development in an underdeveloped society. Still, Cuba had rapidly transformed her important economic institutions. However, individuals without previous experience, technical know-how, or reliable information were directing an economic system. In part, Cuba's difficulty stemmed from an initial economic strategy. The regulated national and international market had made the co-existence of idle land and labour rational from the viewpoint of the large-scale capitalist farmer. By abolishing capitalist production these constraints on land and labour utilization were exploded. It was now argued that an expanded and diversified agriculture could increase and stabilize employment while providing foreign exchange for expanded industrial development. This in turn would absorb a high and rising proportion of urban unemployment. The theory broke down, however, as the import content of the new industries turned out to be higher and their productivity lower than expected, while agricultural productivity in the new crops were disappointingly low and sugar production dropped precipitously. As a result a growth strategy, designed to reduce Cuban dependency, resulted in a tendency toward 'economic stagnation via a growing strangulation of foreign trade.'[21]

As a consequence production bottlenecks arose with greater frequency and other economic problems became apparent: A serious supply problem led to rationing in 1962; shortages increased the political and economic resistance of the peasants, which in turn led to the Second Agrarian Reform in 1963 that nationalized all land-holding above 165 acres; the re-emergence of bureaucratic in-

---

[19] *Obra Revolucionaria*, No. 30, 1961.

[20] These were Charles Bettelheim's estimates. See Carmelo Mesa-Lago, *Availability and Reliability of Statistics in Socialist Cuba*, University of Pittsburgh, 1970, p. 50.

[21] Based on B. Pollitt, "Employment Plans, Performance and Future Prospects in Cuba", Overseas Studies Committee Conference, 1970 University of Cambridge, 1970, pp. 11-12. Also C. Romeo, "Acerca del desarrollo economico de Cuba", *Cuba Socialista*, December, 1965.

efficiency led to a breakdown in economic coordination. As a result, the economy seemed to be running *por la libre,* that is without effective controls.[22] The first response to these problems was an abrupt revision of Cuba's developmental strategy — a return to agriculture and sugar as the turnpike to development, a turn that was to have serious implications for Cuban economic organization.

Some Cuban leaders and foreign advisors began to argue that Cuba's economic difficulties were rooted in Cuban economic organization. What began as a response to circumstances was transformed into 'the Great Debate' over fundamental issues of ideology and revolutionary principles.[23] The participants included most of the members of the Council of Ministers.[24]

In opposition to central direction and control in the industrial sector, another system of economic organization was emerging in agriculture under the direction of Carlos Rafael Rodriguez, and in foreign trade under Alberto Mora. This system of self-finance or self-management was given official sanction in 1962. In order to understand the basic differences between the two systems it is necessary to distinguish between them in their ideal form.[25]

Under the system of self-management enterprises are juridically independent. They trade their products with different enterprises through the market and profitability is the basic measure of their success. Although each enterprise has considerable financial independence, it has to cover its current expenses through banks that provide interest bearing credits. Bank loans are closely supervised so that the banks play a critical role in evaluating and contolling the enterprise. Basic output and investment decisions are set by the Central Planning Agency, but within the aggregate constraints enterprises have independent decision-making functions. Most significantly, managerial incentives and labour income are based primarily on material incentives.

---

[22] For a description of this earlier period see Edward Boorstein, *The Economic Transformation of Cuba,* Monthly Review Press, 1968.

[23] For a compilation and discussion of the Debate, see Silverman (ed.), *op. cit.*

[24] See Dumont, *op. cit.,* esp. pp. 115-133. The debate included some outside observers, and Dumont was one of the first to criticize centralization.

[25] For a good description of the two systems see Sergio de Santis,"The Economic Debate in Cuba", *International Socialist Review,* August 1965. Neither system ever functioned in this ideal form. Nor did the system of self-finance become operational except in a restricted form during the 1963-1965 period.

Under the system of central budgeting, enterprises are more seriously circumscribed by the national plan. Rather than being legally independent, each firm is considered a part of a larger productive unit — the public sector as a whole. Therefore, the movement of products from one enterprise to another is an intermediary step, and products acquire the characteristics of commodities only when they leave the socialized sector and are sold in the market (i.e., in the private sector, to consumers or to other countries). Profitability plays no role in the evaluation of the enterprise, and all net income is deposited with the Treasury, which centrally allocates funds to various enterprises. Each enterprise is directed by the central plan, and, as its function, fulfills the targets set by the plan. Rigorous financial control is established through a central organization, *Empresas Consolidades,* that coordinates the accounts of enterprises in a particular sector (e.g. textiles). Finally, moral rather than material incentive is emphasized as the prime form of motivation. Thus, in the system of central budgeting, the 'administration of things' provides greater possiblility for eliminating mercantile and economic incentives. In 1963, two systems of economic organization and ideology were emerging, representing different sectors of the Cuban economy. A confrontation was inevitable. The central issue was the viability of market socialism as an organizational model during the transition to communism.

The Great Debate over economic organization represented two divergent views concerning the transition to socialism. While each group accepted comprehensive planning, they disagreed about the economic laws regulating the socialist transition and the institutional forms that best correspond to those laws.[26]

Supporters of a great reliance on the market, decentralized economic organization and decision-making and material incentives, argued that the law of value operated in all sectors of the Cuban economy. In their view, so long as the productive forces were unable to provide for the distribution of consumer goods according to need, the stage of commodity production could not be willed away through changes in juridical forms. Centralized organization designed to circumvent the market were beyond Cuba's current level of technological and administrative capacity. Consequently centralization would result in the misallocation of resources, inefficiency, bureaucracy and ultimately in the breakdown of planning. Economic

---

[26] For a more complete discussion of the debate see my introduction to *Man and Socialism in Cuba: The Great Debate, op. cit.*

organization was an aspect of the relationship to production and could not be 'higher' than the historically determined level of the productive forces.

The Guevarist opposition rejected both the 'economism' of their argument as well as the applicability of the law of value to the transition to socialism. The basic elements of their argument were: First, the law of value was not merely an expression of a universal problem of relative scarcity but an historical phenomenon that reached its fullest development under the capitalist mode of production. Therefore, changes in juridical relationships that resulted from the socialization of the means of production did affect the law of value. Second, the pursuit of socialist values required interference with the law of value and the implicit ethics of the market-place Once the law of value was distorted through planning, how could you determine what it was? Third, the ethics of communism based on non-market relationships could only be realized under a centralized system of administration. But Guevara never fully explored the connection between centralization and worker-participation in decision-making. Fourth, contradictions between the relationship to production and the forces of production were inevitable during the transitional phase. But they could be overcome by the development of administrative and technical skills and through the growth of revolutionary consciousness. Thus, Guevara's aim was to consciously use the process of socialist economic development as a force to create a new socialist morality.

Fidel never formally entered the debate, although in 1965 he seemed to display impatience with the controversy when he argued "our obligation as revolutionaries is not to theorize in the fields of philosophy." Moreover, in the same speech, his support of material incentives seemed to suggest opposition to Guevara.[27] Nevertheless, beginning in 1966, Cuba moved decisively to adopt Che's organizational model and by 1967 all *organismos* were operating under radicalized versions of central budgeting. Fidel not only adopted Guevara's ideas but carried them forward more rapidly and in ways that went beyond the arguments of his comrade.

[27] See Fidel Castro's speech "Criterios de Nuestra Revolución", *Cuba Socialista*, September 1965. In this speech Castro reveals a pronounced long-term commitment to moral incentives that probably accounts for Gerassi's suggestion that Fidel supported Che's position (see *Venceremos* Clarion, 1968, p. 20.) But Fidel's pragmatic approach strongly suggested the need to use material incentives. In the same speech he argued that it would be idealistic to assume that the large majority of workers cut cane from a sense of duty Therefore, it is logical to use economic incentives for work that is of critical importance. As a consequence Mesa-Lago in his book, *The Labour Sector and Socialist Distribution in Cuba*, Praeger, 1968, p. 124, suggests that Fidel rejected Che's thesis.

The Radicalization of Economic Organization: Phase III

1966 marked the beginning of a new phase in the evolution of economic organization. During the earlier period, economic organization was linked to the practical problems of nationalization, social justice and the transition to socialism. The new period seemed to signal a conscious effort to develop a communist society and create *el hombre nuevo* (The New Man).

During this phase the transformation of social consciousness (social character) was linked very closely to organizational forms. Market socialism was regarded not merely as a contradiction in terms, but a road to capitalism. Thus Fidel argued:[28]

> The problem is not in equalizing salaries and placing emphasis on the distribution of incomes. If one limits oneself to that, one does not yet break with the conception of a society founded on money. What we wish is to demystify money and not rehabilitate it. We propose to abolish it totally.
>
> Man will liberate himself completely from his lust for money only when his necessities are able to be satisfied outside his wages. But it is not possible to prepare the advent of this period of communism of abundance while continuing to apply the method of the old society.

The emphasis upon the money motive has had special consequences for economic organization.

1. The New System of Economic Management:[29]

The introduction of the new system of economic management in 1967 radically extended Che's system of central budgeting. The new system of economic management eliminated transactions between *unidades* within the socialized sector. Under the guidelines set by the annual plan, firms entered into direct contractual relations but no monetary or credit relations were involved. Records of receipt and transfer of goods were kept but no payments were required. Mercantile relations still occurred in foreign trade, in final sales to consumers, in wage payment, and in the private sector but in the latter three cases they were, as we shall see, seriously limited. Since *unidades* received materials for production without monetary exchange, a major function of banks and the Treasury was eliminated. Domestically, the major purpose of financial planning was keeping the wage fund in balance with the value of consumer goods — a task

---

[28] Junta Central de Planificación, *Sobre el Salario y la Organización del Trabajo*, Havana, 1968. See also R.S. Karol, *Guerrillas in Power*, Hill & Wang, 1970, pp. 342-345.

[29] Based on Junta Report, *op. cit.*, Juceplan, *La planificación en Cuba, op. cit.*, and interviews with Cuban economists.

made exceedingly difficult because all taxes were eliminated under the new model. Moreover, the de-emphasis of money undermined consciousness of financial controls.

The new system of direction raised significant problems for economic control and measurement. Under this system traditional economic measures became obsolete. Thus, analyses based on production costs and revenues were useless and misleading. This was due to two related factors. First, the price freeze and rationing had destroyed any real relationship between value and price. Moreover, the value of final goods was designed to reflect social rather than market factors. Second, labour policy called for the separation of the relationship between wages and output (work). Thus, the new system of economic management had to confront the complex problem of devising new economic measures that were applicable to this economic model (an exceedingly complex task that has not yet been achieved).

The immediate consequence has been to place prime importance on physical rather than value measures. As a consequence, Cuba's reliance on accounting, including cost accounting, has been virtually eliminated, and in its place the system has turned logically to statistical analysis of data, such as delivered output, consumption of raw materials, inventories, etc., expressed in physical units. The goal is to develop a statistical system that would facilitate highly centralized planning.

The new system of economic direction is a logical extension of centralization of economic planning. Therefore, Cuba has moved rapidly to introduce advanced mathematical techniques into its planning apparatus. The latest computer technology is planned to process information and coordinate decisions. Indeed, a visit to the top levels of the planning hierarchy leaves an impression of a relatively technically advanced system. Yet, even on this level contradictions are apparent. By 1968, Cuba had not yet codified her principal products and activities, essential elements of input-output analysis. But, more significantly, a unit of account of economic cost, which makes aggregation and comparison possible, had not been developed. In practice, monetary measures are still used to estimate costs, and shadow prices are employed to calculate the 'actual' cost of production, particularly to account for changes in the price of imported materials that play such an important role in Cuban production costs. But even this procedure is still in its infancy and is only employed for selected goods. Ultimately, Cuba's organizational model is leading economists to experiment with a non-monetary measure of relative costs such as man hours of labour time. Cuban economists have begun experimenting with a unit of account that would translate all output in terms of a unit of simple labour necessary to produce a given quantity of sugar — a commodity that accounts for approximately 85 per cent of export earnings.

Ideologically, Fidel has argued that the commodity myth must be exploded if man is to fully appreciate the social and community implications of productive relationships. Human labour would then be expressed in real terms, rather than in money, its fetished commodity form. But monetary measures still remain the simplest way to deal with the complexities of modern economic relations. And, more significantly, the real test of demystification lies in the real relationship to production that the new system has introduced. And to this we shall shortly turn.

2. Technical versus Political Cadres

The new system of management had special significance for administrators and technicians, particularly at the *unidad* level. On the one hand, the leadership placed increasing emphasis on revolutionary and political commitment. President Dorticos argued:[30]

> We don't conceive...the possible usefulness of an economist that is not absolutely and fully identified with the objectives of this revolution and with its defined conception...
> And consequently, it is just and valid to affirm that we don't think an economist is either useful or usable if in addition to being a good technician he is not, *above all*, a good revolutionary in theory and in practice... It is a task that can be understood not only with an adequate technical preparation but moreover with an attitude and a positive presence before the difficulties that can only be developed by an independence from personal temperaments with the presence of revolutionary faith and of an absolute conviction in the correctness of the Cuban revolution.

On the other hand, the Cuban revolution has stressed the importance of technical development and education. The shortage of technical and administrative cadres has always been singled out by Fidel and Che as the major constraint on economic development. Of course, the ideal administrator should be technically competent as well as a revolutionary. Yet, at this time Cuba's model places special importance on political rather than technical criteria in the management of the production unit.[31] Thus, in 1969, it became obvious that little economic analysis took place at the work place.

---

[30] Unpublished speech presented at Economic Institute in Havana 1969.

[31] For a recent discussion see *Cuba Internacional*, February, 1970, p. 30.

Statistical data were sent to the *Empresa,* or regional level, for analysis, comparison, aggregation. Thus, economic control and responsibility were removed from the production units and transferred to technicians who were less likely to be militants.

This procedure was consistent with the functional requirements of the model. Since material incentives no longer guided managerial and worker behaviour, the major function of management was to mobilize worker participation in the major economic efforts of the regime; freed from 'paper work' and 'money illusions', the manager can concentrate on the problems of work and social consciousness.

But there is a relationship between social consciousness and economic control and responsibility, a factor that has not been fully appreciated in the development of Cuban economic organization.

3. Moral versus Material Incentives

A motivational system based on economic rewards and penalties was inconsistent with the new system of economic management and centralized planning. As a result, Cuba moved rapidly to eliminate many of the remaining material incentives that had been part of Che's central budgeting system. The separation between work and wages was rapidly introduced. Thus, bonuses or penalties for fulfilment or non-fulfilment of work norms were eliminated. Piece rates were rapidly phased out and, where they were part of traditional seasonal work patterns, attempts were made to develop steady year-round employment. Income differentials were narrowed through efforts to reduce the high salaries for new entrants in the labour force and to raise the income of the lowest groups.[32] There were strong tendencies to reduce the use of economic penalties to enforce labour discipline, and the system of work norms, while still in effect, seemed, at least in 1969, to be loosely enforced. How could one norm a worker's conscience? Organized efforts in 1969 led to the virtual renunciation of overtime pay. The salary scale developed prior to 1966 providing differentials was still in effect, but restrictions on personal consumption reduced their motivational significance.

Conscience or moral incentives were the means through which work and sacrifice would be induced and economic development fostered. Essentially moral incentives have been used as a lever for mass mobilization and to convey the idea that work is a social duty rather than a means of personal advancement. In Cuba, the 'moralization of work' has replaced the carrot of material incentives as the

---

[32] The highest salary cited was 300 pesos for engineers.

means of modernization. Thus economic development would grow simultaneously with social consciousness, social commitment and egalitarianism; essential elements in constructing communism.

The renewed emphasis on moral incentives, particularly in 1968, was reflected in new experiments with socialist emulation. The emulation system that had emerged after 1962 was suddenly abandoned in 1966. Bureaucratic and complicated regulations had provided few possibilities for worker participation or recognition of particular problems within individual enterprises. Moreover, the Stakhanovite aspect of the system led to competition among managers for prizes and status, and motivated them to falsify reports.

The transition to a new system began in 1966 and 1967 with the development of industrial efficiency plans. General goals were set up by individual ministries. These general targets were then translated into concrete plans by individual firms. After six months of experimentation, a decision was made to tie the efficiency plans to socialist emulation. The previous bureaucratic structure and complicated point system was abandoned. Although competition between plants was still occasionally practised, the central idea was self-emulation where individual workers and *unidades* set their own *compromisos* (goals) and tried to fulfill them. In 1968 emulation plans were connected to historic periods in Cuban history, culminating, on July 26, with the possibility of winning the Moncada flag. Thus, theoretically, every enterprise could win a flag. Winning did not mean being better, but rather, fulfilling one's *compromisos* (i.e. efficiency plans).

The role of Cuban trade unions (CTC-R) seemed unclear in 1969. They were assigned a major task of fulfilling socialist emulation goals. But their bureaucratic structure and limited function in the plant seriously undermined their effectiveness. There was considerable speculation that Cuba would soon eliminate or replace the trade unions whose function seemed unclear under the new system of management. Experimentation was underway to establish an Advanced Workers Movement that would replace the older system of selecting vanguard workers. In 1969 the Advanced Workers Movement had replaced the local trade union in some factories. These experiments were aimed partly at revitalizing mass participation in the work centre. But in general these efforts were mainly concerned with mass mobilization and increasing work efficiency rather than worker participation in social and economic decisions.

But moral incentives have radically extended the original commitment to social equality and ruralism. First, rationing reduced the consumption patterns that had separated upper income groups from lower income groups. While, paradoxically, scarcity tended to magnify small differences, in general, shared austerity also reduced the disparities in the distribution of consumption and guaranteed minimum standards of living for the entire population. Second, the new orientation de-emphasized private consumption and expanded collective goods and services made available free or with slight charges. This included the continued extension of education, medical and health care as well as free local public telephones, transportation for funerals, weddings, recreation and sporting events. Collective meals were served at work centres and schools. Rent, which was already abolished for many consumers, was eliminated for all families with *per capita* incomes under twenty-five pesos per month. Fourth, mass mobilization has significantly affected the Cuban social structure and re-emphasized the rural bias of the revolution. Large 'armies' of volunteer labour participate in the *Zafra* and in thousands of micro-projects. Youth and communist brigades have been created. Mass education has been increasingly concerned with problems of economic and technological development and students, teachers, intellectuals, and urban workers have been intimately involved in rural development; thus reducing occupational and regional distinctions. The plans to bring the schools to the country, and, more recently, to remove the university from its urban base and connect more closely to the work environment, are all part of the same pattern.

But these policies are not seen as ends in themselves. Thus education, economic and technological change are essential prerequisites for a communist society. Only in the technologically and economically advanced society would the 'moralization of work' end. The work ethic — work as a social duty — would be replaced by the identification with work as a creative activity.

4. Revolutionary Offensive: The Death of the Private Sector

It is inconceivable that Cuba's organizational model could operate effectively within an economy having a significant private sector. Yet in 1966, the beginning of the radicalization process, a considerable private sector existed. (See Table No. 1) Thus a large proportion of the labour force was not only outside the economic organizational model but working in the private sector, either in retail trade, service, light industry or agriculture. This not only undermined the centralized planning system but provided an ideological alternative to

Cuba's radical model. Indeed, under the condition of severe shortages, the private sector provided an illegal source of consumer goods and was competing successfully for scarce resources and labour. Thus, the prototype of the 'consumer goods society' worked within the heart of the Cuban system, playing on the inherent contradictions and inefficiencies within the socialized sector.

On March 13, 1968 the Revolutionary Offensive was launched to eliminate the remaining private sector,[33] and to significantly limit

TABLE No. 1

Distribution of the Labour Force between the Private and Public Sectors

January, 1965

Total Labour Force	2,492,919
Unemployed	376,293
Employed	2,116,626
Public	1,355,259
Private	761,367
By Sector	
Industry	
Public	281,755
Private	105,425
Construction	
Public	93,404
Private	20,247
Transport	
Public	71,585
Private	10,987
Communications	
Public	11,690
Private	979
Commerce	
Public	208,661
Private	53,606
Agriculture	
Public	364,508
Private	304,299
Other Productive Activities	
Public	8,608
Private	70,238
Services	
Public	287,085
Private	202,516

Source: Ministry of Labour, *Balance de los Recursos Laborales*, January, 1965.

[33] "La Nacionalización de los Establecimientos Privados en la Ofensiva", *El Militante Comunista*, June, 1968. See also *Granma* Weekly Review, March 31, 1968.

the role of private enterprise in agriculture as well as to intensify the ideological campaign for revolutionary commitment. It demonstrated Fidel's commitment to radicalize the revolution despite serious economic difficulties. Thus, he rejected the NEP alternative, that is, market socialism. But the Government added to its difficult organizational problems the necessity of planning and managing the many small enterprises in services and retail trade.[34] In many cases this simply meant the reduction or termination of neighbourhood stores.

The move to end private enterprise in agriculture has also become part of the Revolutionary Offensive — but this has proceeded more cautiously and less publicly. In 1968 the Cuban Government revealed that private agricultural production was supervised by and included in the nationwide development plans; what Dumont has called the Third Agrarian Reform. Dumont summarized the process as follows:[35]

> Until 1967 a controller of ANAP (National Association of Small Farmers) asked peasants their forecasts with respect to planting. In the year 1967 the ANAP suggested modifications that seemed desirable. In 1968 he gave them orders established by the regional agricultural plan. In 1968 there began a campaign of exclusive-delivery to the State of all available production. First presented as purely voluntary, it was then made obligatory with the publication of sanctions against those who did not participate.

Moreover, peasants were forbidden to hire their own labour. In effect, peasant land-holdings were incorporated within the large *granjas*. In exchange, the State provided labour, machinery, and technical advice. A campaign was initiated during this period for peasants to voluntarily sell their land to the State. Model projects such as San Andres were also given considerable publicity. They have been held up as examples of the voluntary integration of the *campesino* into socialist agriculture. But, rural workers are permitted one hectare of land for subsistence, which has influenced their effort.

As a result of the Revolutionary Offensive, Cuba could report that in less than a decade it had become the socialist country with the highest percentage of state-owned property. Yet, the Revolutionary Offensive and its strong ideological undertones reflected deeper underlying social and economic forces, to which Cuban economic organization was a response.

---

[34] For a critical view of this approach see Mandel, *op. cit.*, p. 81.

[35] René Dumont, *Cuba: Est-il Socialiste?*, Paris, 1970, p. 92.

Ideology and Reality

1. Economic Organization and Socialist Accumulation

In part, the radicalization of Cuban economic organization was a response to problems immanent in the Cuban model: the spontaneous growth of the private sector and the corresponding rise of the black market; the exposure of corruption at the highest levels of the army and trade unions; the persistent growth of bureaucracy as well as the apparent contradiction between demands of the accounting procedures of Central Budgeting and the available cadres at the base. These problems were not unrelated to the growth of criticism among some members of the old Communist Party within and outside Cuba, who saw both Cuba's domestic and foreign policies as romantic and naive. But in particular, response to economic problems was necessary as GNP in 1966 declined by more than four per cent.[36] The radicalization of Cuban economic organization was closely linked to the decision to intensify the rate of economic development. The unfolding economic strategy of the post-1966 period reflected a determined effort to confront the persistent problem of economic stagnation and inefficiency.

The new strategy originated in 1963, when a deepening balance of payments crisis forced a shift away from industry to agriculture as the leading economic sector. Essentially, the strategy called for capital accumulation through sugar exports. This would provide needed foreign reserves — first, to develop agriculture in which Cuba had a comparative advantage, and later, after increasing agricultural productivity, to transfer this surplus to industrial development. The greater potential yield in agricultural investment was explained primarily in 'terms of the productivity-increasing potential of applying advanced techniques to activities such as cane and animal husbandry, where previously considerable long-term practical experience coexisted with a traditional primitive technology.'[37] The post-1966 period marked a rapid increase in the rate of capital accumulation, leading symbolically to the production of ten million tons of sugar in 1970.

The most significant effect of the policy was to rapidly convert Cuba's labour surplus into labour shortage. The unemployment problem disappeared and a new problem of discovering sources of labour reserves emerged. This was particularly troublesome because

[36] Mesa-Lago. *op. cit.*, p. 51.

[37] Based on Pollitt. *op. cit.*, pp. 12-13.

the initial income policy of the Government had set in motion a large migration of labour from rural to urban employment, particularly services. In part, this was the result of the growth of small towns and state farms in the interior of the country where social and educational services were rapidly expanding. The reduction in the number and productivity of the traditional cane cutter — a seasonal worker — was particularly troublesome. Thus the rural poor were either moving to the higher income centres of the towns or taking part of their increased income and economic security in additional leisure. The rapid expansion of the service sector from one quarter to one third of the labour force, a sector with considerable disguised unemployment, reflected the rapid expansion of the bureaucratic apparatus, as well as the expansion of social services. (See Table No. 2)

Moreover, the increase in the rate of gross investment from an average 18 per cent in the period 1961-1963 to 31 per cent of GNP in 1968 required a reduction in personal consumption. As a result, rationing — established in 1962 — was extended to include virtually all consumer goods, as well as a reduction in the variety and quantity of commodities available for personal consumption. By 1969 personal consumption of durable goods virtually disappeared and most non-food items, such as clothing, were distributed irregularly. Thus, Cuba's strategy implied a rapid expansion in employment co-existing with a planned reduction in *per capita* personal consumption. It was this apparent contradiction — the need to increase work, expand and shift the labour force while reducing personal consumption — that set the stage for Cuba's distinctive growth strategy: economic development with moral incentives.

TABLE No. 2

Active Population by Productive Sector in Cuba, 1958-1965

(000's)

	1958/59	1960/61	1965
Agriculture	813.0	862.0	838.0
Industry and Mining	378.5	411.8	390.0
Construction	82.8	71.7	123.0
Transport	80.6	86.5	90.1
Commerce	284.3	265.5	258.8
Services and Others	558.3	572.7	846.1
TOTAL	2,197.5	2,270.2	2,546.0

Source: Republic of Cuba, JUCEPLAN, Central Statistics Department.
Resumen de Estadisticas de Población, No. 2, Havana, 1966, p. 120.

First, in 1966 Cuba was faced with a decline in agricultural labour at a time when extensive growth of this sector was planned. Reversing rural-urban migration through a programme of resettlement made little sense since economic plans called for a technological revolution in agriculture that would shortly reduce agricultural labour requirements. Therefore, the short-run solution required the redeployment of urban labour to agriculture, particularly during planting and harvesting. The type of labour required was the most menial and unskilled. Material incentives would have had to be unusually high to induce urban labour into these occupations. Moreover, the use of wage differentials made little sense because the transfer was frequently of workers from more skilled and productive activities to less skilled, that is, from industry to agriculture. The moralization of work under these circumstances is quite rational and reliance on unpaid voluntary labour is reasonable. Since 1962 Cuba has increasingly relied on this method to mobilize labour for agriculture. In 1968 perhaps 15-20 per cent of the agricultural labour force was made up of non-agricultural labour.[38] Such a transfer of labour could only make economic sense if it was based on moral rather than material incentives. Moreover, such a transfer of labour inevitably disrupted other sectors of the economy. Under these circumstances of extremely tight factor supply, market socialism was untenable.

Second, the planned reduction in personal consumption made expansion of employment possible, only through the worker's heightened sense of social commitment and conscience. Furthermore, the already low level of available consumer goods made increased capital accumulation possible primarily through the expansion of unpaid labour. Therefore, Cuba seemed to be in a stage where the dangers of 'primitive accumulation'—a period in capitalist development where force was used to extract the economic surplus—was possible.

Yet, if additional labour can be supplied voluntarily, that may be a more consistent translation of the concept of primitive accumulation in a socialist society than that used in the Soviet experience. The translation of primitve accumulation to socialist accumulation was an essential element of the organizational model. But if moral incentives fail then the ominous necessity of coercion must be faced. While the commitment of the Cuban population to the revolution has reduced the reliance upon force, *conciencia* is also a scarce resource and the

[38] More than fifty percent of the labour force was working in agriculture in 1969. See *Granma*, April 1, 1969.

failure to use it efficiently may be one of Cuba's fundamental problems.

Finally, the sharp decline in personal consumption made reliance on material incentives politically dangerous. An emphasis on material incentives during a period when workers were asked to increase hours worked, and to reduce personal consumption, would merely serve to heighten the sense of economic sacrifice and exaggerate economic distinctions and privileges. Politically, under these circumstances an emphasis on collective efforts toward social goals was more reasonable.

2. Cost of Social Conscience

The ideological preoccupation with the commodity fetishism problem and its relationship to economic organization becomes comprehensible when related to Cuba's economic strategy. But it is precisely the contradictions between Cuba's economic strategy and economic organization that have challenged Cuba's ideological goals. Conversely, ideology has frequently become a rationalization for economic and social policy. In order to fully understand these contradictions, as Charles Bettelheim has suggested, "it is necessary...to bring to light the real social relations that are revealed and hidden, at the same time, by the forms of representation and the elaborated ideological notions based on them."[39]

Cuba's economic strategy made the reliance on material incentives and market relations inoperable. In a system of organization based on moral incentives which eliminates the direct connection between individual performance and reward, the individual's motivation for increasing his economic performance must come from a heightened identification with the goals of the nation (internalization of social goals). Paradoxically, over-zealous political leaders can undermine this commitment. This had become in 1968-1969 a serious problem since economic decisions at the base were politically rather than economically motivated. This problem had been compounded by an over-ambitious economic strategy associated with the ten million ton goal which overburdened Cuba's fragile economic controls and planning structure.

Economic controls, through a system of planning, must serve as a substitute for the market and economic incentives. Yet, if national output and efficiency do not increase, a cynical attitude may develop which undermines the worker's identification with the system — an

---

[39] Charles Bettelheim, "The Transition to Socialism", *Monthly Review* December, 1970, p.5.

essential ingredient of the model. As of the moment, effective planning and economic controls are extremely weak in Cuba. Economic decisions depend on a bureaucratic planning structure that must translate information about physical output collected from the base into operational instructions. Managers under this system are seriously circumscribed from making independent decisions based on economic analysis (nor do they often have the skills to do this). As a result, the data collected have little meaning to management and are therefore frequently inaccurate and under-utilized. This is reflected in the hostility sometimes expressed about the useless information that is sent up to the *Empresas* or Ministries that, the managers felt, is rarely used. On the other hand, instructions from above are frequently beyond the competence and skills that exist at the local level. Moreover, Havana-based administrators have no real knowledge of local problems. Despite romantic feelings, a man with a sixth grade education has difficulty collecting and using the simplest statistical data. This is particularly problematic in such critical sectors as agriculture where large-scale state farms have become the basic organizational unit. As a result, success is frequently measured simply by fulfilment of gross output targets expressed in physical terms and by the conservation of scarce raw materials. The fragile planning is further undermined by 'overcommitment' of resources, frequently a product of revolutionary enthusiasm and the uncertainty of foreign supplies. The inevitable has occurred: first, shortages and bottlenecks have reduced industrial capacity and worker productivity; second, the decision-making process has been plagued by bureaucracy, so that a parallel planning apparatus that bypasses the existing bureaucratic structure has been created to ensure the fulfilment of special or urgent strategic economic goals; these special plans are under Fidel's personal direction. Third, there has been a large turnover of managerial and administrative personnel. Problems similar to 1962 have re-emerged.

To meet these inefficiencies, managers have frequently called upon the worker's conscience, that is, labour's willingness to work overtime without pay. Thus, moral incentives have served to compensate for the inefficiencies and irrationalities of the economic organization. Indeed, moral incentives often foster the irrational uses of labour and capital, since managers do not feel compelled to complete tasks that could be done during the normal work day. Nor do they feel compelled to explore sources of inefficiency. Administrators frequently considered overtime or voluntary work costless, and were often perplexed when asked whether they had wasted *conciencia* in fulfilling their goals. The same attitude was prevalent in agriculture. Since no production unit assumed the cost of voluntary work, more labour was freqently demanded than was needed in order to guarantee results. Often, the irrational use of moral incentives results in problems of worker apathy and discontent. The cost of *conciencia* (Cuba's most precious resource) needs to be considered.

3. Conscience and Compulsion: Some Dilemmas of the Cuban Model

In the face of these difficulties Cuban economic organization has undergone some significant changes. First, the search for organizational efficiency has led to some imitation of the military model. The military is the most efficient organization in Cuba and considerable talent has been shifted to this sector. Recently, military techniques have been used in organizing large production units and directing large units of labour. Command Posts have been set up throughout Cuba that resemble the operational headquarters of an army. These techniques should not be confused with regimentation. Their purpose is to establish more effective controls over the organization and deployment of labour and capital, particularly in agriculture. Moreover, labour brigades have frequently employed military techniques and schedules. However, the model has not effectively dealt with the problems of bureaucracy, particularly in developing greater responsibility and self-reliance at the production level. Nor has it effectively helped foster real participation in the decision-making process. Inefficiency and the absence of effective control still plague Cuban economic organization.

A second response to inefficiency is reflected in labour force controls. According to Risquet, the Labour Minister, previous labour legislation that penalized workers with discharge and loss of salary had become outmoded.[40] At first, increased moral pressures were to be used. A labour file was created for each worker where merits and demerits are to be entered after his work record has been discussed at semi-annual assemblies. The second phase was the promulgation, in 1971, of an anti-loafing law aimed at dealing with absenteeism and bringing all able-bodied men between the ages of 17 and 60 into the labour force. The penalties for absenteeism ranged from working under the vigilance of other workers and revolutionary organizations,

[40] *Verde Olivo*, August 17, 1969, pp. 12-13.

to working in a rehabilitation centre for up to one year.[41] Thus Cuba's economic model posed the serious issue of using coercion in pursuing economic development.

In an interview in Havana, Regino Boti argued that after a socialist revolution a period of primitive accumulation may be inevitable. A socialist revolution inevitably leads workers to reduce their efforts because they think that the end of employer control means less work. Therefore, he argued, all socialist revolutions face the inevitable dilemma between economic development and consent. In Cuba this problem has been complicated because the initial welfare and redistribution policies of the Government had retarded the rate of investment and created illusions about the relationship between work and economic development. The question therefore, Boti argued, then becomes how do you get workers to increase their efforts and discipline. Thus Boti's analysis raised some critical questions: Does Cuba's experiment suggest that compulsive work requirements are the inevitable consequences of an organizational model based on socialist values? Is low worker productivity and absenteeism functionally related to Cuba's radical efforts to eliminate material incentives? The economic problems that were admitted in a remarkably candid speech by Fidel in 1970 have reopened these questions.

Our analysis suggests that the roots of Cuba's economic problems must be found in deeper sources than moral incentives. In the first place Cuba's economic strategy required massive increases and deployment of labour. This created an overcommitment of available labour resources. Part of the difficulty can be explained by the particular nature of surplus labour in pre-revolutionary Cuba. In large measure under-utilization of labour was a seasonal problem. Thus, during the months of peak labour requirements, the 'reserve army of labour' was sharply reduced or disappeared. The revolution over-estimated the labour surplus.[42] Consequently, increasing numbers of outside workers, students, and the military, are needed to fulfil agricultural targets, disrupting production schedules in the industrial and service sectors. One of the results is the need to exhort workers to work longer hours or move, when needed, to critical sectors. But these efforts are frequently frustrated because of bottlenecks of poor planning. Thus, workers may spend many hours in the factory or in agriculture but considerable time is wasted or

[41] For complete text see *Granma*, Weekly Review, March 28, 1971, p.2.
[42] Pollitt, *op. cit.*, p.20.

misused. And despite the large increase in land cultivation, "season after season,...the administrators of numerous state farms were obliged to decide which harvests should be sacrificed entirely, or, at least, which crops should be harvested outside their optimal time-period at the cost of a decline in their volume and/or value."[43] Such pressures on labour resources lead to uneconomical hoarding of labour and a work ethic that may contradict the goals of the revolution. It creates a cynical attitude on the part of workers toward the Government's exhortations about labour discipline. The process of primitive accumulation is not a 'law' of social development but rather a function of policy decisions.

A second aspect of the strategy required a reduction in personal consumption while expanding (relatively) employment. Under these circumstances it is quite logical for workers to take part of their real income in the form of reduced effort and increased leisure. Increasing aggregate personal consumption has nothing to do with a system of differential economic incentives. As Ernest Mandel, a defender of moral incentives, has argued, 'raising the producer's standard of living is a major way to stimulate output and raise labour productivity."[44] Ideological pre-occupation with the disappearance of money is, to a degree then, a rationalization of austerity.

The decline in money as a medium of exchange reflects a decline in real personal income, that is, shortages of consumer goods. Its consequences show up in worker resistance and cynicism. Thus, shortages tend to undermine the system of moral incentives by undermining social conscience.

Moreover, rather than diminishing in importance, scarcity reinforces the desire for material goods. True, rationing does provide a more equitable distribution of subsistence than would exist under a free market and many basic services are virtually free. But under conditions of severe shortages, small decreases and additions to consumption assume great importance. As a result informal markets exist where goods are bartered or traded at unofficial prices. The decline in consumption is related to the high rate of planned investment. Unlike the shortages that emerged in 1962, Cuba claims that the present phase of austerity has been planned. But there is a relationship between rate of capital accumulation and the rate of compulsion.

Third, Cuba's development strategy required a highly centralized organizational model where material incentives were

---

[43] *Ibid.*
[44] Mandel, in Silverman (ed.), *op. cit.*, p.81.

inappropriate. Economic incentives could not move hundreds of thousands of workers into the *Zafra*. Political rather than technical cadres direct the productive process under the new system of economic management. Thus far, the results have seriously undermined effective economic control. There is considerable evidence that a highly centralized economic organization is beyond Cuba's present administrative capacity. Political enthusiasm is no substitute for technical and organizational knowledge. This is reflected in the high rate of turnover of politically-committed administrators. Nor does the winning of the Moncada flag necessarily imply economic efficiency.

But what types of economic controls are compatible with moral incentives? The issue becomes apparent when confronting the problem of labour discipline. Economic planning depends on a reliable labour force. High labour turnover and absenteeism are inimical to planning and efficiency. But since economic rewards and penalties have been rejected, only social pressures, and ultimately compulsion, remain as methods to deal with these problems. Policies that lead to premature controls and direction of the labour market may lead to unnecessary compulsion. A supporter of Che's defence of moral incentives cautioned that "to abolish the private ownership of labour power before the society can assure the satisfaction of all its people's basic needs would actually introduce forced labour."[45]

In the face of these contradictions there is a natural tendency for the Government to increase the use of ideological instruments to develop greater expression of social commitment. This is the basis of the Revolutionary Offensive and the 'radicalization' of Cuban ideology which has virtually declared a moratorium on public debate over economic and social policies. These developments have resulted in the externalization of revolutionary ethics. But a system of incentives that relies on directives from above becomes just another form of repression. As Alberto Mora, a participant in the debate over moral incentives warned:[46]

> We must at the same time assure that the superstructure is so organized as to prevent the substitution of the money motive by the power motive.

Thus, worker-resistance is also reflected in the absence of real participation in decision-making. While mass organizations such as the Committee for the Defence of the Revolution and the Federation of Cuban Women have recruited large numbers of para-professionals

---

[45] *Ibid.*
[46] Mora, in Silverman (ed.), *op. cit.*, p.334.

in the extensive dissemination of health, welfare and child-care services, these organizations remain primarily transmission belts for centralized party decisions. Mass meetings are used primarily to gain support for policy decisions already made. Fidel seemed to understand this shortcoming when he recently said:[47]

> We have been able to unleash the energy, interest and will of millions. Now we must channel this energy into greater participation in decisions that affect their lives.

The economic crisis of 1970 has opened a new phase in the discussion about economic organization. Castro's speeches, since July 1970, have revealed considerable frankness about economic and social problems. These initial problems are, after all, part of an early process of experimentation; Cuba's organizational model is only five years old. Certainly an insignificant period to test its efficacy; nor do productivity statistics include the large investment in training and education. Nevertheless, if our analysis is correct, Cuba faces a serious dilemma in the immediate future. Some modification in Cuba's ambitious economic strategy and organization to provide greater local responsibility will be necessary, if the link between socialist consciousness and economic development are to be encouraged and the connection between economic development and compulsion dissolved. This will also require a greater concordance between ideology and reality.

There are some indications that the demystification process has already begun as *praxis* once again triumphs over ideology. Thus, 1970 seems to mark the beginning of a new phase in the relationship between moral incentives, economic organization and economic development. This new chapter will have much to instruct us about the relationship between socialist economic development and *conciencia*.

---

[47] Fidel Castro Speech in *Granma*, Weekly Review, August 25, 1971.

THE REDISTRIBUTION OF CONSUMPTION IN CUBA

David Barkin*

I. Introduction

The choice of the distribution of consumption as the subject of this paper is a reflection of the growing disenchantment with the traditional focus on the rate of growth of aggregate output. It is also a product of our conviction that underdevelopment cannot be overcome unless the mindless race to imitate the consumption patterns and productive structures of the wealthier countries ends; in most poor countries growth creates 'modern' goods for the elites but their production is not generating sufficient employment opportunities and improved welfare for the majority of the population.

While few economists would now argue that the distributional considerations should be ignored, little progress has been made in integrally incorporating them into empirical or even theoretical treatises. Dudley Seers (1970) pointed out what is becoming increasingly apparent, even to the most reluctant of analysts:

> ...it is very slipshod of us to confuse development with economic development and economic development with economic growth, it is nevertheless very understandable. We can, after all, fall back on the supposition that increases in national income, if they are faster than population growth, sooner or later lead to the solution of social and political problems.

Our focus on distribution is directly related to our interest in finding a better way to understand the development process. Aggregate growth is obviously insufficient as an indicator and our search naturally leads us to answer three questions posed by Seers:

> "What has been happening to poverty?
> What has been happening to unemployment?
> What has been happening to inequality?
>
> If all three of these have declined from high levels, then beyond doubt this has been a period of development for the country concerned."

The interest in distribution stems not only from the obstacles that the concentration of wealth may create for further development. While it is true that some believe that the lack of adequate demand for more consumer goods which concentration causes may be an important stumbling block to further development in Latin America, others point to the need to confront the

---

*Work on this paper was conducted while I was a Research Associate at El Colegio de Mexico and was supported by a grant from the Joint Committee of Latin American Studies of the Social Science Research Council and the American Council of Learned Societies.

issue of redistribution simply on the grounds of social justice. Still others are preoccupied by the potential social unrest that might arise from the growing gulf that separates the two parts of many nations: the rich and the poor. The examination of the distributive aspect of economic growth, therefore, is a response to the need for more information and analysis of mechanisms which are being used to increase economic growth and spread its fruits more broadly.

By selecting consumption we suggest that monetary aggregates are poor measures of individual welfare and that the mix of available consumption goods aids in explaining how many nations are able to grow without developing. Although we do not explore this issue in detail here, it seems apparent that the decision to provide most people with a guaranteed minimum standard of living facilitated the task of achieving full employment; the issue was changed from whether work can be found for people to how can they be most productively employed. In addition an effort was made to supply as much as possible on a collective basis and to emphasize the importance of services rather than goods in raising living standards in order to attempt to resolve the problem of improving human welfare without unduly sacrificing long-range growth by diverting foreign exchange or investment resources.

The focus on living standards does not imply the complete disregard of the growth potential of the Cuban economy. In fact, elsewhere I (1972) have suggested that the present development strategy may be the most efficient one to follow in order to obtain a satisfactory economic structure both in the medium and long term. The present policies for distributing consumer goods must be examined in the light of the ability of the Cuban economy to continue producing these goods and to increase their variety and volume in the coming years. These production programs cannot, however, be readily understood without some reference to the new distributive policies which are reshaping consumption patterns.

The analytical basis for the examination of the redistribution of consumption in a centrally controlled economy is, unfortunately, almost non-existent. Present economic theory limits itself to discussing the way in which factors of production (labor and capital) are rewarded in proportion to their contribution to production. There is no hint in the literature about how analytically to approach the problem of income distribution when the state plays a determinant role in distribution of consumer goods. Nor is there much consideration of the possibility that a more equitable distribution of income may facilitate faster growth.*

While moving systematically to eliminate any vestiges of the pre-revolutionary hierarchical class structure, the Cuban leadership during the past

---

*cf. Reder (1969), Mincer (1970) and Bronfenbrenner (1971). Mesa-Lago (1970) discusses Cuban attitudes towards distribution in the context of socialist debates on the subject; his presentation, however, covers the period up to 1965 before the Cubans adopted non-material incentives and provides no analytical basis for examining the changes occurring since 1959.

twelve years has tried to assure a basic minimum standard of living to all people. To achieve this, the very nature of the goods produced and available for consumption on the island has changed; luxury goods, perhaps more broadly defined than ever, are no longer available even to those who might have the money to purchase them. Greater emphasis has been placed on services like education and medical care which are provided by the government on a collective basis. Individual consumption varies little from family to family as a rationing system is used to distribute production among the people.

In the first days of revolutionary government economic conditions in the countryside were improved. People's stores, guaranteed prices, additional jobs in construction, higher rural wages and improved social services were all part of a program to lessen the glaring inequalities that then persisted. Subsequently urban housing and land policy reform complemented agrarian reform. Economic planning called for increased productive capacity of basic consumer goods like rice, meat and dairy products, while also increasing the size and scope of collective public services like education and medical care. Attention was also directed towards broadening the access to recreational and cultural activities.

These programs are part of an explicit attempt to minimize the long-standing disparities between classes which were especially notable in both the rural-urban contrasts and within the urban areas in the pre-revolutionary society. They are designed to ensure that everyone has the opportunity to enjoy a basic minimum level of consumption and access to those public services which the government decided were essential to the new pattern of living which was being created.

This new style program stresses non-material incentives to individual activity instead of the more traditional material rewards based on the productivity of labor and capital. This choice was the result of a combination of pressures resulting from scarcities throughout the economy arising from the highly concentrated development effort as well as from an attempt to break the direct relationship between an individual's productive effort and his family's standard of living.

The scarcities which arose shortly after the assumption of the revolutionary government were due to the rapid increase in demand for many consumer goods which were previously beyond the means of many people; goods like milk, meat and eggs were rarely consumed in the lower classes during the previous regime and the rise in demand quickly outdistanced the ability of the economy to supply these goods. Rationing was the only mechanism consistent with the egalitarian precepts of the revolutionary leadership.

Egalitarianism is a common thread that dates back at least to Castro's self-defense of the attack on the Moncada barracks in 1953;

> ...two essential articles from our Constitution...which
> the first popularly chosen government...will have to respect...
> are one that requires the proscription of the latifundio...
> and another that orders the State to employ all the means at

its disposal to provide employment to all who lack it and to
assure each manual or intellectual worker a decorous standard
of living...

The reforms proposed within the then prevailing economic structure were designed to create full-employment so that everyone would have the means to enjoy a satisfactory standard of living. With the transformation of Cuba into a socialist state, a new philosophical approach to work was expected to transform it into, as Ernesto 'Che' Guevara said,

...a new condition; man as a commodity ceases to exist,
and a system is established for the social fulfillment of
social duty. The means of production belong to society, and
the machine is only the front line where duty is performed.
Man begins to free his thought from the bothersome fact that
presupposed the need to satisfy his animal needs by working.
He begins to see himself portrayed in his work and to understand its human magnitude through the created object, through
the work carried out. This no longer involves leaving a part
of his being in the form of labor power sold, which no longer
belongs to him; rather it signifies an emanation from himself,
a contribution to the life of the society in which he is reflected, the fulfillment of his social duty. (Gerassi, 1968,
p. 394)

But these declarations of general policies were highly conditioned by the imbalance between the inability of the economy to supply more than a minimum of consumer goods to the whole population and the efforts of the revolutionary government to improve the standard of living of the working classes. The combination of measures which were adopted reflect the effort to achieve full employment and provide a minimum standard of living for all while initiating a broad development program; such a program inevitably requires a sacrifice in material living standards for the small group of people in the upper, and perhaps middle classes if it is to be really effective in mobilizing all available consumption resources for redistribution.

The Cuban experience is particularly important in the light of the growing preoccupation with the distribution of income in other Latin American countries. The common problem in many Latin American countries of finding ways in which to absorb workers productively into the economy provides a striking contrast to the Cuban situation, where the problem is to raise production levels to satisfy better the needs of all the people who are presently employed; present Cuban policy is aimed at inducing those people who are working to be more productive and to stimulate others to enter the labor force to perform tasks which are required but presently cannot be completed.

II. Rural-Urban Contrasts in Pre-Revolutionary Cuba

On the eve of the Revolution income was most inequitably distributed. Not only was there a great gap between those people relying on their labor for their livelihood and those receiving income from property holdings, but there was also a huge chasm between groups within the labor force itself. The labor force

> was split into two groups which can be distinguished with a sharpness that is surprising in view of the smallness of the country and the moderately high per capita income...The rural workers received low incomes and were badly housed and largely uneducated...On the other hand, the urban worker, when he happened to be employed, was often relatively well paid (Seers, 1964, pp. 21-2)

It is not necessary to repeat the well-known description of pre-revolutionary society; the stark contrasts between rural and urban people permeated all aspects of life; housing, medical care, food, education and job opportunities. Wage disparities between rural and urban workers were large: in 1957 the annual per capita income for rural agricultural wage workers was about $91 in contrast to a national average of about $374. Needless to say, these differences in earning power were reflected in poorer nutritional levels and greater illness among people in rural areas. Housing conditions were also quite wretched in rural areas, further reinforcing the general poverty of the rural proletariat. (Agupacion Catolica Universitaria, 1957)

Rural-urban contrasts were even more marked in education. A 1950 report noted that:

> Some progress was made in the thirties and forties, particularly in a start towards secondary education...But the general trend in the school system as a whole has been one of retrogression...Rural areas are much worse off educationally in all respects. Where rural schools do exist they are almost exclusively of the one room type in which the same teacher must teach all the primary grades. The educational content is not well suited to the problems of rural living.

The international commission went on to warn that the public school system was in danger of becoming a "poor man's school" and that in general, "The Cuban people have not been getting their money's worth for the relatively generous amounts that they have been willing to spend on education." (IBRD, 1951, pp. 404-5, 434)

Not surprisingly, unemployment was also a great problem in pre-revolutionary Cuba. Although it varied greatly throughout the year -- as agricultural demands changed -- about 16 percent of the labor force was unemployed in 1956-57 (Seers, 1964, p. 12); underemployment was also common and 20 percent of the labor force was reported as 'partially' or 'temporarily' employed or engaged in unpaid family labor.* When people were able to work, however, their work week was considerably longer than 40 hours: almost 50% of all wage-jobs required seven-day weeks and 35% of those surveyed reported working a six-day week. One knowledgeable student of the subject commented:

> That wage-labour should have been <u>willing</u> to work 7 days a week when given the opportunity to do so stemmed, of course, from the fact that such opportunities were limited. Indeed, for a prolonged period of the year it seems likely that a substantial proportion of the agricultural wage-labour force was unable to secure an income from wage-work sufficient to provide basic subsistence for themselves and their dependents. In the months when work was available, it was thus in many cases necessary to earn not simply a <u>subsistence</u> income but a <u>surplus</u> with which to subsidise consumption over the months when it was not. (Pollitt, 1970, p. 88)

These comments about wages, working and living conditions and the availability of basic services like education only give an indication of the situation in rural areas. It does not adequately describe some of the problems of people living in urban slums but it is probably not necessary to emphasize that the differences between the urban rich and poor were also great. The lower classes were, in fact, in dire straits. The economic stagnation of the fifties in combination with the relative deterioration of the educational system provided a very bleak outlook for the rural workers and peasants, the unemployed and even some of the people working in the service sector of the economy.

III. The Tools of Redistribution

Although Castro has frequently referred to the substantial class differences in Cuba and pledged to eradicate them, the lengths to which he has gone to do so were not easily predictable before the revolutionary forces rose to power. Almost from the first day the new government took actions which led to a dramatic redistribution of consumption away from the urban areas and towards the peasants and landless rural workers. The differences

---

*Pollitt (1971) suggested that these figures may be somewhat misleading. "The speed with initially 'abundant' supplies of underutilized agricultural wage-labour were apparently exhausted suggested that this 'abundance' had been exaggerated. In fact,...<u>there was no great, easily-tapped' reserve army of unemployed workers during the months of peak labour requirements</u>."

Contradictory evidence from the 1956-57 survey referred to in the text suggests that one-third of the unemployed people during the harvest season were in Oriente province, itself a sugar producing area, and also next to Camaguey, the island's largest sugar producing region. It is universally agreed upon that during the 'dead season' there was a great deal of real unemployment.

inherited from the highly stratified class structure still have not been entirely eliminated and they will not be in the short-run. Castro (1 May 1971) explained that "equality of satisfaction of needs is the product of a highly developed society" not of one in which "productive forces and the material base" still must be developed. To minimize these differences a cumulative redistributive process is constantly being reinforced with new measures dictated by a pragmatic mixture of ideology and necessity. In this section we shall explore the principal means by which this redistribution is being effected.

Two different types of measures were taken: a reallocation of resources between investment and a redistribution of consumption goods among the population. Economic growth was a primary concern of those responsible for designing a new development strategy but egalitarian considerations transformed full employment and the provision of a minimum standard of living for everyone into important and unpostponable objectives. Investments rose dramatically from less than one-fifth of national income to almost one-third during the sixties as economic planners attempted to restructure the economy to meet future demands and increase productive capacity. (Barkin, 1972) The remaining resources are used to produce or acquire mass consumption goods and foodstuffs; luxury goods and consumer durables, common in the homes of the upper classes prior to the Revolution, became virtually unavailable.

The reallocative measures were designed to raise the country's productive capacity and reorient it to respond to the needs of a new structure of demand from the whole population. They aim to facilitate more rapid capital accumulation and technical innovation as a means of increasing production now or in the future. The redistributive measures were designed principally to transfer control of already existing resources to different groups of people in a more equitable manner.

Few measures had only dynamic allocative effects or static redistributive impact. This is, in itself, an indication of the pervasive nature of the effort to restructure society and redistribute opportunities among people and, more importantly, among formerly well-defined social classes. Although the division must, in the last analysis be arbitrary, our criterion is based on whether or not the particular measure appears to be primarily designed to increase production (allocative) or to redistribute existing or planned increments in production (redistributive).

In order to implement these measures a great deal of emphasis has been placed on the reorientation of individual motivations from material incentives to another system based on 'morale' or non-material incentives. It would be difficult to understand the adoption of and insistence on honorific titles, flags and other symbolic rewards for individual and group contributions to national productive efforts if it were not accompanied by a concerted effort of conscientization and strong measures to redistribute consumption and guarantee minimum standards of living.

Allocative Measures

Perhaps the two most notable and evident changes which have had an important effect on living standards from the beginning of the revolutionary period are the increase in and dispersion of educational and medical facilities throughout the island. These services were previously highly concentrated in Havana and generally available only to the upper classes. A concerted effort has been made during the past 12 years to expand the scope of these programs and to ensure their availability to everyone. This is not the place to reflect on the importance of these services for future economic development, per se, but the expansion of educational opportunities, the achievement of almost universal literacy and the reduction of many environmentally induced illnesses do provide greater opportunities for people from less priviledged backgrounds to aspire to high technical and administrative positions. (Bowles, 1970)

Education. Education is important for the freedom it gives the individual to participate in society. By facilitating greater occupational mobility it is much easier to break the formerly important intergenerational links which tied the socio-economic status of a child very closely to that of his parents. It is important, in this respect, to note that the benefits from education are only permissive; that is, they do not assure a person access to higher incomes or consumption levels or more important jobs. The availability of education itself does not guarantee the creation of a more egalitarian society but when it functions in conjunction with other institutions that ensure the availability of jobs to those leaving school it opens new channels for social and economic mobility in a society anxious for change. (Barkin, 1971)

The first step along this path was the massive literacy campaign undertaken during 1961 to completely erradicate illiteracy. Although the Cuban rate of illiteracy was lower than other Latin American countries, there was 24% illiteracy on the eve of the Revolution. In the first years of the new government, the level of literacy was raised to about 97% (UCLA, 1970) and in spite of the common problem of defining functional illiteracy, it appears that the rate is still above 95% one decade after the massive initial program.(Castro, Nov. 12, 1971)

Part of the reason for this is the rapid and all-embracing expansion of the school system. More than one-quarter of the population is in school and about 7% of the gross national product is presently devoted to education; this is among the highest proportionate amounts spent on education by any country. (Bohemia, 26 July 1970, p. 37) Not only has there been an important extension of the primary school system which now provides opportunities for well over 90% of the school-age population, but there has been an even more dramatic rise in attendance at secondary and higher educational levels. These opportunities are provided throughout the country and are planned in close coordination with the changing structure of the labor force to ensure that the school system is providing the necessary labor for the national development effort. At the university level, for example, there has been a change from a basic emphasis on liberal arts and humanistic careers to engineering, technical and medical faculties; teacher training students represented almost 40% of the university population in 1969 while ten years earlier they accounted for less than one-quarter of the total. (UCLA, 1970)

While the system is still not all-encompassing and there are still many problems with early drop-outs especially in rural areas at the primary level, educational opportunities in Cuba are fairly broadly distributed. The widely and almost universally observed handicap against children from rural areas still exists in Cuba because of the relative lack of educational facilities which is being slowly corrected. (Castro, April 4, 1972) In many cases, the rural schools are more comprehensive than the urban ones because many of them are boarding schools directly concerned with preparing students for careers in technical occupations. (Leiner, 1970; Leiner and Ubell, 1972) At the moment the great shortage of trained manpower assures rapid advancement for those who successfully complete their education and are able to use it effectively in productive activities. (Bowles, 1971)

Medical care. Like education, health services have also grown rapidly in recent years. The quantitative expansion of medical facilities operated and financed by the State is important but even more impressive is their dispersion throughout the island. Although the country was greatly handicapped by the initial large-scale emigration of many trained medical personnel -- 2,583 out of 6,300 qualified physicians in Cuba in 1959 left between 1959 and 1967 -- the expansion of training (there are now about 7,000 physicians in Cuba) and physical facilities has been complemented by a change in attitudes about the provision of medical care. Greater emphasis is being placed on preventive medicine which can be administered by relatively easily trained medical technicians and other paramedical personnel; between 1959 and 1967, 17,549 people were prepared for such positions. Much recent effort has been directed to the construction of out-patient clinics with limited hospital-care facilities. These are designed to diagnose illness and channel people who need further care on to better equipped institutions which service several smaller policlinicos. (Orris, 1970; Liebowitz, 1970)

A program of preventive medicine, especially for young people, supplemented the expansion of medical services and produced a substantial change in the nature of illness. Polio, malaria and diptheria are disappearing. Dysentary and other nutritional problems have declined markedly and now rank low as a cause of death in Cuba, although gastroenteritis is still a major concern for health officials. From an economic point of view, good health increases labor productivity and eliminates costly programs of curative medicine. From the individual's point of view it is another element in the program to reduce the disabilities which environment and socio-economic status confer on the poor.

Other collective services. Medical care and educational facilities are not the only collective services available to sizable proportions of the population. An additional general service which is now widely available is the beach resort. Through a rotating system most working Cubans are now able to enjoy a vacation at formerly exclusive resorts. Recreation is also provided by specially arranged tours of cultural and sporting events. Groups like the internationally acclaimed National Ballet of Cuba perform not only in Havana, as was formerly the case, but are taken on tours throughout the island. This reduces the uniqueness of Havana as a cultural center and increases the cohesiveness and sense of participation of the population in the nation's progress.

Individual goods. But the development effort has not only produced collective consumption and investment services like the ones mentioned above. Individual durable and non-durable consumer goods production has also increased, although certainly not in proportion to the increase in demand that has accompanied the general increase in employment and money incomes. In addition to the whole range of non-durable consumer goods which are rationed, there is another group of durable goods, many of which are being distributed by local workers' councils at work centers. Most essential items and some light manufactured goods, e.g., small electrical appliances, are distributed by state controlled outlets as discussed below (cf. employment and rationing). Other goods, like stoves and refrigerators, are distributed in accordance with the needs of new construction and then the remaining production is allocated on a regional basis for local distribution by the workers themselves. Distribution in the work centers will undoubtedly become increasingly important as the production of consumer durables rises in coming years.

On the allocative side, the Cuban development effort has been directed towards increasing the output of certain basic services and consumption goods. After allowing for the satisfaction of this basic demand, however, a large part of the increases in productive capacity installed since the early sixties has been used for the further expansion of productive capacity rather than for the increased production of consumer goods and services. This strategy is designed to ensure the growth of the Cuban economy while at the same time providing a basic minimum standard of living for all people. In this way not only are all people guaranteed access to certain basic services but, more importantly, the intergenerational transmission of social class and economic status has been greatly reduced.

Geographic decentralization. An important part of new investment has been in secondary towns which are thriving. The decision to relocate industrial and agricultural activity provides a means to consolidate present efforts to redistribute income as these industries grow and improve prospects for the continued equalization of living standards among regions. One of the common features of most countries -- and one which is often exaggerated in the developing countries -- is the extreme concentration of economic activity and services in one or more large cities and the almost complete isolation and neglect of smaller towns and rural areas. Thus, even if attempts were made to equalize incomes amongst all groups in the country, the relative isolation of those people living in remote areas would continually frustrate the effort. A mere redistribution of incomes through the taxation and expenditure system is not effective as long as certain (urban) groups have privileged access to the centers of power and production; a market mechanism would rapidly reconcentrate effective control over resources in the hands of a few. (Barkin, 1972)

The Cuban program to decentralize economic activity is being pursued on a number of fronts. (Acosta and Hardoy, 1971) First, and perhaps most striking, is the effort to slow down or halt the growth of the Havana metropolitan area. During recent years there has been little or no additional construction of housing in the area and, with the exception of an expansion of port facilities, little enlargement of productive investments. These measures have been combined with a national effort to reduce the need for transporting basic food stuffs among provinces by attempting to make each of the urban areas more self-sufficient. To this end, green belts have been designed around each of the larger cities to supply vegetables and other foods for the urban population. Another important facet of the physical planning program has been the construction of several new cities in previously low density areas. These permit both a fuller utilization of the country's natural resources and a more rational use of the transportation system. Development planners are preparing at least eight alternative centers for industrial and agricultural programs. This is in addition to the colonization effort being mounted on the Isle of Youth (Pines). The effect of these programs is to restructure the location of economic activity and end Havana's domination of the rest of the country, so characteristic of the pre-revolutionary epoch; for instance, previously, Oriente province was Havana's principal source of greens but consumption of greens in that region was restricted.

The result of these efforts has been a virtual halt in Havana's population growth; since 1965 it has stabilized at about 1,700,000 (up from 1,217,674 in 1953) and its relative size has diminished as the Cuban population has grown. With relocation of economic activity, the increased opportunities for people in other population centers should further accelerate the growth of intermediate cities like Santiago (from 300,000 to 500,000 in the next 15 years), Santa Clara (where the university is expected to grow rapidly and light consumer durables will be manufactured), and Cienfuegos (where a large port and industrial facilities are being constructed).*

The traditional disadvantage of people in secondary cities and rural areas is thus being attacked by de-emphasizing the importance of Havana as a cultural, educational, and economic center. By redistributing services and improving living conditions in other places, and by discouraging

---

*In 1969, the Cubans suggested an even more drastic reorganization of the structure of towns by calling for the gradual disappearance of "centers with minimal services" and the development of "centers with local services which can also serve the surrounding region." In the first type of "community the improvement of social and environmental conditions would be achieved through temporary investments....The new centers...would be based on the transformation of existing communities through mechanization, intensive cultivation, dense road networks and a high degree of transport development." (Cuban delegation to the 1969 F.A.O. Conference, 1970a)

migration to Havana, the government has been better able to implement its program for equalizing opportunities and living conditions.

In summary, the Revolutionary government has taken a series of measures to increase and relocate production so as to provide greater opportunities for people who were previously isolated from the main stream of economic life. These measures are similar to those proposed by development advisors throughout the world. Increased resources for social welfare to benefit the lower classes and weaken the intergenerational transfer of status are standard parts of a development program. Similarly, specialists on regional growth stress the importance of decentralizing activity to accelerate growth and minimize the social costs of agglomeration. It is rare that both approaches, increased production and relocation, are combined as part of a broad program to equalize consumption and opportunities among different groups of people.

Redistributive measures

Agrarian reform. One of the steps taken to redistribute wealth and improve rural conditions in the first days of the new government was the enactment of agrarian reform legislation which was progressively broadened to end the private ownership of all but the smallest viable units of land. Unlike the two prior agrarian reforms in Latin America, in Mexico and Bolivia, the former large estates were not subdivided to create individual plots and rural bourgeoise and/or peasantry; the leadership argued that since Cuba had a long tradition of a rural proletariat, it would be more advantageous and productive to maintain the organizational integrity of these large units and concentrate on their efficient management for the benefit of the nation. (Gutelman, 1967)

As a result, agricultural development in Cuba proceeded on the basis of state planning and operation of the expropriated lands. This permitted a rapid expansion of cultivated land and a program to increase and diversify production to satisfy growing domestic demands, increase exports and substitute for some imports. When combined with the extensive program of public works -- especially feeder roads and dams -- the state's role in the agricultural sector has occasioned a large increase in employment and substantial increases in incomes for the workers who previously had to depend on the work available during the harvest season to support their families during the whole year.* (Cuban Delegation to F.A.O., 1970b)

Thus, the program of agrarian reform and agricultural development which this permitted created the basis for a widespread increase in employment and incomes amongst the poorest segments of the population. In addition, it has had the obvious effect of taking an important source of wealth from landlords who were appropriating the resource and surplus and transferring it to the public sector where it was used as the basis for the financing of the

---

*There are still about 200,000 private farmers in Cuba.

long-term development effort.

Urban reform. Following close on the heels of the agrarian reform law in 1959 was the first of a series of measures designed to deal with the housing problem. Regulations limiting speculation in urban real estate were later supplemented by limits on the rent for families with low and moderate incomes; for landlords with large incomes, real estate earnings were similarly restricted. Initial regulations limited rents to 10% of income and in 1971 this was lowered to 6%; the poorest families pay no rent.

Needless to say, there is still an acute shortage of housing in Cuba; in 1970 Castro estimated the present deficit at about one million units while a United Nations expert suggests that the figure is closer to 1,200,000 units (Acosta and Hardoy, 1971, p. 106) To solve this problem and keep up with new demand would require an annual construction program of about 119,000 units a year for the foreseeable future. Present housing programs which are providing about 30,000 new units a year are clearly inadequate to solve the problem. It is significant, however, that great strides have been made to give first priority to those families living in the slums and shanty towns on the outskirts of the major cities.

The urban reform program allowed most people to remain in the homes in which they were living at the time of the Revolution; as a result much of the de facto stratification which existed prior to the Revolution might be expected to persist. Important exceptions developed, however, as the upper classes fled the country, the government reassigned these homes to priority groups. Many of the most fashionable large homes in Havana were converted into dormitory units for the university students who are now provided with full scholarships for their education. Others were assigned to workers on the basis of need. Thus, with the migration of large numbers of the upper and middle classes, formerly exclusive neighborhoods have acquired a more varied group of residents.

Employment and rationing. As was suggested in the introduction and in the first part of this section, economic development programs during the first decade of the present government resulted in a large increase in employment as formerly unemployed people were absorbed into productive activities. In and of itself, this improved the well-being of a large but formerly marginal part of the Cuban population and transformed them into supporters of and active participants in the national development effort. With the achievement of full employment and an intensified effort to incorporate people who were formerly not even looking for work into the labor force, came a rapid increase in money incomes.* This increase in incomes created a substantial rise in demand for many consumer goods as people who were previously unable to purchase goods suddenly found themselves with

---

*In a recent attempt to incorporate people who were not working, Castro (May 2, 1971) reported that 101,019 people responded to the possibility of severe penalties by joining the labor force.

money. After imports of consumer goods rose rapidly in the early years of the new administration, it became clear that rationing would be necessary if demand were not to be controlled through price rises; Castro (July 26, 1970) rejected inflation as "nothing short of a ruthless sacrifice of those sectors of the population with the least income."* Castro's attitude toward inflation and his determination to destroy the pre-revolutionary class structure, left little alternative to the imposition of rationing.

Although rationing started gradually, it soon spread to all consumer goods and now covers virtually everything available for sale to the individual. Obviously, those goods which are not rationed are in heavy demand and long queues are testimony to the large quantity of excess purchasing power which many people have after buying all the goods permitted them and available under the ration program.** Part of the reason for the excess money is that there are very few families which have only one breadwinner; social, psychological or other pressures are used to encourage every person to join in the productive effort while minimum wages are generally sufficient to support the average family with only one wage-earner. When this is combined with the observations that 1) most children receive at least one free meal at school and many children are in full boarding schools during the week, without a reduction in the family rations, and 2) most workers receive at least one meal at their place of employment in communal dining halls, it is understandable that expenditures for basic food allowances often account for only a part of the total family income. Rents were always kept low in relation to income; medical and educational costs are completely borne by the state and pensions are provided for the aged. Thus, relatively large amounts of "excess" income are exerting latent inflationary pressures on all available goods. The resulting queues for restaurant meals, transportation, hotel accomodations, ice cream, and other unrationed goods are very long; all reading material is sold out almost as soon as it is put on sale as are all other unrationed products. This further heightens the shortage of consumer goods since "nobody who has the opportunity will miss buying a single article to which he has an opportunity to buy" regardless of whether or not he has a need for it.*** Strong government action to absorb the

---

*Rationing -- either directly or through inflation -- is a necessary consequence of a program of rapid economic development like the Cuban one. With rates of savings and investment approaching one-third of gross material product, it would be difficult to obtain the necessary domestic resources without controlling domestic consumption in some manner. Given the strong egalitarian bent of the Cuban leadership, rationing seems like the only possible alternative to try and still work for both growth and equality.

**There is also an apparent shortage of some rationed goods, especially in Havana, which also induces queuing for these products.

***Bohemia, January 1, 1971. This comment was made in an article on the need to raise tobacco prices in order to absorb some excess money in private hands. Most observers who have commented on the black market in Cuba have suggested that in spite of the large amount of excess liquidity that

excess purchasing power and reduce the distortioning effects it has on the distribution of consumer goods is being undertaken.*

The combination of all of these elements, both on the allocative and distributive levels, produces a guarantee of a basic minimum standard of living and availability of services for most of the population. The Cuban approach raises the minimum standard of living as resources permit while limiting the maximum amount which individuals are permitted to earn. Most equalization is achieved by limiting individual consumption and placing an increasingly heavy emphasis on individual participation in collective services. In adopting this approach greater stress appears to be placed on children's welfare; by reducing the intergenerational transfer of class and status positions through education, medical care, and nutritional planning, many more people are available to participate fully in the development effort and the worst effects of poverty are mitigated even if income differentials are not eliminated.

Morale Incentives**

All of these policies are inextricably related to a more recent decision to deemphasize material incentives in favor of 'morale' or non-material approaches to individual stimulation. This approach was originally championed by Guevara in Cuba and was only formally decided upon after a lengthy debate in which people from all parts of the socialist world participated. Castro explained his decision to adopt this approach in his speech of August 26, 1966. (Silverman, 1971)

The new approach was explicitly designed to break the close relation between work and wages that usually prevails in most economies. It focused

---

remains, there has been an effective control of the black market. See, for example, Mesa-Lago (1971).

*This theme was discussed at length in Castro's speech of May 1, 1971. He pointed out that many light industrial products sold to consumers -- plastic shoes and beer were mentioned -- absorb sizable quantities of excess purchasing power. An extensive analysis of recent measures to control the distribution of cigarettes is illustrative of the dual problem of controlling consumption through the price system without losing sight of the impact such measures would have on equality: "rationing was the worst [solution] because ...it creates a vice in someone who doesn't have it...it creates an incredible small scale commercialism." Castro proposed an alternative of maintaining rationing and low prices "to take into consideration our comrades with low incomes" and sell, at very much higher prices, excess quantities. "Some measure [to absorb income] has to be taken, some measure."

**This section only briefly describes the system of non-monetary incentives presently being implemented in Cuba. Silverman (1971) traces its origins and closely examines its operation and some problems which have arisen in practice in an excellent analysis of the subject (1972).

on the responsibility of the worker to contribute to the productive requirements for social development without making his contribution depend directly on his own personal gain from the effort. This was to be achieved through education and emulation campaigns which could emphasize the common cause of all Cubans in assisting in the effort to break out of underdevelopment. Monetary and other material incentives were to be reduced and eventually eliminated; "The Revolution aspires to attain the equality of workers' incomes of those who are earning least." (Castro, July 26, 1970) Overtime pay was to be eliminated and even greater emphasis was to be placed on the contribution of voluntary labor time for productive activities, especially in the agricultural sector. Similarly, greater attention was to be placed on incorporating those who were not as productive as they might be into the productive effort through mobilization campaigns; they are especially directed at women who are being incorporated into activities at an accelerated rate.

Rewards for work were changed from material benefits in the form of extra pay, household durables, vacations, etc. to titles, awards, and special recognition by regional and national leaders. "Vanguard workers," "million-ton cane cutters," and similar titles were designed to instill pride in the best workers; the poorest workers often found their names posted in prominent places. In return the government would respond by providing services on a more communistic basis to those participating in the effort.

In practice, Cuba is still far from fully implementing a system of morale incentives. Castro (July 26, 1968) himself noted that "There are still large inequalities in income, some of them very large....The Revolution hopes to achieve the equality of income...[but it] cannot achieve such equality in one day." Recently he reiterated this point, explaining at length that although the ultimate goal of Cuban development is the achievement of communism -- with the equality that it implies -- it would be counterproductive to move in that direction too rapidly. <u>Consciencia</u>, the understanding of and commitment to the regime of morale incentives, must continually be developed.* "We should not do anything which would go against the development of this collective <u>consciencia</u>....But the road to communism is not only a road of <u>consciencia</u>; it is a road of development of productive forces and the material base." In developing, however, "we cannot simply forget that there are some jobs which are harder than others...that require more skill and responsibility....Sometimes it is hard to obtain workers for a line of activity....We still have to use some springboards; wages cannot be exactly equal...there is no other mechanism during the process of transition from socialism to communism." (Castro, May 1, 1971).

The goal is eventually to transform completely the role that money plays in the economy. It will no longer be "a means of accumulation, nor an instrument of exchange, nor a measure of value...stripped of its historical

---

*The term 'consciencia' was used by Guevara when he formulated his ideas on moral incentives. Its literal translation, conscience, fails to convey the depth of the Spanish word and it is left untranslated.

characteristics, it will be fundamentally a means of distribution."
(Castro, May 1, 1971) But such a transformation is possible only in an affluent society. Up to the present progress has been made in reducing the importance of wages and money incomes as a determinant of the standard of living. Even before the explicit decision to adopt morale incentives was made, the growing quantity of public services available to the population and the limited amount of consumer goods which could be purchased through the ration program had changed the role which money incomes had in determining living standards. The adoption of the new measures are, in part, a logical extension of the prevailing egalitarian ideology. The scarcity of individual consumer goods further reinforces the need to find some alternative way of motivating people; Castro (March 24, 1968) asked rhetorically whether Cuba was "going to stimulate people with money with which they can buy nothing?" Thus, a combination of egalitarian ideals and physical necessity makes the formal adoption of the path of <u>consciencia</u> a natural choice.

IV. Development and the Redistribution of Consumption

The redistributive tools described in the last section are an integral part of an overall development strategy designed to improve standards of living while creating the basic productive capacity to permit continued growth. The initial effort to redistribute incomes from the wealthier groups in the urban areas to the poorer ones in the rural areas was an important move in this direction as were the agrarian and urban reforms. But these redistributive measures were only a means to replace the hierarchical class structure with a new fundamentally egalitarian social and economic structure.

In the first years of the Revolution, the government was faced with the immediate necessity of reducing some of the glaring inequalities which then prevailed. At the same time, however, it rapidly became clear that it would be important to dedicate as large a proportion as possible of all resources to creating additional productive capacity and building up the necessary social and physical infrastructure. To do this all underutilized resources would have to be mobilized and means would have to be found to limit the proportion of total production allocated for consumption purposes.

Relatively rapid and large increases in agricultural production were obtained in the first years by the cultivation of the vast tracts of idle land which were being held in reserve in the pre-revolutionary period. Ambitious public works projects, education and other development programs were also undertaken to increase rapidly employment and incomes in the lower classes. Consumption rose and the lower classes were the beneficiaries of a series of measures which led one commentator to observe that "nothing is too good for the peasants." (Francos, 1962) It soon became apparent that an unbridled expansion of consumption and a broad scale development program could not continue indefinitely for lack of sufficient exports to finance the burgeoning import requirements of a country which produced little of its own food and practically none of its industrial goods. A rethinking of economic development strategy was called for.

The 1963 decision to emphasize agriculture in the first stage of development was the result. A 10-million-ton goal was established for the sugar harvest and subsidiary goals were set for cattle, citrus fruits, and other agricultural products. These programs were to be implemented without changing the basic commitment to create full employment or to move in the direction of a more egalitarian society. Within a few years, the labor problem in Cuba changed from one of superabundance to generalized scarcity; broad-ranging development plans required large cadres throughout the economy and during the harvest season people were diverted from their usual jobs to participate in the collection efforts. (Barkin, 1972a)

The new type of labor problem made the decision to invest heavily in education and medical care extremely important. With reserves of manpower and land quickly exhausted, future growth had to be based on reorganization and mechanization throughout the economy; agricultural technicians, machine operators and people with industrial skills of all types were urgently needed to permit the installation of new productive facilities and the replacement of low-productivity labor with machinery. Education was restructured and expanded to provide training which was more directly relevant to the new productive needs of the country.

At the same time, the fundamental emphasis on agriculture required the availability of large numbers of people for harvesting chores and hastened the decision to decentralize industrial production. By locating new productive facilities throughout the island, new population centers could provide labor at crucial periods with less disruption of the transportation system and the economy as a whole. The decision to assign new importance to secondary cities would also permit large savings in public works projects and urban transportation, and would avoid urban congestion and reduce pollution, in addition to providing for a more efficient use of the national transportation system and a fuller exploitation of the nation's natural and human resources.

Thus, the allocative measures which we described above were all integral parts of the national development effort. They paved the way for the installation of new productive capacity and the raising of industrial and agricultural efficiency. The urban and agrarian reforms complemented these measures by redistributing the available housing supply in a more satisfactory manner and permitting the government to mobilize all available land for national agricultural development plans.

These programs were insufficient by themselves to assure the success of the development effort. Individual consumption had to be restricted if the nation was to continue using most of its foreign exchange and credit for the needed imports of capital equipment and raw materials for industrial production. A large proportion of Cuba's increased productive efforts was directed towards agricultural products which were to be exchanged for needed capital equipment in international markets. Without an adequate mechanism to restrain internal demand for domestically grown agricultural products and the importation of other consumption goods, it would be impossible to undertake the long term development program sketched out during the mid-sixties.

Rationing was imposed and shortly thereafter accompanied by efforts to change individual incentives to a system of non-material rewards. This did not, by any means, require a decline in living standards for most of the proletariat. The ration program afforded everyone regular access to products which were formerly luxuries like meat and milk while assuring everyone sufficient food; children are especially privileged as special school meal programs and infant rations permit young people a greater variety and quantity of food than most others.* The ration program made the adoption of moral incentives almost a necessity as the goods available to reward workers were not sufficiently attractive to induce the personal effort which the new government hoped to evoke. Rationing also facilitated a more rapid movement towards egalitarianism while permitting the Cubans to devote as much as one-third of their material product to new investment projects.

In this paper we have only tried to describe some of the mechanisms which equalized opportunities and/or actual living standards among different groups in the population. We have argued that these measures were rarely adopted with the single-minded purpose of redistribution but rather that they responded to a series of considerations designed to facilitate the achievement of political, social, and economic goals consistent with a broader view of equality within a formerly highly stratified class structure. Although it is not possible to measure the reduction in equality -- and in spite of the large disparities which will continue to exist for some time to come -- it is clear that we can answer all three of the questions posed at the beginning of this article similarly: there has been a reduction in poverty, unemployment and inequality. Therefore in Seers' language, "beyond doubt this has been a period of development" for Cuba.**

---

*The members of the upper and middle classes who elected to remain in Cuba since the Revolution have probably experienced substantial declines in real living standards as food was rationed and luxury products disappeared; personal services were also drastically cut. For additional insight about pre-revolutionary living standards see Agrupacion Catolica Universitaria (1957), Seers (1964), and IBRD (1951). Some indication of present levels of rations is provided at the end of this article.

**Many of the interesting questions emerging from the focus presented in this article cannot, unfortunately, be answered at this time. There seems little doubt that the redistribution of consumption has facilitated the movement towards greater equality while permitting more resources to be drawn off for investment and collective use. Moral incentives were an integral part of the program but it is not clear that material incentives, advocated by some, would have eliminated the problems of low labor productivity and absenteeism. Greater educational opportunity and better medical care do not guarantee social mobility or equality but within the context of geographic decentralization, agrarian and urban reform, and full employment,

In spite of this judgement, it seems premature to draw any conclusions about the long-term success of the economic development strategy or the accompanying social measures; less than ten years have passed since the adoption of the present development strategy and the necessary changes in technology and economic structure which will permit an easing of rationing and greater flexibility in the distribution of individual opportunities and goods and services are just beginning. Changes in social relations came more quickly than the necessary changes in economic relations which will facilitate a correction of some of the existing disequilibria. (Pollitt, 1971) In spite of the problems of implementing it, the Cuban leadership is still following the guidelines of the development strategy outlined above and is making minor adjustments to permit it to function more effectively. (Rodriguez, October 14, 1970)

The changes in social relations already have improved perspectives for the working classes. Most of the impact of the measures discussed in this paper improved their living standards and employment and educational opportunities. This was achieved at the expense of a small, formerly privileged group, most of whom left the island during the first years of Revolutionary government. By focusing attention on the poorest and redistributing consumption from the upper classes, the government was able to improve overall living standards without diverting large quantities of additional resources from the development effort, once the new development strategy was defined in 1963. The program has begun to break the intergenerational transfer of poverty which doomed a child to the status of his parents and has offered new opportunities for people from the lower socio-economic groups to participate fully in the development effort. Clearly, a perfectly egalitarian society is still not on the horizon, but the disparities characterizing the pre-revolutionary society have been greatly reduced.

Equality, and even development, are not the only elements in a national project of nation building. Cuba's experience is important in this respect. The national project of transforming the highly stratified class structure of the pre-revolutionary capitalist society into a classless society along the communist model produces these effects as part of a larger process. They are not the goals of change but rather the means to construct the new society in the image of the "new man." Institutions are being universalized and in the face of greater specialization, the national project calls for less differentiation among people. The lack of conciencia forces many concessions in the name of technological and material advance -- economic growth imposes contradictions on the society which affluence is expected to resolve. But in the construction of a communist society, affluence itself may only be possible with the universalization of conciencia. Controlling the dialectical interaction between evolving economic and social relationships is still one of the major unresolved problems facing the Cuban leadership today.

---

it seems reasonable to assume that the program is contributing towards the reduction of class barriers. Hopefully detailed studies will permit an evaluation of the Cuban experience in this regard, for these subjects are essential ingredients in the quest for development.

Bibliography

Maruja Acosta and Jorge Hardoy (1971), Reforma Urbana en Cuba Revolucionaria, Caracas, Venezuela, Sintesis Dosmil, C.A.

Agrupacion Catolica Universitaria (1957), Porque Reforma Agraria?, La Habana, Cuba, Universidad Catolica.

David Barkin (1971), "La educacion: Una barrera al desarrollo?" Trimestre Economico, no. 152, October, pp. 951-94.

———(1972a), "Cuban Agriculture: A strategy of economic development," Studies in Comparative International Development, Vol. VII: 1 (Spring), pp. 19-38. Also available as Warner reprint R261 and as a chapter in Cuba: The Logic of the Revolution, (1973), Andover, Mass.: Warner Modular Publications, Inc.

———(1972b), "A case study of the beneficiaries of regional development," International Social Development Review, No. 4 (forthcoming).

Bohemia, weekly magazine printed in Havana, Cuba, issues cited in text.

Samuel Bowles (1970), Planning Educational Systems for Economic Growth, Cambridge, Mass.: Harvard Univeristy Press.

———(1971), "Cuban Education and the Revolutionary Ideology," Harvard Educational Review, Vol. 41:4 (Fall).

Martin Bronfenbrenner (1971), Income Distribution Theory, Chicago: Aldine.

Fidel Castro (1953), History Will Absolve Me, La Habana (reprinted by Instituto del Libro, 1967).

———, Speeches, reported in Granma, Weekly Summary, for date of speech given in the text.

Cuba, Delegation to the 1969 F.A.O. Conference (1970), Informe, reprinted in Economia y Desarrollo, no. 1, January-March.

Cuba, Delagation to F.A.O. Regional Conference No. XI (1970b), Informe, (Caracas, Venezuela) reprinted in Economia y Desarrollo, no. 4, Oct-Dec.

Rene Dumont (1970), Cuba, Est-Il Socialiste?, Paris, Le Seuil.

Ania Francos (1962), Le Fete Cubaine, Paris, Juillard.

John Gerassi (ed.) (1968), Venceremos! (The writings of Ernesto Che Guevara), London, Wendenfeld and Nicolson.

Michel Gutelman (1967), L'Agriculture Socialisee a Cuba, Paris, Francois Maspero.

International Bank for Reconstruction and Development (1951), Report on Cuba, Baltimore: Johns Hopkins Press.

Michael Liebowitz (1969), The Cuban Health Care System: A Study in the Evaluation of Health Care Systems, New Haven: Yale University School of Medicine, doctoral dissertation.

Marvin Leiner (1970), "Cuba's Schools, Ten Years Later," Saturday Review, October 17. Available as Warner module M264 and as a chapter in Cuba: The Logic of the Revolution, (1973), Andover, Mass.: Warner Modular Publications, Inc.

_____ and Robert Ubell (1972), "Day Care in Cuba: Children are the Revolution," Saturday Review, April 1.

Carmelo Mesa-Lago (1970), The Labor Sector and Socialist Distribution in Cuba, New York: Praeger.

_____ (1971), "El problema de los incentivos en Cuba," Aportes, April.

Jacob Mincer (1970), "The Distribution of Labor Incomes: A Survey with Special Reference to the Human Capital Approach," Journal of Economic Literature, January.

Peter Orris (1970), The Role of the Consumer in the Cuban National Health System, New Haven: Yale University, M.P.H. Essay (unpublished)

Brian H. Pollitt (1971), "Employment plans, performance and future prospects in Cuba," in Cambridge University Overseas Studies Committee Conference, London, HMSO.

_____ (1970), On Cuba, unpublished manuscript.

Melvin Reder (1969), "A Partial Survey of the Theory of the Income Size Distribution," in Soltow (ed.), Six Papers on the Size Distribution of Wealth and Income, New York: Columbia University Press for the NBER.

Carlos Rafael Rodriguez (1970), Speech, Granma, October 25.

Dudley Seers (ed.) (1964), Cuba, The Economic and Social Revolution, Chapel Hill: University of North Carolina Press.

_____ (1970), "The Meaning of Development," Agricultural Development Council Reprint (630 Park Ave., New York, N.Y.), September

Bertram Silverman (1971), Man and Socialism in Cuba: The Great Debate, New York: Atheneum.

_____ (1972), "Economic Organization and Social Conscience: Some Dilemmas of Cuban Socialism. Available as Warner reprint R262 and as a chapter in Cuba: The Logic of the Revolution, (1973), Andover, Mass.: Warner Modular Publications, Inc.

University of California at Los Angeles, Latin American Center (1970), Cuba 1968: Supplement to the Statistical Abstract of Latin America, Los Angeles: UCLA.

Membership and subscription information for the Union for Radical Political Economics can be obtained by writing to: URPE/University of Michigan/2503 Student Activities Bldg/ Ann Arbor, Michigan 48104

MARVIN LEINER
City University of New York

Major Developments in Cuban Education

"In 1961 Cuba witnessed national mobilization comparable only to a national war effort. Two hundred fifty thousand young people and adults volunteered to go to the remotest parts of Cuba to fight illiteracy. After eight months of intensive, full-time effort, the illiteracy rate in Cuba was reduced from 25 per cent to 3.9 per cent."

In Cuba education is without doubt a major theme which is displayed in posters ubiquitous in the city streets and alongside rural roads: "The Path up from Underdevelopment is Education." "The School Plan is Your Responsibility." Education, together with emphasis on economic growth, is given first priority in Cuba today.

During a year of study in Cuba (1968-1969) and a return visit in August and September of 1971, I observed some of the recent developments in Cuban education. Much of what I saw can be divided into the following ten areas: rapid quantitative growth, curriculum change, politicization of the schools, boarding and semi-boarding schools, development of new materials, pragmatic approach to educational problems, "school to the countryside" secondary programs, concept of revolutionary educational leadership, teacher preparation, day care education.

RAPID QUANTITATIVE GROWTH

In 1964 Richard Jolly presented his study of Cuban education, based upon a 1962 visit there, in Dudley Seer's book, Cuba: The Economic and Social Revolution. He reported that, "The Cuban Government in the education field has acted simultaneously on a large number of educational fronts, mobilizing economic and human resources with a massiveness seldom if ever seen."[1] The rapid growth of Cuban schools and the investment in education was still evident during my visits in 1968-69 and 1971, as the following statistics will show.

In the decade from 1959 to 1969 the number of schools in Cuba increased almost five hundred percent—from 7,783 to 42,460. By 1971 the number of primary-school pupils doubled—from 717,417 to 1,664,634. By 1971 the teaching force (primary schools) increased more than threefold—from 17,355 to 60,592.

Prior to the Revolution there were 2,580 teachers employed on the secondary level. By 1971 the number of teachers had grown to 15,273. The student enrollment on the secondary level increased from 63,526 to 186,667, or nearly three times.

The number of students in industrial-technological schools more than quadrupled in the 1959 to 1969 decade—from 6,259 to 29,975. Agricultural schools increased from zero to 37 institutions with 2,335 teachers and 36,812 students. In higher education the number of faculty members had grown from 1,053 before the Revolution to 4,645 by 1971. Student enrollment increased from

A WARNER MODULAR PUBLICATION

Library of Congress Catalog Card Number 73-5216

10 9 8 7 6 5 4 3 2 1

**The Developmental Economics Series
is under the editorship of**

DAVID P. BARKIN
*City University of New York
Lehman College*

SUGGESTED CITATION:

Marvin Leiner, "Major Developments in Cuban Education," Warner Modular Publications, Module 264 (1973), pp 1–21

All original publications in this series appear first as separate modules. Most modules will appear in one collection; many will appear in several. To facilitate research use, all modules are numbered serially, and each module carries the same number and folio sequence in all incarnations.

25,599 to 45,247 in the same period.

In Worker-Farmer, or adult education, schools a total of 365,720 persons had completed sixth grade by 1969 and 57,844 had completed secondary schools. In the area of special education only one public school existed before the Revolution. In 1971 there were 129 schools with an enrollment of 7,880 students and 1,401 teachers.[2]

One could cite additional data to indicate the tremendous growth in enrollment and number of schools in such specific areas as fishing, sports, arts, etc. One-quarter of Cuba's population goes to school: two million of eight million people are in a program of free, universal education from nursery school through university.

The following figure presents the organization table of the national educational system of Cuba.[3]

CURRICULUM CHANGE

Change in Cuban curriculum occurs in both "upward" and "downward" directions. Consider an educational organizational chart with the Ministry of Education at the top and the students and classroom teachers at the bottom. By "downward" direction I mean change which is initiated by the Ministry and moves downward to the classroom. Most change appears to occur in this direction. But there is also evidence of change initiated upward, by which I mean change introduced in a particular class or school which then spreads horizontally and finally moves upward through the system to the Ministry. Here are two examples.

First, let us consider the introduction of modern mathematics into Cuban schools. To learn the answers to such critical questions as why the course was changed, how it was changed, and how the change was introduced, I interviewed Dr. Maria de Carmen Nuñez Berro, head of the mathematics curriculum from kindergarten to twelfth grade. She emphasized that mathematics is a key curriculum area. If Cuba is to come up from underdevelopment, a mathematically educated population is a necessity. It is required for science, agriculture, medicine, technology; in short, in almost every area of Cuba's projected growth. Berro explained that in 1965 the Minister of Education had asked her to study mathematics programs in other countries to determine the proper direction for Cuba. She became very familiar with such United States math programs as the Madison Project, the Greater Cleveland Pro-

Major Developments in Cuban Education   M264-3

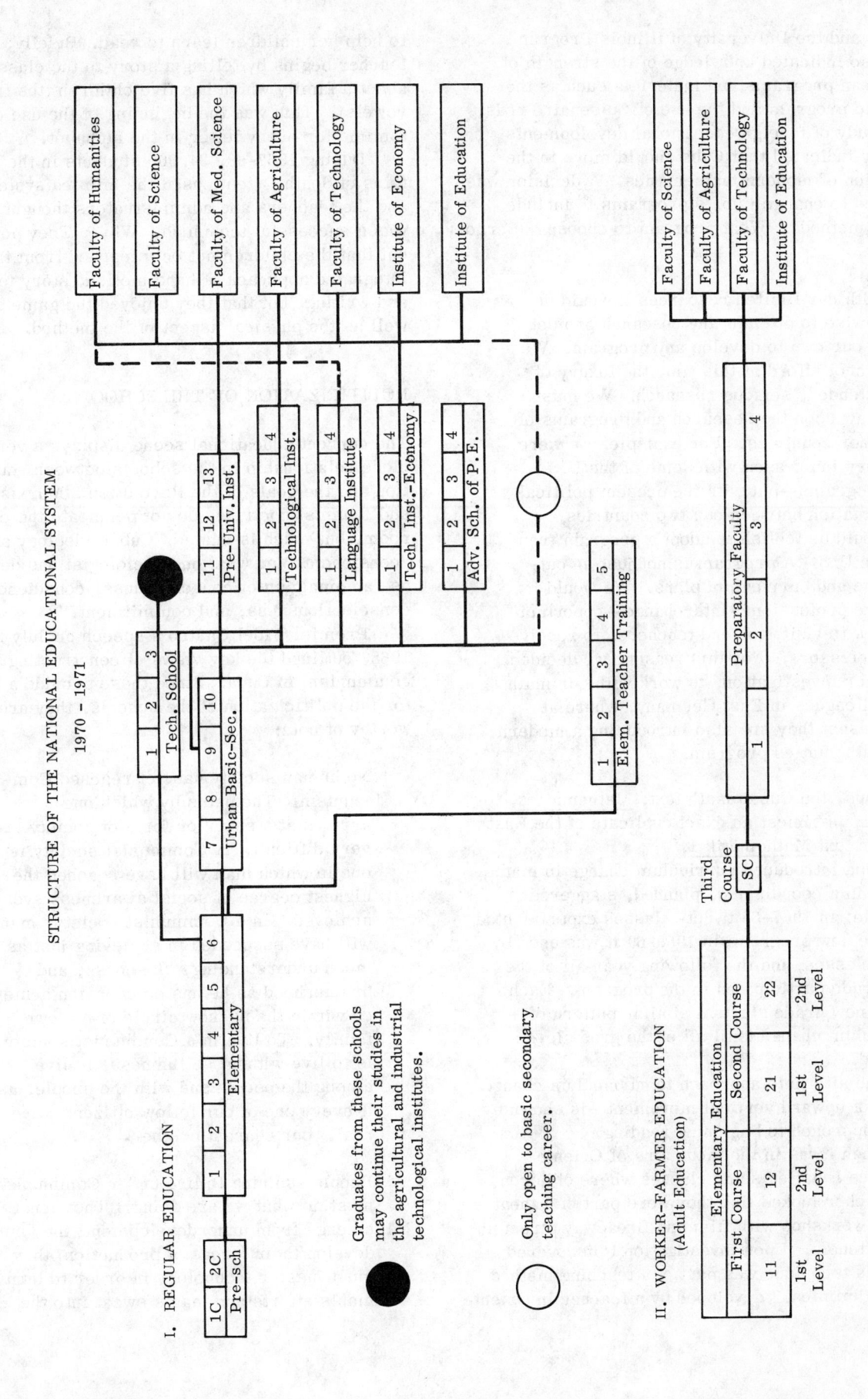

STRUCTURE OF THE NATIONAL EDUCATIONAL SYSTEM
1970 – 1971

I. REGULAR EDUCATION

1C	2C		1	2	3	4	5	6	7	8	9	10	11	12	13
Pre-sch			Elementary						Urban Basic-Sec.				Pre-Univ. Inst.		

Tech. School: 1 2 3

Technological Inst.: 1 2 3 4
Language Institute: 1 2 3 4
Tech. Inst.-Economy: 1 2 3 4
Adv. Sch. of P.E.: 1 2 3 4

Elem. Teacher Training: 1 2 3 4 5

- Faculty of Humanities
- Faculty of Science
- Faculty of Med. Science
- Faculty of Agriculture
- Faculty of Technology
- Institute of Economy
- Institute of Education

● Graduates from these schools may continue their studies in the agricultural and industrial technological institutes.

○ Only open to basic secondary teaching career.

II. WORKER-FARMER EDUCATION
(Adult Education)

Elementary Education			Second Course		Third Course
First Course					SC
11	12	21		22	
1st Level	2nd Level	1st Level		2nd Level	

Preparatory Faculty: 1 2 3 4

- Faculty of Science
- Faculty of Agriculture
- Faculty of Technology
- Institute of Education

gram, and the University of Illinois Program. She also indicated knowledge of the strength of European programs and materials such as the Nuffield program and the use of Cuisenaire rods. Her study of foreign educational developments clearly indicated that Cuba should move in the direction of modern mathematics. A decision was reached to change Cuba's programs to include newer methods. What program to choose? Berro said:

> With our limited resources it would be unwise to attempt any research project of our own to develop any program. We cannot afford at this time the luxury of extended, serious research. We must draw upon the research and programs of other countries. For example, we were very impressed with some of the U.S. programs—but with the present political situation between our two countries, it would be foolish to adopt a program from the U.S. A program is not just an outline and curriculum plans. We would like professional interchange—opportunities to visit, to send teachers, to receive professors. For this reason, we decided, after investigation, to work with our math colleagues in East Germany, where at present they are also introducing a modern mathematics program.[4]

Thus, the Cuban math text, Mathematica, for grade 1, is almost an exact duplicate of the East German text Mathematik 1.[5]

Cuba introduced curriculum change in mathematics in a coordinated, planned, staggered schedule. In 1967-68 twenty classes experimented with the new program; in 1968-69 it was used by 1,000 classes; and the following year all of the first grade participated in the program. Each year a new grade starts a similar pattern of curriculum change until all of the grade levels are reached.

The alternate approach to curriculum change —that of upward vertical movement—is shown by a new approach to beginning reading.

When I was in the mountains of Oriente Province I visited some classes where children and teacher looked like they were part of a theatre games workshop with film and Broadway director Mike Nichols. Upon investigation I discovered that this technique was part of a teaching method called "mimica," developed by a teacher in Oriente to help her children learn to read. Briefly, the teacher begins by telling a story to the class about a family which has five children (the five vowels). This was the beginning of the use of pantomime for every letter in the alphabet.

During 1967-68, 34,000 students in the mountains of South Oriente used the mimica system, and the teachers and administrators thought that it was a successful technique. Why? They pointed out that the children not only learned from the integrated approach of hand motion, story telling, and writing, but that they enjoyed the game as well as the physical aspect of the method.

POLITICIZATION OF THE SCHOOLS

The current educational scene displays a very close relationship in the schools between education and the goals of the Revolution. Marxist and Leninist doctrines do not permeate the classroom, but much is made of Cuban ideology and "consiencia," or what one sociologist has defined as "an amalgam of consciousness, conscience, conscientiousness, and commitment."[6]

Premier Fidel Castro's speech on July 26, 1968, outlined the key views of constructing communism in Cuba. Since these provide a basis for the politicization of the schools, they are worthy of note:

> No human society has yet reached Communism. The paths by which one arrives at a superior form of society are very difficult. A Communist society is one in which man will have reached the highest degree of social awareness ever achieved. In a Communist society, man will have succeeded in achieving just as much understanding, closeness, and brotherhood as he has on occasion achieved within the narrow circle of his own family. To live in a Communist society is to live without selfishness, to live among the people and with the people, as if every one of our fellow citizens were really our dearest brother. . . .
>
> People aspiring to live under Communism must do what we are doing. They must emerge from underdevelopment; they must develop their forces of production; they must master technology in order to turn man's efforts and man's sweat into the

miracle of producing practically unlimited quantities of material goods. If we do not master technology, if we do not develop our forces of production, we shall deserve to be called dreamers for aspiring to live in a Communist society. . . .

The problem from our point of view (however) is that Communist consciousness must be developed at the same rate as the forces of production. An advance in the consciousness of the revolutionaries, in consciousness of the people, must accompany every step forward in the development of the forces of production. . . .

And above all we should not use money to create consciousness. We must use consciousness to create wealth. To offer a man more than is expected is to buy his consciousness with money. . . . As we said before, Communism certainly cannot be established if we do not create abundant wealth. But the way to do this, in our opinion, is not by creating consciousness through money or wealth but by creating wealth through consciousness.[7]

Thus, according to Cuban ideology, the old society developed an approach which was motivated by money, by fear of poverty. The new man, on the other hand, will work for the common good. For this he will sacrifice, he will work with dedication. From this kind of altruism will develop a spirit of cooperativeness and humanity.

In order to determine what effect the official ideology was having in the classroom, I used the fairly simple technique of the open-ended question. The same questions were posed to a variety of students in all parts of Cuba.

One composition topic I offered to a number of classes in the upper grades was, If I Had Five Wishes. I instructed the teachers simply to ask the children to write. If the student asked about the assignment, the teacher was to refrain from prejudicing the classroom by examples. She was to tell them simply to write any five wishes they would like to come true.

The following is from a fifth grader in the mountains in Oriente:

My Wishes

My wishes are that my country will continue being free as it is and also that it will come out of underdevelopment.

I also wish that the people of Vietnam will gain their complete liberty so that our Vietnamese brothers will be free and happy.

I also wish that our center will be the best, maintaining the strictist discipline, studying and working better each day.

Before any thing else I wish to get excellent marks at the end of the semester.

Besides all of that I wish that our country will be able to complete the plan goal, that is to complete the ten million tons of sugar for 1970.

With certain variations all the compositions included several common themes:

1. Study. (Sometimes combined with personal goals, e.g., the wish to become a teacher or an engineer.)
2. Achievement of national goals—usually ten million tons of sugar (in Oriente they would add two million tons of coffee).
3. Some international reference to other people in Latin America.
4. Invariably a reference to Vietnam. (If any nation is glorified in official propaganda it is the heroism of the North Vietnamese and the National Liberation Front.)

The other open-ended writing assignment I gave to students asked them to describe what they thought their life and work would be like at age thirty. This assignment was given to high school students.

Here are typical selections from Makarenko Institute students (teenagers in the primary-school teacher-training program).

My life and work at age 30 would seem better. Why? I've already finished school and I would be teaching in the Institute or I'll go to the province where I'm appointed. I will teach those children who don't know, I will serve the revolution wherever necessary.

My work will be even better. I will help

my country in its development even more. My parents, seeing the success I've had with my studies, feel proud and advise me to continue. Since they couldn't study with the same ease with which children now go to the Revolutionary Government schools. These schools didn't exist before, especially in the rural areas; now all children, whites as well as blacks, have the same rights to study and improve themselves. At 30 years of age there will be teachers in Cuba who are capable of going to other countries to teach those children who don't know—underdeveloped countries which don't even know what schools are. I am 16 years old and in the third year of the institute.

My father is a dock worker and my mother is a housewife. Both my mother and father completed the 6th grade. My dream is like a gift, a morning star which will tell me what will happen when I'm 30. In my present life I'm 18 years old, in future years I aspire as all women, to get married, have kids, and a happy home, simple but peaceful.

I also aspire to work with children, each time to teach more about life, to emphasize with my example morals, ethics, love for our country.

That it is necessary to die for a just cause that they do it as Che did, and as I will do if it is necessary.

The themes of commitment and sacrifice are repeatedly expressed in the compositions. "To go where the revolution needs me" is a most frequent expression.

When questioned about the obvious reflection of the official Cuban revolutionary ideology in the schools, the Cuban educators were most direct in their response. One educational leader at the Ministry of Education, Abel Prieto Morales, said that when he was in Italy, someone at an educational conference asked him: "Is the school in Cuba an instrument of the state?" His answer was, "Yes, of course, just as it was before the triumph of the Revolution, and as it is in the present day in Italy."[8]

BOARDING AND SEMI-BOARDING SCHOOLS

Cuban internados (boarding schools) and semi-internados (semi-boarding schools) currently offer room for 250,000 students in the internados and 160,000 at semi-internado schools where free clothing, lunch, and dinner are provided.

Cuba plans to change all junior high schools to boarding schools. Forty new ones were opened by September 1972. The revolutionary government has set 1980 as the goal for 1,000 junior high boarding schools in the country. If this target date is kept, almost every youngster of junior-high age will have the opportunity to attend one of the new schools.[9] If this effort is combined with the preuniversity boarding schools already in existence and the semi-boarding schools on the elementary level, it will be, I believe, the largest boarding school effort in the history of education. The cost, of course, is tremendous. Economists who have examined Cuban investment in education estimate that the cost of maintaining a scholarship or boarding student (with clothing, food, housing, and staff) is ten to fifteen times higher than educating a nonboarding school primary student.

Boarding schools are considered by educational leaders to be a key to creating the new Cuban man. First, boarding school students live together and develop attitudes and values consistent with Cuban revolutionary goals.

Secondly, they provide a full curriculum which includes physical education as well as academic subjects, or the training of the whole body and mind.

Thirdly, students from rural, isolated areas develop skills in arts, science, and technical areas in urban centers.

Fourth, the new semi-internado schools become part of a consolidated rebuilding effort in rural areas where school becomes part of a central town development which consists of the school, a polyclinic, a social center, and new housing for the campesinos (peasants).

DEVELOPMENT OF NEW MATERIALS

The production and distribution of new materials for Cuban schools, including books and audio-visual aids, is another development in Cuban education. Since the Revolution books from other countries have been translated and used.

I had forgotten to take with me to Cuba my

trustworthy pocket English-Spanish Dictionary, the University of Chicago Press edition. While I was there a new paperback book with a handsome Picasso printcover was published by the Cuban Book Institute. When I opened it, I found an exact reproduction of the University of Chicago book, including the same introduction.

This is true of other texts, too, such as L. J. Cronbach's Educational Psychology and Myra McFadden's Sets, Relations and Functions: A Programmed Unit in Modern Mathematics.

In 1967, for what others consider obvious economic considerations, Premier Castro renounced all copyright laws. He suggested that the literature of the world belonged to the people of the world. Authors should be "proud" that their works are being used.

During the last few years the Ministry of Education has also been productive by publishing its own texts. During the past five years 28 texts were created under a new policy which calls for the development of books by collectives. According to this policy, a first-grade reader or seventh-grade math text is created by a team of technical specialists, consultants, teachers, and students. The students are involved in testing the book and criticizing specific content. New Cuban texts do not credit individual authors. Instead, a paragraph cites a particular collective in primary education or secondary education or a specific unit of the Ministry.

Partial analysis of the curriculum materials indicates that, although the general quality of layout, illustrations, and content vary with different books, many texts are of a fairly good standard. Unfortunately, some texts, such as the first editions of the Math 1 and Math 2, use difficult language which is above the level of many children in the grade, or they include too much on a page. However, the new system with the built-in feedback of the collective has the advantage of pilot-testing and incorporating teacher-suggested corrections before publication.

When considering materials or aids, it is impossible to ignore Cuban national television. Almost every secondary-school classroom is equipped with two TV sets. Lessons are broadcast each day for four hours on every secondary-school subject.

A staff of 162 teachers and consultants works on TV lessons and 92 technicians and directors assist in production. Primarily, TV is used to help overcome the shortage of teachers and to raise the quality of instruction by exposing students and teachers to talented teachers. The massive, integrated use of TV is unique not only for an underdeveloped country like Cuba but for economically advanced nations as well.

FLEXIBLE APPROACH TO EDUCATIONAL PROBLEMS

Flexibility and change, as a result of constant self-criticism of existing practices, are characteristic of contemporary Cuban education. Witness the alliance with East Germany in mathematics and the reproduction of texts from anywhere in the world. Similarly, study-abroad programs offer teachers and national and local leaders an opportunity to visit and live in other countries in order to gain knowledge about foreign programs.

Young psychologists I interviewed study and are familiar with Piaget, Erikson, and Bruner and are attempting to develop new curriculum approaches consistent with contemporary psychological thought.

To illustrate what I call the "learn-from-experience" approach, here is a Cuban report to UNESCO referring to developments in economic education: "In the evening session we have established the '3 by 5' plan, and students attend classes only three times a week as experience had shown that they did not attend five days of the week as required."[10]

SCHOOL TO THE COUNTRYSIDE

In 1968 Cuba instituted a new program called "escuela al campo" (school to the countryside) for secondary-school students which calls for each school to move to a country campamento, or camp. For forty-five days they work in the fields and, in addition, do schoolwork, participate in physical education, sports, and recreation, and have political discussions.

A Ministry of Education report cites the benefits to be gained:

> a) The plan by means of its various activities, and basically through productive work, is a powerful instrument for the moral and ideological training of our youth. Through work, character is trained, will is strengthened, creative activity channeled, and real discipline is firmly based.

b) It contributes to the development of a real agricultural consciousness in accordance with the reality of the economic development of our nation.

c) Although this plan was not conceived for economic but rather educational purposes, it helps to solve production problems.

d) The plan, with its problems of living together in the camps, initiates the students, in a concrete form, into organizational practices and self-government on the basis of group cooperation and work, and it also helps to develop collective tendencies and weed out individualist ones.[11]

I visited several schools in the countryside and lived in two for two weeks, interviewing students and observing teacher and student behavior. A key characteristic of the working program was student involvement, including participation and self-government. Most groups contained a unit organization, called a brigade, of approximately ten students. The brigade leaders, elected by their peers, worked with the student school leadership to develop a self-governing council. Student leaders headed areas of production, education, recreation, and politics, while the brigades were evaluated on the almost parallel bases of work, study, organization, and discipline.

Students were also responsible for cleaning and service in the dormitories and the kitchen. In addition, they were responsible for the beautification of the campamento, including building benches, developing mural displays, creating a miniature park, and the like.

In 1971 a new direction was established on the junior high school level: the establishment of the "escuela en el campo." According to Cuban educators the new program brings together the ideas of "two great thinkers: Marx and Marti."[12] The daily program combines "intellectual work and manual work." Each new junior high school, with an approximate capacity of 250 boys and 250 girls, is located in the countryside. The boarding-school students work half a day on their own agricultural areas, which are located near the school. The other half of the school day is concerned with academic subjects which include the following: mathematics, Spanish, geography, history, English, physics, chemistry, biology, physical education, and industrial arts.

The "escuela en el campo," reports the new Cuban journal, Educación, is a school which responds to "pedagogical conceptions and the realities and necessities of Cuban life" (my emphasis —ML). In short, the new school provides higher levels of opportunity to work and study by not making "work time" a separate, forty-five-day experience. It is now an integral part of the school day.[13]

CONCEPT OF REVOLUTIONARY EDUCATIONAL LEADERSHIP

The "school to the countryside" is related to another Cuban educational development: the revolutionary concept of educational leadership.

Both teachers and principals in the school to the countryside live in the dormitories and, together with students, work in the fields. Interviews with students and teachers revealed a common view of the effective leader: a person given greater responsibility, not greater privilege; one who works harder and provides a model of dedication.

Parenthetically, there is no tenure in Cuba. If a principal does not meet the guidelines of accountability, measured by promotions, attendance, and other variables, he returns to teaching or perhaps is appointed director of a smaller school.

At this juncture it is important to note the 1961 Cuban literacy campaign. In 1961 Cuba witnessed national mobilization comparable only to a national war effort. Two hundred fifty thousand young people and adults volunteered to go to the remotest parts of Cuba to fight illiteracy. After eight months of intensive, full-time effort, the illiteracy rate in Cuba was reduced from 25 per cent to 3.9 per cent.

The 106,000 "brigadistas," or student alphabetizers, who participated in the 1961 campaign now play a key role in educational leadership at all levels. The fifteen year old who went to the rural hut of a campesino in 1961 was the twenty-four year old principal of an elementary school in Las Villas; the fourteen year old who was an alphabetizer in Pinar Del Río is now a teacher trainer. In interviews, these "battle" veterans spoke about their day in the Sierras. The "battles" they referred to were their literacy campaign experiences with poor, uneducated families in distant, isolated mountain settings.

TEACHER PREPARATION

Growth in student enrollment and the increase in the number of schools required high priority for teacher training. The Makarenko Teachers Institute, with boarding schools in each province, offered primary-grade teacher training.

Until 1968-69, all first-year students of education attended a mountain school in the Sierra Mountains in Oriente. This school in Minas Del Frío was purposely built in one of the most rural, remote parts of Cuba in order to emphasize the environment and to train teachers in primitive, isolated conditions so that they were ready for the toughest possible teaching assignments. In 1969-70 teacher training was decentralized with each province controlling its own five-year program. Today teacher training is directly under the aegis of the Ministry of Education.

Student teaching is particularly stressed, with the third, fourth, and fifth year given to daily student teaching. At the Makarenko Institute I noted that preparing for teaching was tantamount to becoming a revolutionary. Naturally, this means serious commitment. Students studied from early in the morning until late at night. Self-government permeated practically all aspects of their lives—study, the dormitory, recreation, and military training.

Instructors in academic areas were young graduates of the program guided by veteran "asesoras" (consultants). At Tarara, the large teacher-training center outside of Havana, each morning a fleet of small buses exited with student teachers for 259 student-teaching centers in Havana.

Unlike student teaching in the United States, each student was in charge of his own class. There was no cooperating teacher, but the principal was a supervisor from the Makarenko Institute. The supervisor-principal visited her ten or eleven student teachers every day to discuss lessons and problems and evaluate their work.

DAY-CARE EDUCATION: CASE STUDY IN CUBAN EDUCATIONAL STRATEGY

The tenth major educational development in Cuba is the strong emphasis on day-care education. I have given a description of the history, organization, and program of Cuban day-care centers in a previous publication.[14] The growth and development of day-care programs provides a case study of how the Cubans have overcome the obstacles of underdevelopment to provide what is implicit in the definition of a modern society: equality of opportunity for all.

Nursery schools admit children from as young as 45 days old up to kindergarten age, five years old. However, most of the schools I visited had few children under one year old. The centers are organized to include monthly meetings with parents which help them with child raising. These sessions include such topics as hygiene, food, prevention of illness, and behavior problems.

With a strong concern about health, teams of doctors, dentists, and nurses from the Ministry of Health provide regular examinations and care for the children. The schools provide three meals a day, with emphasis on balanced nutrition.

Now in the process of change, the programs are placing greater focus on guided activities for play, language skills, music, and art.

The Cubans enunciate three basic tenets which determine the structure and policies of day-care centers; namely, the liberation of women, the development of the new socialist person, and the economic and social benefits for the community at large.

In Cuba today it is clear that the first priority which went into organizing nurseries and kindergartens was—and still is—the liberation of Cuban women in order to enable them to participate in the economic life of the country. "Women's participation in the Revolution is a revolution within a revolution. And if we are asked what the most revolutionary thing is that the Revolution is doing, we would answer that it is precisely this: the revolution that is occurring among the women of our country."[15] That is Fidel Castro voicing one of the primary goals of Revolutionary Cuba.

As in most parts of the world, women in Cuba were an oppressed section of society. Traditionally, before the Revolution women were relegated to serve as maids in the homes of the wealthy, to serve in vassalage to the interests of United States and other foreign tourists and residents. When not participating actively in the economy, working-class women, even those who were educated, often found little or no access to the mainstream of economic life of the country. The role of women in pre-Revolutionary Cuba was typical of Latin America in general. Machismo—the Latin notion of male chauvinism and aggressive maleness—permitted women only the chance to dote on her man.

The Latin cult of machismo dictates that

women be enigmatic, saintly, and unreal, and that her life be lived through her strong, earthy, virile male. He, on the other hand, can fulfill his sexual fantasies apart from her, but he must fight—even to the death—in defense of her purity. Together with a host of other upheavals, the Cuban Revolution sought to alter the role of the woman in the society, to destroy the traditional condition in which women found themselves.

Schools became central to the alteration and remain so. "Society has a duty to help women," Castro pointed out on May 1, 1966. "But at the same time society helps itself considerably by helping women because it means more and more hands joining in the production of goods and services for all people. As it is known, one of the means to make it possible for women to work is the creation of day nurseries."[16]

It is important to note here that Castro insists that Cuba concentrate on the liberation of its women in order to play a key function in what Cubans hope will be the emerging strength of their economy.

Early childhood education in Cuba in particular offers women (as mothers) an alternative to traditional child rearing. Day care permits mothers to leave their children in the custody of an early childhood staff so that the mother may participate in the wider economic life of the nation. Moreover, Cuban nursery schools are flexible enough to render services for a broad spectrum of working mothers. Most offer care for children who are under one year old. Open seven days a week, twenty-four hours a day, these centers for babies and small children are structured so that women who work late can either pick up their children after dinner or later in the evening or they can leave their children there all week and take them home weekends only. Despite the considerable hostility toward these new day-care facilities in the beginning, the current demand for early childhood schooling far outstrips available space.

Whether or not Cuban women are prepared for liberation and, more importantly, whether or not Cuban men are prepared to deny their tenacious machismo are yet to be discovered. Certainly the national policy favors the liberation of women—if only in those special circumstances which permit women to leave the home and their traditional child-rearing functions in order to work. Early childhood education in Cuba is there, in part, to serve that goal in practical terms.

Much has been written about the "new socialist man" in Cuba and elsewhere in the socialist world. Scholars have analyzed the nature of this phenomenon from various perspectives. Theodore Hsi-en Chen, writing about the New Socialist Man in China in the Comparative Education Review, reports,

> According to the Communists, the old society breeds individualistic and selfish persons motivated by feudalistic and bourgeois loyalties. They think of personal benefit and personal ambitions. Their narrow family loyalties encourage selfishness and the neglect of what is good for the general public or the state. The new man will be collectivist, utterly selfless and ever mindful of his obligations to the revolution and the Communist party. Until the old man is replaced by the new, the proletarian way of life cannot prevail and the new society must remain a dream.[17]

According to Chen, the characteristics of this new man will consist of absolute selflessness, obedience to the Communist party, ideological study, love of labor, versatility, and expertise in socialist construction. With only minor variations on that theme, the New Cuban Man (according to Cuban leadership in early childhood education) will exhibit similar traits.

To train children to their future role as new socialist men, collective consciousness begins the moment the child enters the Circulo. When a Cuban baby is placed in a playpen, he is put into no standard United States model with only room enough for himself—or at most two toddlers. The Cuban playpen—or more appropriately, "corral"—permits at least six infants to play together in a space equal to the size of a small room. Based on the Soviet or Eastern European model, the corral, raised on legs coffee table high, offers children the chance to interact with their asistentes practically face-to-face. Far more rationally designed than the American playpen, it avoids the tedious effort of adults in attendance to bend to floor level to assist children. Struck by the creatively designed Soviet playpens, Urie Bronfenbrenner of Cornell University notes,

> In fact, the pens are at different heights depending on the stage of the child's development—higher for supine babies than for the crawlers who begin to pull them-

selves up by the bars. But even more striking to the Western eye is the fact that each playpen is the size of a small room, and contains not one but half a dozen infants. Soviet children must learn to live in a collective society, and they begin to do so in the first year of life.[18]

So, too, must the Cuban infant.

Group play, as distinct from individual activities, takes precedence. A group of Boston educators in a visit to Cuba during the summer of 1970 found group activity dominated the classroom.

> In older children's rooms in day care centers most activities seemed to center around a child working as a member of a group or for the good of others. Much of the child's time is spent in circle games and activities. Often, one child or the teacher is in the center and the other children work as a group.[19]

Encouraged to design activities to stimulate group play, asistentes in the Círculos lead children into social and play patterns to help them develop collective attitudes. Asistentes are to make special efforts to see to it that all children participate in the program designed for the collective.

THE MANPOWER DILEMMA

How is day-care education instituted to accomplish the goals outlined above if there are no trained personnel available?

The question is a fundamental one for developing countries and for developed countries who are attempting to introduce day care or other "revolutionary" educational changes on a massive scale.* Cuba provides a case study in an area where there are no previous models. The Cubans have worked out their own solutions to staffing day-care centers.

The Paraprofessional Solution. After my first visit to Cuba I reported, "The exodus of the country's middle class on those flights from Havana to Miami had nearly depleted whatever meager literate resources Batista had ungraciously left behind. Never before had a socialist revolution permitted its fat cats to flee in such numbers and with such license."[20] Cuba's educated class fled from the Revolution as from a burning building. As Jolly reports:

> In the first three years following 1959, it seems likely that about 250,000 Cubans left. A very substantial percentage of these were professional workers. About one third of the doctors emigrated, as did perhaps 15 percent or more of the stock of technical and professional personnel.[21]

It has been noted above that following the Revolution, the nation's educational agenda expanded exponentially: the lack of trained personnel immediately became critical. As Consuelo Miranda commented:

> At the same time that our need for teachers and professors increased with the expanded educational opportunities offered by the Revolution, the number of qualified teachers decreased sharply.[22]

Even those who had been educated and who had not

---

* During the year 1971 there was much political and educational discussion in the United States about increasing day-care education for low-income families. It is interesting to note that a number of the new, projected proposals for day-care training are out of necessity similar to current Cuban practices.

On December 23, 1971, the Director of the Office of Child Development (a division of the U.S. Dept. of Health, Education and Welfare), Dr. Edward Zigler, announced that a new type of position would be created—a worker called a "Child Development Associate." This person would be someone who did not have four years of college but had had training in concepts of child development. Dr. Zigler stated: "We could say that every day-care teacher needs a bachelor's degree and the supply would never meet the demand. . . . It is very easy for people to insist you have the very best, but then you often wind up with unrealistic demands. If you did this with day care, you would not upgrade quality, you would drive day care underground. With unrealistically high standards, you could make services worse." New York Times, December 24, 1971, p. 16.

left Cuba were so hostile to the Castro regime that many refused to participate in its new educational programs.

Lacking a pool of educated young people to join the new early childhood educational system, the Cubans turned elsewhere. They tapped the resources of their largely uneducated teenage population and older women whose previous experience had been in their own homes raising their own children. Consequently, the pioneer asistentes in Cuban day-care centers had meager training and very low scholastic levels. At Fidel's suggestion the círculos at first employed manejadoras—or nursemaids—who had served middle-class children. As anyone who lived in pre-Revolutionary Havana could testify, the parks of wealthy sections of Vedado, Miramar, Country Club, and Baltimore fluttered with these white-uniformed, uneducated girls from the farm.

These women who came to work in the círculos and jardines of Cuba carried only their own experience in their baggage. With little or no formal schooling and hardly any experience in early childhood education, they brought with them the tattered belongings of their childrearing practices from home. Out of the threadbare patches of necessity Cuba clothed its day-care centers with a paraprofessional staff. It was unprecedented in the annals of education.

In the beginning, while ostensibly a sixth-grade education was required, in order to satisfy the demand for staff the círculos at first permitted women to work in the centers without even achieving that simple standard. This was particularly true for centers in the countryside where the general level of education was lower than in the cities. Only recently have the standards been raised to the point where an eighth-grade education is required to become an asistente.

Because of the low level of educational background, day-care paraprofessionals are neither called nor considered teachers. The centers do employ kindergarten teachers who work under the direction of the Ministry of Education. These professionals have traditional classroom duties for children of kindergarten age. A typical círculo employs one teacher to approximately twenty asistentes.

In 1969 círculo asistentes earned $82.47 per month, regardless of longevity. Provided with free uniforms and shoes, they work six days a week routinely and often on Sunday they do "voluntary work," either at the círculo or elsewhere. Those who are on the 6 a.m. to 2 p.m. shift eat breakfast, snack, and lunch at the school. Workers on the 11 a.m. to 7 p.m. schedule receive lunch and afternoon snack.

At first, asistentes were offered minimal remedial-training courses. Often even these were cut short in order to fill posts at círculos which were opening at a faster rate than training schools could supply. As the círculos matured, asistentes were required to achieve greater scholastic proficiency. Some outstanding asistentes were taken from the círculos and sent to school for a year to study liberal arts, child care, child psychology, nutrition, etc. Upon returning to her círculo, she was then expected to guide the others.

On a visit to one training school for asistentes in Havana, called the <u>Escuela: Formación y Supermación de Círculos Infantiles,</u> I observed that work in the day-care centers was balanced with studies at the school. Each group was composed of twenty-six students who worked together for three months at a time. Classes were held Tuesdays through Saturdays with Mondays set aside for "productive or agricultural work."

Círculos with normal working conditions, rather than model schools, were chosen for student teaching. The schools were close to the student dormitory, which housed forty asistentes, or nearby the student's home. Not every asistente-in-training slept in the center's dormitory. Three students from the training center were assigned to each círculo.

Of the 109 women who entered the program, only forty-six remained after eight months. While some dropped out of their own accord, many students had been persuaded to leave after consultations with the cooperating círculo personnel and training staff. Some left simply because they did not like children; others were asked to leave because they did not seem to have the "basic equipment" for work with children; still others quit because they discovered that the work was intensive and physically hard. Not displeased with the high drop-out rate, the school believed that its program permitted those who were not suited to the work to leave before they actually came to a círculo full time. The training center acted like a strainer through which poor students slipped out as the hard spray of daily experience pressed on them.

At this training school I witnessed a Spanish class taught by Dr. Edilia Blanco Sanchez, whose major responsibility was not as a Spanish teacher in a school for asistentes but rather as a consultant on technical and professional training at the

Ministry of Education. Because of the existing shortage of adequate personnel at all levels of the Cuban educational system, she was pressed into teaching service. Using the following letter which Ché Guevara had written to Fidel Castro, she wove into the lesson grammar, revolutionary idealism, Cuban history, and the needs of the círculo.

Havana, Year of Agriculture

Fidel:

At this moment I remember so many things: when I met you at Maria Antonia's house; when you asked me to come; all the excitement of getting ready.

One day they came and asked who was to be notified in case of death, and the real possibility of this struck us all. Later we learned that it was real, that in revolution (if it is a genuine one) you either win or die. Many comrades have fallen along the path to victory.

Today everything seems less dramatic, because we are more mature, but the fact repeats itself. I feel I have fulfilled that part of my duty which bound me to the Cuban Revolution on its own territory, and I bid farewell to you, to the comrades, and to your people, who are now mine.

I formally renounce my duties in the national leadership of the party, my post as minister, my rank of major, and my Cuban citizenship. I have no legal ties to Cuba, only ties of a different kind which cannot be dissolved as official positions can.

When I look back over the past, I believe I have worked with honesty and dedication to assure the triumph of the Revolution. My only serious mistake was not to have trusted you more from the first days in the Sierra Maestra, and not to have understood soon enough your qualities as a leader and a revolutionary. I have lived through some magnificent days, and at your side I have felt the pride of belonging to our people during those radiant yet sad days of the Caribbean crisis. Not often has a statesman acted more brilliantly than you did during those days, and I am also proud of having followed you unhesitatingly, identifying with your way of thinking, and realizing the dangers and principles of our position.

Other nations are calling for the aid of my modest efforts. I can do what you are unable to do because of your responsibility as Cuban Leader. The time has come for our separation.

I want it to be known that I do this with a mixture of joy and sorrow: Here I leave behind the purest of my hopes for building, and the dearest of my loved ones, and I leave a people that has accepted me as its son. This deeply hurts a part of my spirit. In new fields of battle I will bear the faith you instilled in me, the revolutionary spirit of my people, the feeling that I am fulfilling the most sacred of duties: to fight against imperialism wherever it may be. This comforts me and more than compensates for any regrets.

Once again, let me say that I absolve Cuba from any responsibility, except for that which stems from the example it has set. If my final hour comes under distant skies, my last thoughts will be for this people and especially for you. I thank you for your teachings and your example, and will try to be faithful up to the final consequences of my acts. I have always identified myself with the foreign policy of our Revolution, and I continue to do so. Wherever I may be, I will remain conscious of the responsibility of being a Cuban revolutionary, and will act as such. I have left no material possessions to my wife and children, and I do not regret it; I am happy it is this way. I ask nothing for them, since the state will provide for their needs and their education.

There are many things I would like to say to you and to our people, but I feel it is unnecessary; words cannot express what I would want them to, and it is not worth wasting paper.

Ever onward to victory. Liberty or Death!

I embrace you with all my revolutionary fervor.

"Ché"[23]

The instructor commented to me in conversations after the lesson that she proudly utilized an important historical, revolutionary document—Ché's letter—to teach word analysis and reading comprehension skills. This, she said, was "pedagogy that drew upon the revolution" for lesson content.

Most training in the early days and even today is provided by continuous in-service courses. Given to all asistentes who have not completed acceptable levels of formal education, these classes offer asistentes fairly rudimentary concepts of child development and growth.

Divided into three areas, in-service training prepares asistentes in what the círculos call cultural, technical, and political categories. Organized under the Worker-Farmer educational courses, the "cultural" program provides women with their minimum sixth-grade educational requirement. "Technical" sessions are held under the leadership of the director of the school and offer training in materials, teaching, psychology, and other day-care matters. For the "political" section, study circles cover current events and discuss materials presented by the Communist Party, the Union of Young Communists, and the Federation of Cuban Women. These groups meet about every fifteen days while the children nap in the day-care center. At first these improvement courses were offered at night, but the hardships of getting out after hours at the close of a long day at the círculo proved insurmountable. In-service training is given not only to those who deal directly with the children, but to cooks, cleaning women, and others who work in the círculo as well.

In 1970 the círculo leadership concluded that better training and higher qualifications were necessary if standards were to be raised. To this end they opened three new, four-year day-care-training schools, Escuelas de Educadoras. The one in Oriente trains círculo personnel for that province as well as for part of Camaguey. Another, based in Havana, serves students from the provinces of Havana, Pinar del Río, the Isle of Pines, and Matanzas. The third, in Las Villas, covers that province together with the other part of Camaguey. New entrance requirements prescribe a minimum eighth-grade education. Students are accepted between the ages of fourteen and twenty-five.* Applicants must also be members of the Federation of Cuban Women, "since we cannot have anyone lacking Revolutionary conviction involved in the formation of the new generation."[24] By autumn 1971 the Oriente and Havana schools had begun their second year; the school in Las Villas had just started to accept students. The círculos campaigned for students by visiting secondary schools throughout Cuba to inform them of the new program. Eighth-grade students were invited to visit círculos, and as a result some 225 were registered. The limited number of students enrolled in the new Escuelas de Educadoras reflects the círculo leadership's intention of keeping these schools as small pilot projects until they can be properly evaluated and adequately staffed.

The curriculum not only offers the day-care workers-in-training courses related to future professional activities, but provides a general education, including the usual liberal arts and sciences. Mastery of a musical instrument is essential.

Professional courses include general, early childhood, and developmental psychology as well as educational vocational psychology. Pedagogical studies cover the teaching of reading and arithmetic (which has been experimentally initiated in some círculos). In addition to taking courses in art, dancing, music, etc., students are taken to concerts, ballet, and exhibits.

Asistente training begins in the second year when they observe at day-care centers. In their third year they do some supervised activities; and in the fourth year students undergo daily, intensive training and practice. In this last year asistentes-in-training spend fifteen days in the day-care center and fifteen days at school. They practice at the same círculo throughout the final year. Under the direct supervision of the head of the círculo, before graduation each student will have had at least sixteen or eighteen weeks in a day-care center with full responsibility for a group of children. Note that the regular asistente is present at all times during the student's sessions at the center.

Current plans call for a coordinator to be assigned to the círculo to facilitate the integration of asistentes in the center. The director will continue to supervise students day-to-day.

Asistente training at in-service courses during the círculo day, and even in the more advanced level four-year schools, concentrates on

---

* Until 1971 applicants for the training program for asistentes were accepted up to the age of 30.

establishing an understanding among the women who work with children for the need for warm, affective relationships between the child and his caretaker. Acknowledging that the educational level of the asistentes often is not advanced enough to grasp more sophisticated psychological theories, the in-service círculo classes are content with modest lectures in simple language. They cover basic steps in child development—sensory-motor, language, and social behavior. Examples are drawn from asistentes' experiences within the círculo.

Dr. Consuelo Miranda, in addition to writing most of the orientation articles for personnel, is director of the asistentes' educational section in the training school. She commented,

> We explain that these characteristics develop simultaneously but we separate them so that the asistente can understand each process better. We caution them that any thing they do can affect not one, but all these aspects. We explain these things in a non-scientific vocabulary.[25]

Psychology is taught as one way of establishing an affective relationship between asistentes and the children. Miranda suggested ways in which this may be explained to the unschooled asistente:

> Now how can you do this? When the child cries, you don't let him cry. Mothers don't do this. When he cries they go see what is wrong. This is what you must do. If he is cold, you must cover him; if he is hot, you must move the crib to a cooler spot; if you think he is tired of the position he is in, you must move him; if he is hungry, give him food; if he is thirsty, offer him water; if you think he is frightened, carry him, hug him a little, cuddle him, hold him close to you and say sweet things or sing, and then put him back in the crib. This relationship must be established, very directly, because what we are teaching them is very clear, things that belong to the various periods of psychological development, but taught, as you can see, without nuance, stripped of scientific vocabulary—as if it were a conversation. If we were to explain this in other terms, they would not understand it.[26]

Contemporary psychologists understand that a basic requirement of children is to establish relationships with adults who care for them. Naturally, this is equally as vital for the child whether the adult happens to be his mother or the woman who cares for him at a day-care center. We know that if the child does not feel loved and properly cared for, he will not develop the kind of trust required for his socialization into the group. If the child receives consistent and understanding attention from the day-care worker, he will be better equipped to deal with others. With trust in others comes confidence in oneself. Therefore, the chief criterion in selecting day-care center workers is that they be warm and affectionate, capable of dealing with children in loving, maternal ways.

Naturally, the jardines also expected their day-care workers to be as warm and generous as círculo asistentes—if not more so. If jardin psychologists discovered that those who were seeking employment were rigid or authoritarian, they would not be accepted. Prospective teachers were given psychometric tests to determine the quality of the teacher's personality and to weed out those who the jardines felt would be harmful to the children. Sanchez explained,

> But even after all the tests, what counted most was our interview. We were interested in the picture which emerged when we met them face-to-face. During the interview we could determine whether the person was reasonably intelligent and whether her personality was suitable.[27]

Turning an uneducated teaching staff into an effective group of paraprofessionals is not an easy task for the círculo leadership. Ideally, women who work with children should have an appreciation of childhood development and psychology so that their interaction with children will be based on a clear understanding of what is to be expected from children at different age levels. In practice, however, asistentes are often ignorant of the basic development needs of children, despite their best intentions. For example, Santander relates an incident which occurred in a Camaguey school:

> When I tried to explain that a toddler of two and a half should be taught to dress and undress himself and fold his clothes and put them away, one of the women said to me, "Poor little things. How can I

make these little children do it. It's so
hard for them. It is much easier for me
to do it for them." Then I had to explain
that teaching the children to do it for
themselves would be much more work
for her, but that it was the only way they
would learn and develop. Some still
insisted that they felt sorry for the little
ones, and that they preferred to dress
and undress all the children, even though
it was a lot of work for them. I had to
spend a good deal of time explaining to
them what that meant in terms of retarding the children's development at that
point, and preventing them from moving
on with the next steps in the program.[28]

Underscoring the lack of well-trained personnel in Cuba, a jardin psychologist lamented, "The
academic background, the level of those who work
in day-care centers is very low."[29] Realizing
that it would be impossible to hire only those
teachers who have achieved acceptable levels of
scholastic ability, the jardines and the círculos
depend on their assessment of personality and
accept only those who, at least, will not cause
emotional damage. "If they had an education as
well it would be ideal; but since they do not at
least we try to select those who are healthy."[29]

The jardines, in their search for the "healthy"
day-care worker, attempt to screen out those who
exhibit obsessive characteristics. "We reject the
obsessive person because they are always concerned with whether the child will fall and what if
the child gets dirty; they inhibit children."[29]
Those diagnosed as depressives and impulsives
were also rejected—depressives because they
limit the child's ability to express joy and impulsives because they agitate children by screaming
at them. Applicants considered "pacific" were
embraced. Recalling one woman who came to
work in a school who at first glance might have
been rejected by more formal acceptance procedures, a jardin psychologist said:

At one school we have an older woman,
the first one to work in the plan. A lady
of about fifty, she resembles a grand-
mother; she is calm, peaceful, relaxed,
and affectionate with the children. She
may have a sixth grade education, but
what she brings, in terms of how she
relates to the children, is quite positive.[29]

Garrity observed that asistentes "seemed
like women who were relying on their common
sense to deal with groups of children and didn't
have any storehouse of ideas or activities or
theories to fall back on."[30]

The círculos, too, understand that educated
professionals may not be essential ingredients for
the best preschool educational system. As
Miranda points out, women who work with children
need not have the security of advanced educational
backgrounds to deal effectively with children.
Unschooled paraprofessionals do not often view
the children with the cold-bloodedness of educators who feel that their responsibility to children
is a duty and not a pleasure. Miranda said,

A woman without so much professional-
ism, but who offers great affection, is
of much more help. I'm not interested
in whether or not people who work with
children are university graduates. If
you employ someone who has achieved a
degree, she may turn out to lack affection and human warmth. Who wants
them, even with their higher education?[31]

In the Cuban professional journal, Psicología
y Educación, two young Cuban educational psychologists, Sergio León and Franklin Martínez,
outline four principal elements which determine
the character and personality of children: biology,
culture, environmental stimuli, and interpersonal
relationships. Among these influences the last,
"the personal history of the experiences of the
individual with others," is the most significant
"since personality is, in its major part, a product
of social learning in the interaction of the child
with the family, other members of his group, and
social attitudes." León and Martínez indicate
that the formation of personality through these
interpersonal relationships takes place during the
child's first five years of life.

Clearly, those individuals who are employed
at the círculos and in other early childhood programs exert marked influence on the development
of the personalities of the children in their charge.
It was with this in mind that León and Martínez
undertook to find out what kind of people ought to
be permitted to work with young children. To this
end they developed a series of tests to discover
the right kind of person and to exclude those who
do damage to the child's developing personality.

First, León and Martínez describe four crucial factors necessary for the healthy development of children: (1) Solid, positive, consistently affective relationships between the child and his parents or the person in charge of the child. (2) Stimulation of independence, curiosity, and freedom to play and explore with adequate affective support. (3) Socialization and education through learning based on good affective relationships and respect and guidance of the child's initiative. (4) A good pattern or model of conduct which allows the child to acquire positive characteristics and reactions by imitative behavior or indirect learning.

Based on these criteria, the Cuban researchers defined the kind of person who could best be expected to promote these essential bases of good personality development. People who work with children should be able to establish "solid, pure loving relationships." They should be able to stimulate and reward "independence, autonomy and curiosity" by tolerating the child's exploration, experimentation, and free play with loving approval. Adults should be able to put themselves in the place of the child; that is, understand that the "child is not an adult" and know the child's "limitations and possibilities." Finally, "aggression and rejection should be absent as much as possible" from the personalities of those who are to work with the young.

The questionnaires and tests developed by these workers were originally designed for preschool teachers. To my knowledge, these tests have not yet been administered either by círculos, the jardines, or the Ministry. Nevertheless, they are of interest because they reflect the kind of concern Cubans feel in this area. Note that these psychologists in their absolute focus on the needs of the children in the classroom purposely ignore some of the character traits which the Revolutionary ethic requires of all its citizens. As Leon and Martínez remind us, their object is to focus on only one aspect of the potential teacher's personality, and that is the person's "vocation" to work with children. According to these Cuban researchers:

> We are not considering other factors of the individual's personality except those related positively or negatively to such work. This means, for instance, that in answer to the question, "What are the three things you like to do best?" If the subject answers, "Do productive work," that answer—although from a political and social point of view is very positive—has a neutral value [inasmuch as we] are not interested in registering militancy but ability to work with children.[32]

The following expressions would be considered positive and would lead one to believe that the prospective candidate would work well with children: "I chose this work because I like children." "I like children; I feel happy with them." "I would like to be a teacher." "I love my children and I have the highest feelings for them."

These expressions, on the other hand, are considered negative by these psychologists and would indicate that the candidate would not be suited for such work: "Most children are silly." "I chose this work because I needed any kind of work." "Preschool is easy to work in." "Marriage, the home, and children are absurd."

These examples are considered neutral and would not be used as a basis on which to judge the character of a prospective teacher: "I would like to study sculpture and painting." "I like classical music and the movies." "I like foolish conversations." "Children are born to be happy."

All of the answers—positive, negative and neutral—were actually selected at random from those given by people seeking jobs as teachers.

In selecting the right person for the classroom, educational systems elsewhere in the world rely in large measure on objective scholastic-achievement tests, the number and variety of education courses one has physically sat through, and an hour count tallying up to an arbitrary total of days, weeks, and perhaps months as a student teacher. Yet these basic questions about personality traits of an early childhood worker must be raised by educational systems. Is her character suited for working with children? Is she kind? Does she understand the needs of children? Does she feel affection for children? Will they put their trust in her? It is not enough for someone to have taken all the proper courses, passed all the tests, and put in all the hours. Without a fundamental sense of caring and a healthy disposition towards children, the teachers who are chosen might be at best as ineffective as another leg on the teacher's desk, or at worst as damaging as a policeman's nightstick.

It is to Cuba's credit that in principle the day-care leadership appreciates the critical importance of this issue. Whatever educational route the Cuban day-care centers finally take—whether directed learning, laissez-faire, or some other mode—the quality of the teacher will tell. No system has any chance of success if those who work with children are funneled into the classroom as faceless numbers on a teacher's license.*

Once selected, the asistente is offered literature on the role she should play. Stressing affective relationships, one report by Miranda recommends that asistentes show their faces to babies in the crib as much as possible and manage to say a few words to each child as often as they can, even though the words themselves may be of little consequence. The report suggests that asistentes try to make the children laugh whenever they can. They should become familiar with and be able to distinguish the child's different types of crying and how he shows anger and fear. In general, asistentes ought to be able to know and interpret what the child needs when he calls for it. Miranda says that this can be achieved by caring for the child with love. "There is no possible excuse for letting a child cry a long time without going to his side and trying to calm him."

As the child matures, asistentes are instructed to be resourceful in developing activities for children to play by themselves when they are not involved in group play. Asistentes who offer children toys must first teach the child how to use them and then participate in the game for a few minutes. After the age of three, group interaction becomes important for the child's own attempt at socialization. As a matter of fact, Miranda notes, "separation from the group constitutes a punishment for the child whose conduct is not adapted to the group in one way or another." Miranda cautions asistentes to be careful in their use of this sort of punishment. "It is not advisable to abuse this punishment, but in certain circumstances the asistente can separate the child from the group when he disturbs the rest. . . ." The report concludes with an admonition to all asistentes, reminding them of the critical importance of warm, open relationships between children and adults:

> Inasmuch as coldness and lack of affection produces disturbances characteristic of anaclitic depression which leads to serious consequences in the child's future life, every assistant should offer love and tenderness to the children in her care. . . . For her children she will be the "adult" who directs and gives security to their first social contacts, the "adult" who will not fail the little one, but who will attend him lovingly in every moment.[33]

Rosenham, remarking on the similar Soviet emphasis on warm teacher-child relationships, reminds American educators, "as we revise our own curricula for young children, that care precedes technique, that positive regard is a necessary ingredient for intellectual maturation."[34]

Finally, it should be noted that both in the circulos and the jardines the asistentes are all women. Cuba, therefore, does not depart from the traditional view of women being the only source of staff for very young children. Lamenting the lack of men in day care, Sanchez said recently:

> It is a great deficiency. We ought to have men in day care. But if you consider the world wide custom of relegating childcare to the mother, the lack of men in the center is not hard to understand. The feeling that women should have control over infant rearing is first of all purely biological in that she provides the infant's food. Once past this stage the mother is seen as the source of kindness, warmth, and protection; this feeling having grown for centuries. Nevertheless, it is important for the child to be influenced by a man. The presence of a man in the household, especially in Cuba, is very important.[35]

The preponderance of female figures in all of the child's varied environments at school and at home prevents boys from receiving routine access to male models. The lack of men in school and at home during most of the day is not Cuba's problem alone. But it does not appear likely that the current leadership will alter this situation. When asked whether men can be hired as círculo asistentes, Marta Santander replied emphatically, "We don't need to place men in the círculos!" Her reasons? Children in day care receive enough attention from men in the street, in their home, and especially from men who come to the center to do such chores as gardening, plumbing, and maintenance. And perhaps more important:

---

* Reportedly, 30 per cent of those women who enter the círculo asistente program fail to live up to the personality requirements set by the leadership.

> There are many fronts of work in this country and men are very much needed. There are many jobs women can do, but many others she can't. The man working with children would have to be a young man. But young men are working on other important things.

Naively, she assumes,

> Men are not going to work with children when women can do it. And in any case, since children need affection and special care, it's hard to find this in a young man.[36]

Even today in revolutionary Cuba stereotypic roles seem to be the order of the day.

Experience with the use of paraprofessionals in other countries offers only fragmentary indications of their success in the classroom. Studies in the United States with very small groups lead researchers to believe that paraprofessionals can serve many useful functions.[37] While no clear evidence is available which indicates that an essentially untrained staff can be effective in preschool education, the Cuban experience shows that if large-scale day care is to be implemented rapidly, school systems can call upon the untapped resources of people in the community at least to initiate the early phases of the program and perhaps they can continue to be effective as the program matures.

For Cuba there was no real choice. If they were to embark on their ambitious program of day care, they could not wait while they trained their population to care for the children in the day-care centers in a manner that would meet minimal standards in more advanced countries. Cubans were in the midst of a Sisyphian dilemma. If they rolled the stone of backwardness up to near the peak of the mountain marked by the achievement of a sophisticated staff, they would only discover that new demands for more personnel would force the stone down again so that they would never have enough "qualified" people to do the job.

An overview of the above ten selected educational developments (including a more detailed case-study description of the day-care education personnel problem) indicates these points:

1. During the past 14 years Cuba has made a major national investment in the universalization of education.
2. Education is one of Cuba's key vehicles to expose young people to "the revolutionary experience." The boarding-school development and "school to the countryside" and "school in the countryside" are examples of new modes to promote revolutionary ideology, provide for student involvement, and improve academic performance.
3. A key aim of Cuban school organization is to bridge its rural and urban segments. Schools, therefore, emphasize the values of countryside and work.
4. Cuban school leadership has concentrated on quantitative problems and is now turning with increased concern to the problems of the quality of education. Of course, the relationship of quantitative and qualitative problems cannot be easily separated. For example, the very establishment of new schools in some rural areas and schools in special education is a "qualitative" change when previously such schools were nonexistent.

Although I have not completed my analysis of the interaction of students and teachers in classes visited, initial evidence from my tapes of classrooms indicates that large numbers of classrooms were teacher-dominated and skills in critical thinking were not emphasized. However, as Beeby has noted, underdeveloped nations suffer from the facts of their underdevelopment: insufficient and inadequate teachers, rigid approaches, lack of planning, disorganization, unsatisfactory and limited materials. As nations develop into modern societies certain barometric educational indicators parallel societal progress. Beeby states that:

> Any attempt to reform the work in the classroom is most likely to succeed if it is a part of a nationwide movement for the improvement of social and economic conditions, if it is known to be warmly supported by the Ministry of Education at all levels as well as by the teachers' own organizations, if steps have been taken to make the parents understand the changes, and if the teacher can be made to feel himself less isolated in his classroom.[38]

The above factors were clearly evident to me during my visits to schools in all parts of Cuba. Although beset with numerous problems (e.g., the exodus of many of the middle class, including many teachers), the important current barometrical educational readings for emerging Cuba are most positive. The development of new curricula, programs, and materials, the strengthening of teacher training and inservice training, and the search for new educational models are some of the signs I cited in this brief report. They indicate that Cuba is coming to grips not only with the quantitative challenges of a developing nation, but the qualitative future of radical educational change.

REFERENCES

1. Dudley Seers, ed., Cuba: The Economic and Social Revolution (Chapel Hill: The University of North Carolina Press, 1964) p. 181.

2. Fidel Castro, "Address at Congre, January 5, 1969," Granma Weekly Review (Havana, Cuba) January 12, 1969, p. 2; XXXIII International Conference on Public Instruction, OIE-UNESCO (Havana, Ministry of Education), September 15-23, 1971, p. 9; JUCEPLAN, Boletin Estadistico (La Habana: 1970) pp. 212-229.

3. XXXIII International Conference on Public Instruction, p. 5.

4. Interview with Dr. Maria de Carmen Nuñez Berro, Coordinator of Mathematics, Ministry of Education, Havana, in Cuba, 1969.

5. Herbert Butzke and Joachim Sieber, Matamática, Primer Grade (La Habana: Instituto Pedagogico Makarenko, 1968). The German edition was Lehrbuch Fur Klasse 1 (Berlin: Volk und Wissen Volkseigener Verlag, 1968).

6. Joseph Kahl, "The Moral Economy of a Revolutionary Society," Transactions, April 1969, p. 32.

7. Fidel Castro, "Address at Las Villas on the 15th Anniversary of the Attack on the Moncanda, July 26, 1968," Granma Weekly Review (Havana, Cuba), July 26, 1968, pp. 3-5.

8. Interview with Dr. Abel Prieto Morales, Ministry of Education, Havana, in Cuba, 1969.

9. See Rafael Sanchez Lalabret, "40 nuevas secondarias en el campo para 20 mil jovenes mas," Bohemia, 15 de Septiembre 1972, pp. 38-45; Fidel Castro, "Speech at the Inauguration of the Comandante Pinares Junior High School in the Countryside," Granma Weekly Review (Havana, Cuba), October 3, 1971, p. 3; Arthur Gillette, Cuba's Educational Revolution (London: Fabian Society, 1972), p. 32.

10. Report to the XXXI International Conference on Public Instruction Convoked by OIE and the UNESCO (Havana: Ministry of Education, 1968), p. 42.

11. Ibid., p. 54.

12. See "Una Experiencia de Pedagogia Revolucionaria: La Escuela en al Campo." Educación, Ministerio de Educación, La Habana, Cuba, Ano 1, no. 1, Abril-Junio 1971, pp. 11-23.

13. Ibid., p. 13.

14. See Marvin Leiner, Children Are the Revolution: Day Care in Cuba (New York: Viking Press, 1973).

15. Fidel Castro, Speech at Santa Clara on December 9, 1966, in Linda Jennes, Women and the Cuban Revolution (New York: Pathfinder Press, 1970), p. 5.

16. Fidel Castro, Speech on May Day (May 1, 1966) in Martin Kenner and James Petras, eds., Fidel Speaks (New York: Grove Press, 1969), p. 187.

17. Theodore Hsi en Chen, "The New Socialist Man," Comparative Education Review, February 1969, p. 88.

18. Urie Bronfenbrenner, "Introduction," in Henry Chauncey, ed., Soviet Pre School Education, Volume I: Program of Instruction (New York: Holt, Rinehart, and Winston, 1969), p. xii.

19. Nancy Garrity, "Cuba as a Case Study: The Role Played by Education in the Socialization

of the New Man" (Tufts University, unpublished thesis, 1971). For a more detailed description of Cuban efforts to develop a socialist consciousness on the day-care level see Marvin Leiner, Children Are the Revolution: Day Care in Cuba.

20. Marvin Leiner, "Cuba's Schools, Ten Years Later," Saturday Review, October 17, 1970, p. 59.

21. Seers, op. cit., p. 177.

22. Interview with Dr. Consuelo Miranda, director of training program, Instituto de la Infancia, in Cuba, August 1971.

23. Ernesto Ché Guevara, "Letter to Fidel," reprinted in Venceremos! The Speeches and Writings of Ernesto Ché Guevara, ed. by John Gerassi (New York: The Macmillan Co., 1968), pp. 410-411.

24. Miranda interview, August 1971.

25. Ibid.

26. Interview with Dr. Consuelo Miranda in Cuba in 1969.

27. Interview with Lela Sanchez (leader of Jardines Infantiles), September 1971, in Cuba.

28. Interview with Marta Santander, Director of Educational Programs, Círculos Infantiles, August 1971, in Cuba.

29. Interview with team of psychologists working with the Jardines Infantiles (1969), in Cuba.

30. Garrity, p. 15.

31. Miranda interview, 1969.

32. Sergio León and Franklin Martínez, "Creación de un instrumento para medir vocación para trabajar con niños menores de cinco años," Psicología y Educación (La Habana), Julio-Diciembre 1968, pp. 25-62.

33. Miranda interview, 1969.

34. David Rosenham, Preface to Soviet Pre School Education, Vol. II, Teacher's Commentary, Henry Chauncey, ed. (New York: Holt, Rinehart and Winston, 1969), p. xi.

35. Sanchez interview, 1971.

36. Santander interview, 1971.

37. See Merle B. Karnes, R. Reid Zehrbach, and James A. Teska, "A New Professional Role in Early Childhood Education," Interchange 2, no. 2 (Ontario: Ontario Institute for Studies in Education, 1971), pp. 89-105.

38. C. E. Beeby, The Quality of Education in Developing Countries (Cambridge: Harvard University Press, 1966), p. 129.

JORGE E. HARDOY
Instituto di Tella
Buenos Aires, Argentina

Spacial Structure and Society in Revolutionary Cuba

"There is ... a definite connection between the governmental program of particular socio-economic groups which control state power at any given time, and the spatial and sectorial distribution of productive investments, social infrastructure and human and natural resource utilization."

INTRODUCTION

The relationship between sociopolitical systems and the urbanization process has been neglected in the social sciences. Nonetheless, in Latin America it is possible to discern, through two thousand years of urban history, a clear relationship between economy, technology, and social structure and the resulting urban patterns and spatial structures. The Aztec, Mayan, and Incan cities, the administrative and commercial cities of Latin America and Lusoamerica, the cities constructed by the French, Dutch, and English in the American colonies, the republican cities and the Brazilian imperial cities, the incipient industrial and commercial cities of pre-World War I vintage, and the great metropolitan cities of the more recent era of import substitution: each has unique characteristics which reflect their gradual disassociation from primary activities and an increasing multiplicity of functions. In other words, the implicit or explicit objectives of different sociopolitical systems, which successively determined the characteristics of Latin American society, were reflected in different spatial structures and urban models.

There is undoubtedly a definite connection between the governmental program of particular socioeconomic groups which control state power at any given time and the spatial and sectorial distribution of productive investments, social infrastructure, and human and natural resource utilization. All investments influence the shape of and use of urban and rural space. As these investments are determined by interest groups with conflicting objectives, it is logical that a country's spatial structure and the internal structure of each area will be determined by a broad range of exogenous and endogenous factors related to the nation's socioeconomic configuration.

A country or province may be very urbanized from a demographic point of view, as are Uruguay, the province of Buenos Aires, Havana, or the state of Mexico; but the urban population tends to be concentrated within a limited area of the total national or provincial territory. The influence of Buenos Aires, of Mexico City, and, in general, of the great Latin American capitals, extends throughout all the respective national territory. This influence is seen in political and administrative policies, in finance, commerce, and culture. A foreigner's vision of most countries in Latin America is conditioned by the capital city. It is a distorted image which does

A WARNER MODULAR PUBLICATION

Copyright © 1973 by Warner Modular Publications, Inc.

All rights reserved. No part of this publication may be reproduced, stored in a retrieval system, or transmitted, in any form or by any means, electronic, mechanical, photocopying, recording, or otherwise, without the prior written permission of the publisher. Printed in the United States of America.

Library of Congress Catalog Card Number 73-5217

10 9 8 7 6 5 4 3 2 1

The Developmental Economics Series is under the editorship of

DAVID P. BARKIN
City University of New York
Lehman College

Translated from the Spanish by Elizabeth Fernandez

SUGGESTED CITATION:

Jorge E. Hardoy, "Spacial Structure and Society in Revolutionary Cuba," Warner Modular Publications, Module 265 (1973), pp 1-16

All original publications in this series appear first as separate modules. Most modules will appear in one collection; many will appear in several. To facilitate research use, all modules are numbered serially, and each module carries the same number and folio sequence in all incarnations.

not reflect the realities of rural backwardness, regional underdevelopment, and underutilization of the resources of entire territories which have been poorly served by the prevailing concentration of political power, productive investment, and national services within the central megalopolis.

Varying sociopolitical systems are reflected in distinct urban ecologies. In the cities of Latin America's capitalist countries, the value of urban land and housing, the codes, and the regulations all reflect different socioeconomic levels in the urban setting. The unreality and injustice of the development policies which sustain the capitalist governments of Latin America contribute to the deterioration of urban conditions. To gain time, capitalist planners insist that underdeveloped economies are economies in transition. They are, if by transition one means the precarious step from a dependent, underdeveloped economy to a more developed one which does not open channels of participation or produce a more just distribution of wealth.

In the cities of socialist countries, ownership of urban land and housing either disappears or acquires a different social meaning. Land is a resource which belongs to all and is not an asset which can be freely bought and sold. Housing is an indispensible social factor in the productive struggle for national goals and its use is a right guaranteed by society, not a privilege. Urban services are accessible by their very existence to all members of society rather than to certain, special social groups which have greater economic power.

Cuba has abandoned the traditional development model used by the capitalist governments of Latin America. Its achievements and failures have been noted, praised, or criticized. There is little knowledge, however, about what the revolutionary government has done and plans to do with respect to the urbanization process. By the beginning of the 1960s, Cuba's leaders had decided to create a new spatial structure which would reflect the needs of the new society which was being born. To this end, Cuba radically altered the spatial structure and the urban model inherited from the former capitalist society. This chapter analyzes this transformation.

URBANIZATION AND SOCIETY IN CUBA

Increasing urbanization throughout Latin America

is the combined result of the natural growth of the urban population and the migration from rural areas into the cities. Immigration from foreign nations no longer influences this growth. Migrations from within the Latin American area are of no importance, either. Those countries with a larger rural population and higher rate of population growth are subject to more rapid urbanization. In order for urbanization to occur, however, other conditions must be present, aside from the simple combination of a comparatively high rate of national population growth and a predominantly rural population. Urbanization requires a minimum level of development, basic transportation and communication systems, and some spatial concentration of productive investments and services.

If, indeed, the indices of urbanization in Latin American countries are equal to those of Europe, these countries nevertheless do not enjoy a comparable degree of development and industrialization. Even those Latin American nations which are highly urbanized present marked regional differences. In all these nations, the growing rhythm of urbanization has paralleled the growing supremacy of the city-port, which originated in the colonial period and consolidated at the beginning of the nineteenth century when the role of Latin America was externally defined as that of a provider of raw materials and a market for already industrialized countries. The spatial structure that evolved in each country reflected the "outward looking" pattern of development imposed by foreign interests and by nationals interested in maintaining the basic characteristics of their economies.

Even in the most economically developed countries of Latin America, poorly industrialized regions with poorly developed public services coexist with modern urban centers which receive the lion's share of productive and social investments. Vast sections of the population in each country barely participate in the domestic consumer market because they still lack effective purchasing power. This situation characterizes virtually the entire rural population; and to the degree that agrarian backwardness continues unabated, a growing percentage of the urban population of rural origin is similarly "marginalized."

Urbanization in Latin America—and until a few years ago Cuba was no exception—has proceeded unplanned and spontaneously, with excessive concentration in certain areas. One observes in almost all the countries of Latin America a hypertrophic capital, a marked absence of dynamic regional centers which could balance the oppressive influence of the principal cities on all aspects of national life, a disintegrated network of rural towns which are too small to justify the provision of essential public services in any socioeconomic system based on individual gain, and a scattered rural population existing without community services and subject to the continual threat of unemployment and underemployment as a result of the prevailing system of land tenure and land use.

In comparison with the other nineteen nations of Latin America, Cuba now has a moderately stable urban pattern. According to the national census of September 1970, only 39.6 per cent of the Cuban population is rural, making Cuba the fifth most urbanized country of Latin America. According to United Nations estimates for 1970, the national annual population growth rate was 1.92 per cent, the fourth lowest of the area, while the rural population grew at 1.10 per cent, the ninth lowest in the area. Furthermore, the United Nations has estimated on the basis of past trends, that by 1985 there will be a decline in the national growth rate, which will be around 1.72 per cent, the fifth lowest in Latin America. Nonetheless, according to United Nation's projections, between 1970 and 1985 the population of Cuba will increase by approximately 2,570,000 persons. Of these, 78.3 per cent, or 2,015,000 persons, will be absorbed into urban areas and 555,000 into rural areas. This means that urban areas must absorb an average of 134,000 new dwellers per year, and rural areas, 37,000.[1]

In present-day Cuba, however, unlike the other Latin American countries, urban and rural development policies complement each other and have affected the spatial structure of the country and the distribution of population. Even though these policies are less than a dozen years old, the proportion of people in cities with more than 50,000 inhabitants has in recent years held relatively stable. A slight rise in the percentage of the urban population can be explained by the planned concentration of important rural groups in new agricultural towns, but not as a consequence of spontaneous migrations from the countryside to the city in search of work, public services, and other benefits.

Regional and urban policies are integrated into national programs for economic and social development. Both have been made possible by the almost simultaneous urban and agrarian reforms, which drastically reduced the inequality of income distribution. By contrast, urbanization in the rest of Latin America is a spontaneous process which comes into being without plans or policies. It is viewed by technicians and by the few politicians and leaders who seriously weigh its implications as an irreversible process and a proof of development. Urbanization within the framework of underdevelopment, however, reflects the lack of other alternatives in the daily lives of millions of rural persons, which is the result of a productive system which is spatially incomplete, socially unjust, and economically dependent. In almost all of Latin America great urban concentrations and relatively developed regions coexist with backward and unpopulated regions, rich in mineral resources, fuels, and uncultivated land.

This was also true in Cuba at the close of the 1950s. On the eve of the Revolution Cuba was one of the more urbanized countries in the world. In 1953, 24.3 per cent of the national population lived in Havana, Santiago, and Camaguey, the three urban centers with populations of over 100,000. This urban percentage was greater than that of Canada, France, Italy, and other industrialized countries and inferior in Latin America only to Argentina, Uruguay, and Chile. In 1958, 28.6 per cent of the national population lived in the three urban centers with populations of 100,000 or over, and 31.9 per cent lived in nine centers with 50,000 or more* (see table 1).

The origin of the principal urban centers of Cuba, as in all Latin American countries, goes back to the colonial period. But even as late as the middle of the nineteenth century the twelve largest cities in present-day Cuba did not form an interconnected network. Their principal activity was based on the export-import trade which was oriented towards the demands of a small market and limited industrialization. Sugar mills proliferated as a result of the stimulus provided by Carlos III in 1763.

> At that moment the construction of a sugar empire began, first over the backs of the slave workers and then of the salaried workers, and side by side surged misery and the greatest and most fantastic native and foreign fortunes.[2]

There were about 100 mills in 1764, close to 500 in 1792, over 800 in 1802, and some 1,500 by the middle of the nineteenth century.[3] The majority of the mills at that time were in the western region of the island, close to the north shore and its ports, in order to facilitate export and equipment shipments. Havana flourished during these decades, stirred more by its commercial activities with the ports of Mexico and Spain than by its small, isolated cities in the interior.

In 1837 the island's first railroad was built. In the following decades more railroads were constructed from Havana, Cienfuegos, Matanzas, Casilda, and other ports towards the interior, providing easy transportation of sugar and thus making possible the extension of lands cultivated with sugar cane. Railroads formed small networks with microregional influence rather than a national network with branches to the principal cities.

The elements of a society dominated by foreign commercial interests remained in the form of a productive system which was based on the latifundia and monoculture, in this case the sugar economy, which created their own social or "cultural" organization. This organization was characterized by the misuse of the land, annual harvest cycles, and a "slavery with invisible chains," as Castro called the social condition before the Revolution; by an unstable economy dependent on the exportation of a product with a world market price it could not control; by a political system dominated by foreign interests—in Cuba's case, North American interests—and the national oligarchy; by a society rigidly stratified and almost entirely marginal to the fundamental decisions which shaped the future of its country; by a fragmented nation, with no sense of national entity or solidarity, which neither comprehended

---

* The three urban centers were Havana, with 1,361,000 inhabitants; Santiago, with 189,200; and Camagüey, with 129,500.

Table 1
CUBA. DISTRIBUTION OF POPULATION ACCORDING TO SIZE OF LOCALITY

Categories	1943 No. of Centers	1943 Population	1943 % of Total	1953 No. of Centers	1953 Population	1953 % of Total	1969 No. of Centers	1969 Population	1969 % of Total
Metropolitan Areas	1	868,426	18.2	1	1,139,579	19.6	1	1,737,954	20.7
500,000 and over	1	868,426	18.2	1	1,139,579	19.6	1	1,737,954	20.7
Large Cities	1	118,266	2.5	2	273,625	4.7	5	873,871	10.4
200,000 to 499,999	-	-	-	-	-	-	1	286,523	3.4
100,000 to 199,999	1	118,266	2.5	2	273,625	4.7	4	587,348	7.0
Medium Cities	14	540,268	11.3	19	747,220	12.6	23	988,795	11.9
50,000 to 99,000	4	242,244	5.1	5	322,752	5.5	9	602,680	7.2
20,000 to 49,999	10	298,042	6.2	14	414,468	7.1	14	386,115	4.7
Small Cities	229	807,774	16.9	216	1,055,491	18.1			17.1
10,000 to 19,999	15	203,034	4.2	19	256,443	4.4	31	436,494	5.2
5,000 to 9,999	21	151,551	3.2	40	251,128	4.3	67	479,262	5.7
2,000 to 4,999	99	322,520	6.8	107	338,412	5.8			
1,000 to 1,999	94	130,669	2.7	150	209,508	3.6		501,113	6.2
Other	-	2,443,831	51.1	-	2,623,114	45.0		3,342,846	39.9
Total	245	4,778,583	100.0	338	5,829,029	100.0		8,360,335	100.0

Sources: For 1943 and 1953: JUCEPLAN, Resumen de Estadísticas de Población, no. 3 (La Habana, 1963), chart 6, p. 11.

For 1969: Estimates by the author, with information prepared by the Institute of Physical Planning in August 1970.

nor understood the great national problems; and by an underutilization of natural and human resources, subordinate to foreign interests.

Cuba's structure reflected this condition. In each period of Cuba's political and economic history, urbanization as a national process, and the city as an ecological space, reflected the prevailing social forces, the level of technology, and external bonds. If we exclude sugar production, Cuba was not very industrialized in the 1950s, even by Latin American standards. In 1957 sugar comprised 81 per cent of the export trade and tobacco, 6 per cent. The U.S. acquired 58 per cent of exported goods and provided 71 per cent of Cuba's imports which were mostly machinery, vehicles, chemical and pharmaceutical products, textiles, metals, foodstuffs, liquor, and fuels. The manufacturing locations of cigars and cigarettes, rum, rope, dairy products, canned fruits, cement, and ceramics, among others, were generally urban, as were those of cosmetics, beer, clothing, glass, and other types of production which depended on imported raw materials. Industry was badly integrated and, with the exception of sugar and tobacco derivatives, it produced consumer goods for domestic use. On the eve of the Revolution, 75 per cent of the value of industrial production, excluding sugar, and 52.8 per cent including it, was concentrated in Havana, a city in which slightly more than 20 per cent of the population lived.[4] Oriente province, however, with 31.9 per cent of the total population, 37 per cent of the total area, and the principal mineral reserves, contributed a mere 15 per cent of the industrial production.[5] Before the Revolution, Havana's port accounted for 90 per cent of the country's shipping and was the main fishing port.[6]

Cultural life was concentrated in Havana, as was the university population. The public University of Havana, founded in 1721, accounted for 87.8 per cent of the country's university students in 1952-53.* Attracted by middle- and upper middle-class housing construction and public works programs, 90 per cent of Cuba's architects worked in Havana on the eve of the Revolution. Approximately 85 per cent of the total circulation of daily newspapers was published in Havana.

Havana was the undisputed political and administrative center of the country. Administrative centralization corresponded to the demographic and economic concentration, a pattern which was repeated on a smaller scale in all provincial capitals throughout the island. The national capital was also the center of transportation, in spite of its eccentric position with respect to the geographic configuration of the island. In effect, approximately 1,400 of the 2,017 private bus lines operated in 1958 were located in the capital city and in the province of Havana.[7] The main department stores were in Havana, as were the best equipped public and private hospitals. Banking was also centered there.

In synthesis, although Cuba had a one-crop, rural economy, it poured its earnings into Havana, to the detriment of the rest of the country. But in 1951 even in Havana 53.8 per cent of families had poverty incomes (less than $70 per month) or minimal incomes ($70 to $149 per month); 94 per cent of the total number lacked saving capacity, spending upwards of 50 per cent of their incomes on food alone.[8] Inversely, 5.4 per cent of the families had abundant incomes of over $500 per month. Wealth was concentrated in the hands of a few, even in the richest city of the island.

The rural situation in Cuba was characterized by its backwardness and the instability of its inhabitants. "The expansion of the latifundia and the consolidation of the monoculture destroyed small properties and eliminated diversified agriculture."[9] On the eve of the Revolution, there were more than 100,000 small agricultural workers, 83.8 per cent of whom did not own the land they worked. Forced to find work in an economy characterized by being seasonal and prone to periodic crises, many of these workers joined the migratory movement to the cities. The isolation of rural housing and its low quality, the absence of communities, and the depressive, chronic unemployment and underemployment of the population were starkly incongruous with the rural origin of Cuba's wealth.

---

* The Encyclopedia Americana 8: 287. The University of Havana had 18,379 students enrolled in 1952-53 and the Catholic University, of St. Thomas of Vilanueva, 523. There were 1,256 enrolled in the University of Oriente and 767 in the University of Santa Clara.

REGIONAL DEVELOPMENT AND URBANIZATION POLICIES

An examination of urbanization in Cuba since 1959 points out how effective state action can be in reorienting a country's spatial organization and the internal structure of its cities in accordance with national development goals. One of these goals was to convert the city into a center of life and work which reflects the values of a society bent on living unselfishly.

Fidel Castro said:

> A communist society means that human beings will have been able to achieve the degree of understanding and brotherhood which man has sometimes reached within the close circle of his family.[10]

In my brief visit to Cuba in 1970, I was convinced that in spite of certain protests for the lack or the rationing of this or that product, rumors of the rationing of some other product, and complaints about the congestion of traffic or the long waits to enter a cinema, bar, or ice cream parlor, there thrives a spirit and cohesion which reflects "the attitude of the people . . . which really does things because it understands them, comprehends them, because it wants to do them."[11]

"Touristic" Havana of prerevolutionary decades has disappeared. In its place stands a society without unemployment or slums, with antiquated and crowded buses, but with beaches open to the people; with unpainted houses but with an urban growth which has been ordered and controlled, once land speculation was eliminated. New parks and a green belt around Havana provide recreational facilities and permit the production of food and industrial crops. Gone are the contrasts between gaudy, well-lit neighborhoods and dark, marginal sections, between neighborhoods with luxurious institutions and discriminating clubs, and others with not even the most basic services, between ostentatious palaces and miserable tenements. Social classes have disappeared; schools, hospitals, and sports events are free; the old clubs are open to all; and some day housing and transportation will be free. Cuba is equalizing itself from the bottom up, and nowhere is this transformation more evident than in Havana for one who has visited the country before and after the Revolution.

Physical changes can be observed everywhere, but they are most dramatic in the rural areas. The importance of the countryside in the economic independence of Cuba is a goal established prior to the triumph of the Revolution.[12] Rural development and the improvement of rural life meant, for the leaders of the Revolution, justice for the most oppressed groups and national unity. The collective effort of the sugar harvest, the diversification of crops, the concentration of the dispersed rural population on plantations, the construction of lakes, roads, and bridges, rural electrification, and the incorporation of new lands into production reflect the fact that the greatest efforts have been concentrated in the countryside. Literacy programs, preventive medicine, and sanitation campaigns were strengthened in rural areas.

All this has been possible, in spite of many limitations and apparent contradictions, because the government of the Revolution has the political power and popular support necessary to initiate plans and require sacrifices. During the first years of the Revolution errors were committed because of inexperience, excessive optimism, latent internal opposition, and the lack of a definite political and economic line. In spite of the position of the leaders and their interest in promoting rural development, some spectacular works were realized in Havana during the first years of the Revolution, works whose validity and design were later criticized. In a housing development of East Havana, imported and domestic criteria for urban planning were employed in the construction of costly cooperative housing. The art schools in Havana, built between 1962 and 1965, were costly and difficult to maintain, as well as unsuited to the projects for which they were intended. The University City of Jose Antonio Echevarria was the last of a series of costly works constructed in Havana whose standards were higher than the Cuban people could afford to adopt. During this period Cuba saw itself brusquely deprived of many professionals and technicians who abandoned the country. The North American blockade cut off supplies of equipment and replacement parts, fundamental in a country which, prior to the Revolution, almost exclusively utilized vehicles and machines made in the

United States. The threats of invasion and the internal situation forced the diversion of resources and people to unproductive activities. The vacillations of the first years reflected the lack of experience, information, and professionals trained in engineering, economics, design, and construction. The planning mechanisms which existed could produce a plan, but did not take advantage of the potential contribution that other specialized groups could make.

Between 1959 and 1962, eighty-three new rural towns were constructed throughout the island. This step, along with the improvement of employment conditions and of rural life in general, tended to consolidate the rural population in areas where their contribution to the productive effort was necessary, avoiding regional disparities between the availability and demand for employment. In 1961 the state was uniting, under its direct control, a large part of the Cuban productive system in order to provide for the distribution of the means of production and technical assistance. Secondary education in the agricultural disciplines was developed and illiteracy was almost entirely eradicated. Campaigns against malaria, dysentery, and infectious diseases in general notably reduced the mortality rate, particularly infant mortality.

In 1964 the National Institute for Physical Planning (IPF) was created to incorporate a territorial dimension into national sectorial plans elaborated by the Central Planning Board (JUCEPLAN). By then the agrarian and urban reform laws had already had their impact. Both had served to reduce the traditional differences between the country and the city and had provoked a redistribution of income, essential aspects for a process leading to a classless society devoid of inequalities.

As a result, the IPF was able to dedicate its energies to the study of the physical characteristics of the national terrain in order to exploit its potentials in line with economic goals which were determined by the JUCEPLAN, and to propose integrated physical solutions for rural and urban areas without fear of pressure from interest groups which were motivated by individual profits. Further, the IPF was encouraged by the growing spirit of community.

For the Central Planning Board, Cuba is a single development area and Havana is a part of that region. The IPF was concerned about the nation as a whole and adopted a flexible system of regional divisions. Although based on the existing spatial structure, it is also being adapted to the new spatial structure which the island is gradually acquiring. The new spatial structure is based on a territorial plan which considers the various types of land, natural resources, topography, industrial works, and infrastructure in each region. Each center or point of this spatial structure, old or new, is based on an increasing knowledge of the characteristics and potential of each region. A hydraulic, topographic, and agro-industrial analysis determines the areas of influence of rural towns and sugar mills, complementing available information about climatological and road conditions. Bit by bit, urban growth plans have been elaborated for the principal cities; they are essentially physical plans which stress the use of land and the most appropriate densities, pointing out the best location for new facilities. This is being done gradually, in accordance with priorities determined by agricultural production goals, by the needs for more rural services, or by the need to keep ahead of the rapid growth of some secondary cities. Equally important was the adoption of local strategies which incorporated a time factor into the urban and rural territorial plans. This permitted the evaluation of the effectiveness of sectorial plans which were either too ambitious or allowed too little time for implementation.

The entire system of physical planning is in continual modification, searching, through a gradual administrative decentralization, for a greater participation at the provincial and regional level. The greatest amount of decentralization can be noted in agricultural activities. Presently, provinces generally have the right to decide on the location of activities within the JUCEPLAN guidelines. This decentralization is reflected in the organization of the IPF.

In each one of the six provinces, the IPF office, like the national one, is divided into urban and rural planning divisions. The urban division is responsible for demographic, population, and human resource studies, and for establishing norms for urban planning and services. The rural division is responsible for agricultural, industrial, and infrastructural studies. Each provincial office coordinates the activities of various regional offices which study agricultural problems and maintain a current inventory of local conditions. In those regions with an important urban center, however, its principal task is the planning of that center, with the collaboration of technicians from provincial and national offices of the IPF.

As a result of the regional focus of national development plans and the territorial dimension which is gradually being introduced, Cuba's spatial structure has undergone important changes. The most notable is the reduced demographic importance of Havana as a result of the decentralization of investments and decision-making. Immigration to Havana has been discouraged; it has been reoriented towards some intermediary centers where new sources of employment and public services have been concentrated. Paralleling this is the stabilization of the rural population as a result of the improvement in the rural standard of living. Havana's population remained almost stable between 1967 and 1970* (see table 1). The development of Oriente province has been important in the decentralization of productive investments, services, and human resources[13] (see tables 2 and 3).

The development of the new industrial centers has had short-term effects. Cienfuegos is being transformed into the island's second port, with technical facilities for the loading of semi-

---

* According to the national census of 1970, the population of greater Havana was 1,755,360. The estimated population for 1967 was 1,700,300. The annual rate of growth in 1965-66 was 0.9 per cent, the lowest among cities of 20,000 or more inhabitants and almost two and one half times below the national growth rate. For more details on the 1970 census, see Gramma Weekly Summary, January 10, 1971.

Table 2
CUBA. POPULATION OF PRINCIPAL CITIES. CENSUS FOR 1943 AND 1953, ESTIMATIONS FOR JUNE 30 OF 1958, 1966, AND 1967

	1943	1953	1958	1966	1967
Cuba	4,778,583	5,829,029	6,548,300	7,799,600	7,937,200
Greater Havana	935,670	1,210,920	1,361,600	1,693,600	1,700,200
Santiago	118,266	163,237	189,200	249,600	259,000
Camagüey	80,509	110,388	129,500	170,500	178,600
Guantánamo	42,423	64,671	76,700	131,400	135,100
Santa Clara	53,981	77,398	83,200	132,900	137,700
Cienfuegos	52,910	57,991	62,700	88,700	91,800
Manzanillo	36,295	42,252	51,100	87,000	91,200
Holguín	35,865	58,776	68,300	90,800	100,500
Matanzas	54,844	63,916	72,900	81,000	84,100
Pinar del Río	26,241	38,885	43,000	64,700	67,600
Cárdenas	37,059	43,750	41,200	64,500	67,400
Sancti-Spíritus	28,262	37,741	44,900	60,500	662,500
Ciego de Ávila	23,802	35,178	40,700	53,700	54,700
Greater Havana as a per cent of national	19.5	20.7	20.7	21.7	21.4
Other 12 cities as a per cent of national	12.3	13.4	13.7	16.3	16.7

Source: JUCEPLAN, Resumen de Estadisticas de Población, no. 3 (La Habana, 1968).

Table 3
CUBA. RATE OF ANNUAL GROWTH PER 1,000 INHABITANTS
OF CITIES WITH 50,000 OR MORE IN 1966 AND 1967

	Provinces	1931-43	1943-53	1953-58	1965-66	1966-67
CUBA		15.9	21.1	21.9	22.1	17.6
Greater Havana	Havana	22.3	27.5	21.9	9.1	3.4
Santiago	Oriente	13.0	34.5	27.7	37.3	37.7
Camagüey	Camaguey	22.2	33.8	29.9	55.1	47.5
Guantánamo	Oriente	35.2	45.3	32.2	30.4	28.2
Santa Clara	Las Villas	29.9	38.6	13.4	46.1	36.1
Cienfuegos	Las Villas	4.4	9.7	14.5	46.9	34.9
Manzanillo	Oriente	15.2	16.1	35.7	50.3	48.3
Holguín	Oriente	34.8	53.3	28.1	83.0	106.8
Matanzas	Matanzas	8.2	16.2	24.5	44.7	38.3
Pinar del Río	Pinar del Río	24.9	42.2	18.7	65.9	44.8
Cárdenas	Matanzas	8.4	17.6	-11.0	52.2	45.0
Sancti-Spíritus	Las Villas	21.6	30.9	32.6	42.0	33.1
Ciego de Ávila	Camaguey	26.4	41.9	27.3	22.5	18.6

Source: JUCEPLAN, Resumen de Estadisticas de Población,
no. 3 (La Habana, 1968), chart 5, p. 9.

refined sugar. A plant for the production of fertilizers, a thermoelectric plant, and an oil refinery—all in different stages of construction or planning—complement tourism as new activities in this city, whose projected population will climb from the 91,800 it had in 1967 to 175,000 in 1995. Cienfuegos is the port of Las Villas province. Nuevitas, a small port on the northern coast of the province of Camaguey, is also being transformed into a new industrial center with a projected 1985 population of 70,000. Nuevitas is in reality a new city. Its port, with facilities for the mechanical loading of semirefined sugar, will be the third most important one on the island. A cement plant, a fertilizer plant, and a thermoelectric plant will fill the needs of Camaguey province. New electrical plants will also be constructed in Nuevitas.

Santa Clara, the capital of Las Villas province, is situated in the geographic center of the island, near the Carretera Central (Central Highway). It is a center for technical education, as well as the principal center for the production of stoves, refrigerators, and other domestic appliances. Processing facilities for agricultural and livestock production will be in Sancti-Spíritu and Camagüey.

The integrated urban-rural development of Oriente province, the farthest from Havana, is designed to provide a counterweight to the traditional concentration in the capital. The development of Oriente is based on farming as well as the processing of local mineral resources. The province will be connected to the rest of the island by a new highway now under construction and by electric railroads. A new network of rural roads will facilitate better communication between urban and rural areas in the region. The regional development of Oriente is based on the promotion of Nícaro-Moa, on the northern coast, and Santiago, on the southern coast. The latter will have a multifunctional character: port, tourist center, industrial center—rum, cement, factories, etc.—university center, and principal center for the province's administrative and service offices. A new city, Levissa, is being constructed, with a projected population of 130,000. Other centers in the province are being industrialized: Manzanillo as a fishing, rice, and hide center; Guantanamo as a center for the textile industry and light metals; Bayamo as a center for the dairy and refrigeration industries.

OBJECTIVES OF URBAN REFORM

Much has been written about Cuba's agrarian reform; almost nothing about its urban reforms. Like the Agrarian Reform Laws, however, the urban reforms were as fundamental for meeting national economic and social development goals as they were for incorporating the entire population into an increasingly better-integrated society.

The precedents of the Urban Reform Law appear, in a way, in Fidel Castro's famous self-defense at the trial following the abortive attack on the Moncada barracks in 1953.[14] This law, in my opinion, has no practical precedent in other socialist countries, where rent is generalized and where private property has not been maintained. I do not know how the commission which proposed the Urban Reform Law proceeded or how it elaborated its considerations and articles. It is evident that the Urban Reform Law was facilitated by previous legislation promulgated in 1959 about rent, savings, and unused lots, and especially by law number 691, of December 23, 1959. In many aspects of the legislation and in the Cuban experience, however, there is an originality and dedication which merit detailed study. After all, along with sugar interests, urban land and housing speculators and tourist organizations—particularly in Havana, Varadero, and other international centers—were among the most fervent opponents of the revolutionary government, and these were supported by many financial and professional groups. It was these interests which created a psychological war in 1959 and 1960, delaying payments and deliberately making mistakes on statements in order to delay the implementation of the Agrarian Reform Laws, speculating on the defeat of the Revolution or the modification of its orientation.

The first Agrarian Reform Law, which changed the rural land tenure system and created some 100,000 new landowners from one day to the next, and the legislation preceding the Urban Reform Law, especially law number 691, which dissuaded speculation and defined the complete and efficient utilization of urban land, were issued practically simultaneously.

Both reforms complement each other and are basic, it seems to me, as political and socioeconomic measures. These actions deprived the great rural and urban landowners of their political and economic power, incorporating important areas of arable land into production and making urban areas available for housing programs and social infrastructure. These measures together with the reduction of rents required by law number 135 of March 10, 1959, the reduction of public service fees, the policy of full employment, the increase in salaries, and the notable increase in educational and health facilities, raised the standard of living for the masses.

Equally important is the spirit of the legislation passed in that first year.[15] Among the provisions of law number 86, February 17, 1959, which eradicated gambling and created the National Institute for Savings and Housing in order to finance new housing, are the following:

> To govern, orient, and educate a nation is an art of patience, rather than effort.
>
> The habit of saving should substitute the habit of gambling.
>
> One of the most useful measures of the revolutionary government is one which would specify a definitive solution to the housing problem, so that the necessity of living under a roof stops being exploitation, as well.

Law number 80 attacks profits, exploitation, and parasitism; it establishes guidelines for the conduct of the new man who is to be forged by the Revolution and be its greatest masterpiece.

In Latin America's capitalist societies, land is one of the most abundant idle resources. In Cuba prior to 1959, the situation was comparable. The great sugar industrialists cultivated only part of their lands; the great cattlemen favored exploitation of an extensive type with low-grade cattle; the production of milk and eggs was very low. In 1957 one-third of the labor force, 700,000 Cubans, was either underemployed or unemployed; the majority were rural people living in abject misery.[16]

The productive and social value of rural land is now recognized. The redistribution of land, while provoking a brusque redistribution of income, stimulated internal consumption, improved the standard of living, and attracted popular support. The state's control of most of the land, achieved with the implementation of the Second Agrarian Reform Law, allowed farming activities to be oriented towards the most suitable locations according to economic goals which were determined by an integrated national plan. In other words, in a planned economy which controls land resources, territorial planning becomes the fundamental instrument for the spatial mobilization of existing and idle resources. Agrarian reform in Cuba, then, not only destroyed peonage but, complemented by regional plans, also allowed more adequate use of each type of land according to its ecological characteristics and allowed planning of the location of public works and social infrastructure based upon the new agricultural and human resources development strategies.

The productive value of urban land is not known. Its social value is often not even mentioned by those who defend the social value of housing and attack the manipulation of rents and construction costs. The value of urban land, however, reflects, as does no other indicator, the socioeconomic segregation which exists in cities of capitalist societies.

> In capitalist countries, land is a negotiable good in a market subject to fluctuations, often sudden ones, which depend on factors independent of the land itself.[17]

In all capitalist cities, land, whether uncultivated or with low-density construction, is an idle resource which impedes the state's ability to provide indispensable services at reasonable prices and to form an adequate urban physical structure. Its fragmentation impedes the use of industrial techniques in construction. Its irrational use is one of the principal factors in the destruction of the natural scenery and of the deterioration of the environment. Undoubtedly, urban land has an equally productive value if we consider that the level of urban mental and physical health and the effective use of urban time depend, more than on anything else, on the adequate physical planning of a city. I do not know of a single instance in which a city with a free market for land and rent has found a solution to these problems.

The Urban Reform Law was issued on October 14, 1960. It is made up of forty-five articles. The first few constitute a declaration of principles and include a program for the construction of housing. Article 1 establishes the right of each family to decent housing and later outlines the three stages of the construction programs. In the last stage, which should have begun in December 1970, each family should receive permanent housing free of charge.

The Urban Reform Law endorsed and extended previous legislation. It banned, for example, the leasing of housing, or any contract which implicated "the ceding of partial or total use of an urban dwelling" (article 2), and declared null and void all existing lease contracts (article 5), thus revalidating the previously adopted law number 26 of January 26, 1959, with exceptions made for housing in resort areas or transient housing. The law established procedures for the buying and selling of housing by its occupants which linked the price to the rent paid by the tenant (article 17) and the date of construction (article 15). In this way, old property owners who received rents of up to $150 per month will receive $150 plus 50 per cent of the difference between this sum and the total rent paid (article 37). Indemnizations acquired the characteristics of lifelong rents, the payment of which is the responsibility of the National Bank of Cuba. No property owner could receive over $600 per month as total compensation for dwellings (article 22). A similar payment scale was created for mortgage holders, as all the mortgage debts were cancelled. The law took into account the plight of small home owners. The occupant of a dwelling had priority in buying the dwelling (article 9).

The law created the permanent Superior Council for Urban Reform, and the temporary provincial councils, with the responsibility of interpreting problems of a civic or social character which resulted from the application of the law, as well as of collecting the monthly payments of new property owners (articles 7, 8, and 9).

The law determined that tenements, ranch laborers' living quarters, and tenement blocks would be expropriated without compensation for the owner, using the rent paid by the occupants for an individual fund which would pay for decent housing given to each family (articles 25 and 26).

The law also authorized the Ministry of the Treasury to issue public bonds destined to substitute for titles or stocks which were in the hands of the national banks, as a mortgage guarantee for dwellings (articles 35 and 36). The transgressors of the law could lose ownership of the dwelling and/or receive prison sentences. The law excluded nonresident foreigners from its benefits.

CONCLUSIONS

Conceptually, agrarian reforms led to urban reforms. Undoubtedly, the leaders of the Revolution had clearer precedents for the goals of agrarian reform and how to implement them than they did for urban reform. Furthermore, since one of the Revolution's social and economic goals was to equalize the standards of living between the city and the country, the investments in housing, schools, sanitation, roads, clinics, etc., have been more important in rural areas than in the great cities. This explains the contrast one observes in the amount of new rural construction as opposed to the abandonment and relative lack of construction in Havana, Santa Clara, and other cities. In a speech in 1965, at a reunion of the secretary generals of twenty-five national trade unions, Fidel Castro once more reaffirmed the priority which the countryside would receive. He said,

> There is much need for housing in the country, both in the cities and in the countryside. Alright now, where should we concentrate the effort to resolve the housing problem? In the cities? No, it truly should not be in the cities. The cities must wait, wait until the development of the construction industry allows for massive construction. . . . The resources we have for housing must be concentrated in the countryside.[18]

The Cuban experience has taught us that urban reform does not have to be reduced to the control of land and housing speculation and the promotion of occupation of unused land. Urban reform must have broader goals. It must permit an urban land use which corresponds to the functions of different points or centers in the spatial structure of a country or region within a program of national socioeconomic development. In other words, an economy planned through policies of urbanization, and regional plans which will gradually include the whole country, are prerequisites for an affective urban reform. If indeed in theory it is possible to attempt to direct the cities' physical growth with only the state's strict control of key sectors of the economy, one of the most distorting factors in the physical aspects of a city will remain; that is, the sale of urban properties with its inevitable reflection in the spatial distribution of the population by socioeconomic levels.

For this reason, the Cuban urban reform is a part of a revolutionary process oriented towards replacing those systems maintained by the traditional institutions of power.

> In provoking transcendental and long-range changes in the social structure of a country, and in seeking to reduce social stratification, mass integration is facilitated, and mass participation is promoted.[19]

Backed by new legislation which established the right to a home over kinship ties, the urban reform has, for the first time in Latin America, facilitated a causal relationship between the new ecological characteristics of the city and the new cultural values of a society seeking to unite moral incentives and an unselfish attitude towards common problems with a centralized form of economic organization.

Certain inequalities persist both in incomes as well as in access to material goods. Many widely accepted objectives are difficult to put into practice. One of these is the eradication of the status attached to the ownership of a fine house or apartment in one of the better located neighborhoods and with better city services, or that attached to owning a house on the beach or at a resort area. This housing, previously occupied by professionals and the old middle class, has remained in the hands of its old owners. The housing left vacant by exile families has been passed on either to family groups designated by their fellow workers, to the National Council of Urban Reform, or to student groups. In the distribution of housing, merit and necessity are the prime criteria. New housing blocks are assigned by the same criteria. It is these new urban housing groups which receive the best and newest services. In this sense, the old socioeconomic separatism has been ruptured. Urban families retain title to their homes. This property may have originated before the Revolution or as a result of previous distributions. Because they cannot be sold, however, the sense of property is restricted. It still implies, all in all, some advantage, as they can exchange property or pass it on to an heir, if the heir has resided in the house since the moment of the old owner's death.

There are still urban tenants who pay no more than 6 per cent of their family income to the state as rent. At the middle of 1970 the third and last stage of the housing program was expected to begin, according to article 1 of the Urban Reform Law, which provides for the end of tenant leases and the beginning of free and permanent housing for every family. This measure was delayed, however. Among the possible explanations for this are 1) the production of housing has fallen about 25 per cent short of needs and 2) the excess money in circulation as a result of rising incomes and limited availability of goods. The elimination of rents would have meant an increase in available currency without any increase in goods on which to spend it. But because rents are neither eliminated nor imposed on old or new landowners who do not pay them, some inequality remains.

The housing deficit is still great, in spite of the fact that the revolutionary government has tripled its annual production in comparison with prerevolutionary years. The lack of availability, together with the rigidity of the exchange system, makes better use of existing housing difficult. A family whose numbers have been reduced by deaths, marriages, transfers, or other reasons continues to occupy the same dwelling. Often, families in this situation have attempted to exchange a dwelling which is difficult for them to maintain, but the slow process and lack of alternatives have dissuaded them. Undoubtedly, the number of transfers is small, as uncertainty as to what type of housing they will be able to get has discouraged people from changing neighborhoods or cities.

The solution lies in an increase in the production of housing, and voluntary brigades have been organized in order to improve the maintenance of existing housing and to contribute to the construction of new housing.

I would like to make one other point. In a capitalist economy, subject to the pressures of interest groups, if one region gains comparative advantages it is very difficult—practically impossible, I might say—to achieve an adequate regional balance. Regional inequalities cannot be overcome in a laissez-faire economy. The existing comparative advantages in central-south Brazil, the coast of Argentina, or the Caracas-Valenia axis in Venezuela, for example, are such that the governments, with their present orientation and objectives, will not overcome these inequalities. Moreover, the inequalities continue growing in spite of government proclamations, plans, and attempts at regional decentralization.

This was the situation in Cuba before the Revolution. It was characterized, as I previously pointed out, by a great concentration of productive investments and general services in the capital city and by a centralization of decision-making. To break with this meant to evaluate and exploit the nation's resources with a national approach. Cuban planners understood that regional development could not be reached through the exclusive creation of new growth poles. On the contrary, regional development was based on an ample and increasing base of technical knowledge about regional resource endowments. The land studies, assisted by excellent aerial and cartographic studies, are the most complete in any Latin American country. On this base they advanced towards the simultaneous integration of rural and urban development. In this process the training of the population has been essential, as it would be impossible to stimulate regional growth and development if the population were unprepared.

One immediate consequence of the new orientation of national growth was the stabilization of Havana's growth. The construction of new public works was intentionally decelerated at the beginning of 1963. Havana is still the main administrative, cultural, and industrial center of the country, but its relative importance has been reduced with the deconcentration of productive investments and educational, clinical, and housing resources. Only the Cordón de La Habana, an agricultural and recreational green belt with new towns and structures which surround the city, can be compared to many public works created in the interior of the country.

On the other hand, intermediate-size cities play a fundamental role in the decentralization policies being undertaken. They are, generally, old rural service centers or minor ports which, at the outbreak of the Revolution, had populations which ranged from an insignificant number to seventy thousand inhabitants. These centers are experiencing high rates of urban growth: Holgúin, an agricultural center; Manzanillo, a fishing center; Nícaro-Moa, the main center for heavy industry in Cuba—all three are in Oriente province; Nuevitas, a new port on the northern coast of the province of Camaguey; Camaguey, the capital of the province of the same name. Pinar del Río, the principal center for services in the western part of the island, and others.

Revolutionary Cuba has planned and constructed more cities and new rural towns than any other Latin American country. The main objective was to urbanize the countryside and, through the concentration of the rural population, to make services, community facilities, and employment available to all. Most of the towns are small, frequently numbering only a few hundred people. If the experience of other countries is valid, it would seem that Cuba's small size would not, for the time being, permit the great variety of activities, the richness of interactions, and the scale of economies which would justify the urbanization of the rural population. There are discrepancies, however, between the political leaders and technicians, which have led to new programs; and it is possible that the original criteria will be exchanged for new ones based upon experience. In this case, as in many others, it is its experimental and continuously renovating character which makes the Cuban urbanization experience a model of so much interest to others.

NOTES

1. United Nations, Department of Economic and Social Affairs, Population Division, Urban and Rural Population of Individual Countries, 1950-1958, and Regions and Major Areas, 1950-2000, (mimeographed) New York, September 22, 1970.

2. Jose Benitez, "Biografia de Una Industria," Casa de las Americas 11, no. 62 (Havana: September-October 1970): 29.

3. Ibid., p. 30

4. Ministerio de la Construccion, Plan de La Habana, Havana, n. d.

5. Maruja Acosta and Jorge E. Hardoy, Reforma Urbana en Cuba Revolucionaria (Caracas: Ediciones Sintesis Dos Mil, 1971), p. 80.

6. Ministerio de la Construccion, op. cit.

7. Acosta and Hardoy, op. cit.

8. Consejo Nacional de Economia, El Presupuesto familiar Cubano. Muestro Estadistico en la Capital de la Republica. Document 162/E1/1 (Havana, August 13, 1951).

9. Acosta and Hardoy, op. cit., p. 44.

10. Fidel Castro, speech on July 26, 1968, Gramma Weekly Summary, July 28, 1968. Reprinted in Kenner and Petras, Fidel Castro Speaks (New York: Grove Press, 1969), p. 319.

11. Ibid.

12. See, for example, Fidel Castro, History Will Absolve Me, (Havana: Book Institute, 1967), especially chapter XIV, pp. 69-73.

13. For more information, see Acosta and Hardoy, op. cit., chapter III, p. 77-108.

14. Castro, History Will Absolve Me, op. cit.

15. For more information see chapter IV, pp. 109-133, in the work by Acosta and Hardoy and in Juan L. Vega, *La Reforma Urbana de Cuba y otras Leyes en Relación con la Vivenda*, Havana, n.d.

16. Based on study done in 1956 by the Catholic University Association, *¿Por que reforma agraria?* For more information, also see chapters 1 and 5 of this book.

17. Jorge E. Hardoy, "The Demand of Urban Land and its Use" (Paper presented to the United Nations seminar on "Policies of Urban Land and Methods of Control over the use of Land," Madrid, November 1-13, 1971), p. 16.

18. Roberto Segre, "Diez Anos de Arguitectura en Cuba Revolucionaria," *Cuadernos de la Revista Union*, 1970.

19. Jorge Hardoy y Oscar Moreno, "Primeros pasos de la reforma urbana en America Latina," in *EURE II*, no. 4: pp. 83-100 (Santiago de Chile: March 1972).

CONTINUITIES IN CUBAN REVOLUTIONARY POLITICS

BY RICHARD R. FAGEN

In the pages that follow I shall not indulge in detailed description or analysis of what the Cuban revolutionary government has tried to do or how it has gone about trying to do it. Rather, I shall address myself to two more basic, interrelated questions: Underlying the welter of plans, programs, twists, turns, and inconsistencies in the revolutionary scenario, is there a foundation of beliefs, behavior, and institutions that might be deemed the Cuban political style? (Style is used here in its dictionary sense of a "characteristic mode of presentation, construction, or execution. . . .") If so, how does an appreciation of this style contribute to an understanding of programs and strategies as diverse as those undertaken by the revolutionaries over the past twelve years? We thus seek stylistic continuities which will aid in ordering the rhetorical and programmatic complexities with which all students of the Cuban Revolution must eventually come to grips.

The most obvious continuity in Cuban politics under the revolutionary government is, of course, Fidel Castro himself. A complex and intelligent personality, an event-making man par excellence, and the most commanding figure in twentieth century Cuban (and possibly Latin American) history, his centrality to the revolutionary process is undisputed by either his

---

Richard Fagen is a professor of Political Science at Stanford, currently on leave as visiting professor at the Latin American School of Social Science (FLACSO) in Santiago, Chile.

enemies or admirers.* But simply to assert Fidel's centrality to revolutionary politics in Cuba is to risk superficiality or tautology in understanding other continuities. In other words, although much of what we see as continuous in the Cuban political style is shaped by the beliefs and temperament of Fidel, the style has a vitality of its own, conditioned by additional aspects of Cuban history, culture, and the revolutionary experience. Thus, in what follows, Fidel—for all his importance—will not be treated apart from other continuities in revolutionary politics.

What are the general characteristics of the Cuban political style? Although each will subsequently be developed at some length, it is well to have them in mind from the outset: (1) the Rebel Army and the guerrilla experience; (2) pragmatism, flexibility, and adaptability; (3) the search for a politics of unity and harmony; (4) the search for appropriate political forms; and (5) human transformation and the search for productivity.

Notice that these characteristics are neither logically exclusive nor all of the same type. If they were, in fact, it would be difficult to justify calling them a style, for the very notion of style suggests an interrelation of different—and sometimes clashing or contradictory—elements. Thus, the Rebel Army and the guerrilla experience are historical realities supplying the revolution with men, models, and certain ways of viewing the past, present, and future. Pragmatism, flexibility, and adaptability refer to ways of doing political business, making decisions, and ordering priorities. And the final three topics may be thought of as problems that have been with the revolution from the outset. Other problems could have been chosen—our list is hardly exhaustive—but these three are profound enough to have shaped revolutionary politics more or less continuously over the past twelve years. Furthermore, they also illuminate basic goals of the revolutionary government, for the continuing struggle for unity, appropriate political forms, and human transformation and productivity is as much a product of Castroite revolutionary ideology as it is an inevitable consequence of the exigencies of national development.

---

* The best portrait of Fidel is still that presented in Lee Lockwood, *Castro's Cuba, Cuba's Fidel* (New York: Macmillan, 1967).

The Rebel Army and the Guerrilla Experience

One of the most enduring features of Cuban revolutionary politics is the continued pre-eminence of veterans of the Sierra in the ranks of top leadership. Beginning with Fidel, his brother Raúl, the comrades-in-arms like Guillermo García and Juan Almeida, not only the Central Committee of the Communist party of Cuba but also many other top bureaucratic and Party positions have been and continue to be held by charter members of the Rebel Army. If members of the urban branch of the 26th of July Movement and the several university factions are also considered legitimate children of the glory and tragedy of the struggle against Batista—as they certainly should be—then the first and second levels of revolutionary leadership are overwhelmingly staffed by persons whose credentials were first legitimized in the guerrilla period. The rise in organizational prominence and then the rapid demise of members of the old Communist party during the early 1960s was only an interlude which temporarily upset the almost total dominance of the guerrilla group. And the presence today in the central leadership circle of Osvaldo Dorticós, Raúl Roa, and Carlos Rafael Rodríguez, three older men with political origins apart from the guerrilla experience, is only the exception that proves the rule. The Sierra and the urban resistance of the late 1950s together gave political education to the overwhelming majority of men and women who now exercise power in Cuba. And of these two arenas, it is the Sierra which above all continues to give a special tonality to the Cuban revolutionary style.

What are the ideas of the guerrilla period, the "guerrilla complex," carried by these men and women into the governance of revolutionary Cuba? Most immediate was belief in the viability and propriety of armed struggle as a way to national liberation, and the particular emphasis given to the guerrilla *foco* in the theory subsequently elaborated by Che Guevara and Régis Debray. So much has been written about this set of ideas, its development in the early 1960s, and its partial test and costly failure in Bolivia, that there is no need to review the matter here. What does bear emphasizing, however, is how heavily (one is tempted to say entirely) the theory rested on the Castroite experience. It was a theory built on an analogy whose primary term was the Sierra Maestra, 1957-1958. Few have violated the rule "thou shalt not generalize from a sample of one" as completely as Guevara, Debray, and their Cuban *compañeros*. The spell of the Sierra was so powerful that it cast a lengthening and finally fatal shadow over some of the courageous men who created the original events. Ten years later, Cuba's realities turned out to be Bolivian myths.

But this unhappy history of one aspect of the guerrilla complex should not be allowed to obscure the importance of a triad of more general and ultimately more enduring legacies of the period: voluntarism, egalitarianism, and ruralism.* Voluntarism is a formal and somewhat colorless word for the expansive sense of efficacy, competence, and personal power generated during the guerrilla period. The struggle against Batista was the stuff of which legends are made. Again and again, Fidel and the tiny band of survivors of the *Granma* narrowly escaped betrayal, defeat, and death. Then, twenty-five months after the initial landing, Batista had fled, his army was in complete disarray, and Castro was undisputed victor in the battle for political and military control of the island. The rebels marched into Havana, overflowing with the conviction that, having routed Batista, there was no developmental redoubt or political rearguard that they could not handle with facility. It is easy to understand why such feelings prevailed, for both in the city and in the Sierra what the anti-Batista forces had accomplished was truly remarkable, a tribute to their courage, tenacity, intelligence, and good fortune.

As might be expected, the initial ebullience cooled under the impact of the chilling realities of developmental dilemmas and international relations. For instance, on July 26, 1970, in the wake of the failure to achieve a sugar harvest of 10 million tons, Fidel opened his speech by saying, "Today we are going to talk about our problems and difficulties, our setbacks rather than our successes."** He then went on at length to list organi-

---

* Voluntarism is here used in its technical sense, denoting a philosophy which conceives human will to be the dominant factor in experience and thus history. This usage has nothing to do with the notion of voluntary labor as used by the Cubans themselves.

** *Granma,* Weekly Review (August 2, 1970).

zational shortcomings, inefficiencies, and economic catastrophes of almost every kind. Yet during the same speech, as he and others have done again and again over the past twelve years, Castro reiterated the basic revolutionary belief that anything is possible, given man's will and man's capacity to make history:

> We are not offering magic solutions here. We have stated the problems facing us and we have said that only the people, only with . . . the determination and will of the people can those problems be overcome. . . . When this Revolution, only ninety miles distant from the ferocious and powerful empire, decided to be free and sovereign and challenged the imperialists, got ready to face all difficulties and started on a truly revolutionary road, many said that it was entirely impossible because of such factors as cultural, political, and ideological influence. But we believed that the battle could be won with the people—and it was waged with the people and won with the people!

Just as the "unbeatable" Batista fell to an irregular troop of several hundred brave men, backed by the bulk of the Cuban population, so current difficulties would give way before the determination and heroism of the masses. The population at large has not always seemed to resonate as profoundly as the leadership to this vision of the power of human will and action, but for the moment that is not the important point. What does seem as true today as it was a decade ago is that, despite increasing recognition by the leaders of the enormity of Cuba's problems, their conviction that they will find a way to beat the odds remains unshaken. With the vocabulary of a Caribbean Prometheus chained to his rock, Fidel continues to hurl invective against his northern tormentor while simultaneously insisting that the revolutionary fire can and must be kept alight.

The second important legacy of the guerrilla experience is egalitarianism. As Guevara emphasizes in his writings on the period, and as is evident from frequent references in the speeches of Castro and others, the mountains taught a number of hard and enduring lessons. One, of course, was an understanding of the plight of the Sierra peasant (and by implication, the plight of all *campesinos*), and a determination to do something about it once in power. But more central to the growth of the egalitarian ethic was the rudimentary experience of living, fighting, and surviving in the mountains. The men of the cities soon learned that the skills and habits bred of urban ways were not those needed in the Sierra. The *guajiro,* at first unappreciated and probably even denigrated for his mountain ways by some of the urban *guerrilleros,* subsequently grew in their affection and respect as they shared his living conditions and multiplied his hazards by their presence.

Furthermore, the always primitive and at first highly mobile life of the guerrilla troop discouraged the growth of internal differentiation and privilege. Guns, hammocks, assignments, and rank were distributed on the basis of performance in the mountains. Uniforms were irregular, to say the least, and the already high level of cultural informality which prevailed in Cuban speech and manners was accentuated among the *guerrilleros.* Thus, there developed as a natural concomitant of the situation in the mountains not only a strong sense of identification with and respect for the local peasantry, but also a basic belief in the rightness of the "career open to talent." The *guerrillero* who marched, fought, and inspired his *compañeros* in superior fashion was the *guerrillero* who rose in esteem and rank. Whether a peasant like Guillermo García or a doctor like Guevara, the guerrilla *comandantes* were all men who had demonstrated that they were *destacados,* outstanding, according to the evaluative criteria used in the Sierra.

The ramifications and manifestations of this egalitarianism have been considerable in revolutionary Cuba. In the elegant social clubs now open to all, in the performance criteria established for entry into the new Communist Party, in the profound attempt to redress cultural and economic imbalances, in the pervasive informality of dress and address, in the spectacle of members of the Central Committee in the fields, sweat-soaked from cutting sugar cane, in numerous other programs and activities of the Revolution, this egalitarianism is practiced and enlarged. But it should also be pointed out that it is essentially an egalitarianism of equal opportunity and shared hardship. It tries to insure that all will reap the benefits of the revolution while sharing fully in its burdens. Not in the Sierra, however, nor in Cuba today is it a non-hierarchical or fully participant egalitarianism. Just as *comandantes* gave orders in the mountains and the troops obeyed or were summarily punished, so in

Cuba since the revolution decisional power has been extremely concentrated and dissent has been rather strictly controlled. The Sierra-born concept of equality does not include a commitment at the national level to participatory and decisional egalitarianism, or even significant sharing. As we shall subsequently see, there *is* in the Cuban Revolution a countertendency of long standing in which participatory forms are sought out and explored; but it is best to consider this apart from the theme of egalitarianism. Thus, in Cuba a radical economic, social, and cultural egalitarianism is married to an authoritarian and hierarchical decisional structure. The marriage does not seem incompatible; in fact, it can be and has been argued in developmental theory that to achieve the former one needs the latter.

Ruralism is a corollary and extension of egalitarianism. The essential tenet of this strain of revolutionary thought is that the countryside is not only where the major developmental struggle must be waged, but also the locus of values and a way of life from which every Cuban has much to learn. Celebrated in this way of life are simplicity, comradeship, loyalty, hard work, tenacity, courage, sharing, and sacrifice—an idealization of the character and behavior of the *guerrillero-campesino*. The programs and formative experiences that flow directly from these beliefs are legion: the literacy campaign of 1961 which brought city youth into contact with *campesinos* for months at a time, the "schools to the countryside" movement in which entire classrooms move to rural areas for extended periods, the *cordón* or green belt around Havana where tens of thousands of urban dwellers have planted and harvested crops, the annual forays of non-agricultural workers into the canefields at harvest time, the extensive programs for young adults on the Isle of Pines.

The growth of such activities is not a simple extension of the guerrilla experience, for subsequent programs such as the literacy campaign modified the manner in which the leadership viewed the possibilities and costs of the movement from city to countryside. But from the very outset there has been a number of constants in the theory and practice of ruralism. First, ruralism contains an implied and sometimes explicit critique of urban values, not just a romantic celebration of the countryside for the virtues it engenders. The kind of egalitarianism which is taught involves a "return to basics," through bringing all Cubans into contact with an environment in which achievements and skills entitling one to status in the more "advanced" sectors of society open no doors and lighten no burdens. Second, ruralism as a way of encouraging individual *formación* and culture change is very much oriented to direct experience. The lessons of ruralism are not learned from books or from discussions, but rather are intended to alter consciousness through extended and profound personal confrontation with rural life and work.* Finally, although it implies a critique of certain urban values and a celebration of life-styles associated with the countryside, there is nothing primitivistic about ruralism. That is, the dirt, poor housing, and general impoverishment that comprise the common lot of many, if not most, rural residents are considered unacceptable, whatever salutary effect experiencing such conditions might have on the consciousness of urbanites. Ameliorating this backwardness has from the beginning been a primary challenge facing developmental planners in Cuba, but an equally longstanding subsidiary challenge has been to modernize the rural areas without destroying what are thought to be the beneficial aspects of rural character and social relations.

Pragmatism, Flexibility, and Adaptability

Even those who sympathize fully with the Revolution are forced to admit that Fidel and his lieutenants have taken Cuba —and at times the world—through a dizzying and often contradictory scenario of promises, programs, alliances, and adventures. What are we to make of a political system in which the leadership welcomes Israeli technical aid while outspokenly supporting the Palestinian guerrillas, first claims that sugar cane cultivation has distorted the economy and then plants more cane than ever, rehabilitates prostitutes and moralizes public life but officially acknowledges and runs the *posadas* or hotels to which men take the women whom they cannot take home? The list could fill pages and be extended into every domain of government activity.

---

* For further elaboration of this theme see Richard R. Fagen, *The Transformation of Political Culture in Cuba* (Stanford: Stanford University Press, 1969), especially pp. 148-150, and 169-179.

What explanations can be offered for this complex tangle of twelve years of Cuban public policy? One answer is that we are seeing little more than the Cuban variant of the contradictions and illogic that characterize the public acts of any government. Another easy and frequently expressed hypothesis is that Cuban policy stems from the projection onto a national and sometimes international stage of the antic and inconstant (or, in another view, the forceful and fertile) disposition of Fidel Castro. Both perspectives on the Cuban situation capture a fragment of the truth, for surely the Cuban government has utilized its guaranteed minimum allotment of illogic, and Fidel Castro's disposition and perspectives are, without question, a key input into public policy.

But closer to the heart of the matter is the fact that with the exception of a few closed or non-negotiable questions and issues—national sovereignty, public ownership, the right of Castro's group to rule—almost all other aspects of both the theory and practice of revolutionary governance can be considered "up for grabs." Of course this core of non-negotiable issues is of great importance, and many programs and policies of the government flow inexorably from it. But equally impressive are the issues that are left open: Almost the entire institutional and organizational life of the Revolutionary government, including such key aspects as the role of the Communist Party, is unfettered by conventional constraints of theory or dogma.* Similarly, the basic structure of economic relations has been hammered out in practice without either the benefits or the constraints imposed by a theory (much less a detailed plan) of the economic system. A powerful strain of pragmatism and experimentation thus constantly intrudes into public life. The operating rule in many policy areas—touching subject matters as different as hemispheric armed struggle and agricultural policy—seems to be, "try it; if it doesn't work, abandon it and try something else." The passion and conviction with which the revolutionaries

---

* The bankruptcy of the old political institutions greatly reinforced this characteristic of Castroism. The current leaders have been relatively free to experiment with political forms because the old order left hardly any legacy of legitimate or even quasi-legitimate institutions and organizations. The contrast with Chile is striking.

embark on a new course of action, the belief that "this time the way has been found," leads observers to overestimate the importance of doctrine and dogma in the Cuban decisional style. It is, however, with just as much passion and conviction that yesterday's plans and programs are discarded. The passion is a matter of political temperament, while the endless experimentation is a matter of political style; the latter is more basic.

The policy consequences of these elements of style are most visible in the large arenas of international and domestic affairs. A foreign policy which embraces diplomatic and commercial exchange with governments and groups as diverse as mainland China, Spain, Britain, the South Vietnamese National Liberation Front, Israel, Egypt, France, the Soviet Union, and the Vatican cannot be accused of dogmatism or inflexibility. When informal but friendly relationships with governments such as the current Peruvian military junta are added to this list, what emerges is the outline of a foreign policy quick to adjust, within the limits imposed by the core values mentioned earlier, to elite perceptions of Cuban national interest and to the exigencies of the world situation. Similarly, the gross dimensions of shifts in agricultural and industrial policy during the first decade of the revolution reveal not the implementation of a grand design, but rather the awkward and costly gropings of an inexperienced, anti-theoretical, but pragmatic and relatively open-minded group of leaders. Fidel's oft repeated statement that "the Revolution is our great teacher" captures the empiricism of the style, but it fails to emphasize the costs of learning through experimenting in such a rough and society-wide fashion.*

On a smaller but pervasive scale the consequences of these elements of style are manifest in revolutionary attitudes toward the planning and implementation of programs. From the outset of the revolution, extensive developmental programs were launched, without the detailed planning and organizational work that would subsequently be necessary to keep them going. From

---

* In fairness to Castro, it should be pointed out that on a number of occasions he has spoken at length about the consequences of the inexperience of revolutionary leaders and the costs incurred in learning-by-doing. See, for example, his speech on the failure of the 1970 harvest, *Granma*, Weekly Review (August 2, 1970).

the revolutionary point of view, the important thing was to begin; the planning and organizational work would come after, not before, this commitment-through-action. It was believed that the act of trying, the struggle itself, would open up possibilities and generate resources that could not have been imagined or counted on before the battle was joined. The negative corollary of this belief is that too much thought given in advance to the possible consequences of a program tends to erode revolutionary will and courage. Thus, "planning doth make cowards of us all" could almost be taken as an early motto of the revolutionary leadership, despite the seeming anomaly of such a belief in the bosom of a revolution already committed to massive state intervention in society and economy.

Although time has softened the hold that this view of planning and organization once exercised over the leadership, it has by no means been rejected. In the flurry of activity occasioned by the planting of the green belt around Havana in 1967 and 1968, for example, some elementary facts of agricultural life were overlooked. As impressive as the mobilization of *habaneros* was during the clearing and sowing of the land, follow-up care in weeding, watering, and harvesting was often neglected. Additionally, in the frenzy of ground-breaking and planting, insufficient attention was paid to matching crops to soils and methods of cultivation to climate. As a result of these and various other shortcomings, the green belt did not turn out to be the showplace that the leadership had hoped it would be. In the kind of cost-benefit calculus used by the revolutionaries, the *cordón* is probably adjudged a success because of the political and formative, if not the productive and nutritive, fruits that it has yielded.* Yet not to be overlooked, although difficult to assess, is the attrition in popular support occasioned by this all-too-familiar experience: Workers who have invested part of their leisure time, their sweat, and their stock of revolutionary good will in the planting of a field of coffee trees, do not suffer easily the spectacle of that field three months later browning

---

* The *cordón* was undertaken in part to break the black market dealings and economic autonomy of the small farmers in the area, while simultaneously incorporating them into the Revolution through both material and organizational incentives. In this the *cordón* seems to have been successful, at least when aided by the *ofensiva revolucionaria* of spring 1968.

in the tropical sun, unirrigated, untended, and dying. Thus, impressive investments of time, energy, and resources are frequently eroded for lack of careful planning and organization. The ambivalent Cuban posture toward planning and organization, so attractive and liberating at one point in the developmental process, often produces waste and debilitation later on. The Cubans' genius for "inventing" the revolution as they go along has not yet been fully harnessed to the machinery of planning, organization, and management necessitated by the developmental road on which they have set out.

The Search for a Politics of Unity and Harmony

Like many other aspects of the revolutionary style, the search for a politics of unity has roots deep in the pre-revolutionary experience. The enduring heroes of the last 100 years of Cuban history, beginning with Maceo and Martí, all preached an inclusivist variety of nationalistic thought. In the Cuban nation that they envisaged, identifications and divisions based on race, class, region, or birth would all be subordinated in a harmonious social order. Eligible for inclusion in the national society was any man or woman who put Cuba, *la patria,* above self or sector. This idealized vision of an inclusive and integrated society nurtured Fidelista formulations of the revolutionary future, giving to them a distinct ring. In fact, from his "History Will Absolve Me" speech through his most recent pronouncements, Fidel's thought has been remarkably free of the rhetoric and the conceptual apparatus of conventional Marxist class analysis. He and others, of course, do draw distinctions of many sorts between the friends and enemies of the Revolution, but these are distinctions based on behavior in the contemporary context, not on class or other bases of social stratification.

More important than the distinctions that are drawn, however, is the continuous quest for a politics of unity. Cuban leaders believe that social, cultural, organizational, and ethnic schisms are in some basic sense "unnatural," the product of an imperfect past and a still imperfect revolutionary experience. This vision of natural harmony (once certain contradictions are overcome) is also present in classical Marxist thought, but the Cuban view is much more immediate and unencumbered by the formalities of doctrine and the notion that harmony can prevail only after the working out of a long historical process. Thus, the egalitarianism and ruralism previously described blur class lines without ever coming to grips theoretically with the "class problem." The efforts to form a revolutionary political party (the ORI, the PURSC, the PCC), while often tumultuous and conflictual, have from the start been based on the premise that persons of the most diverse political backgrounds—and many with no political antecedents at all—could be integrated into a Marxist-Leninist organization. Similarly, the continuous though seldom publicized effort within the University of Havana to unite historically contentious and fragmented students and faculty in the common revolutionary cause bespeaks not just an attempt to control dissent and harness developmental resources, but also a belief that university conflict has been rendered obsolete by the triumph of the Revolution.

Other manifestations of the continuing search for a politics of unity can be seen in areas as diverse as the regime's hemispheric vision, doctrine of mass organizations, relations with artists and intellectuals, and attitudes toward black nationalism. Despite the diplomatic and economic isolation brought about through the U.S.-engineered decisions of the Organization of American States, Cuba has continued to express solidarity with "the people" of the hemisphere. At times this expression has been symbolic and poetic as in the following verse:

> Brazilian brother: your hand.
> Argentine carpenter: your hand.
> Panamanian port worker: your hand.
> Honduran banana worker: your hand.
> Bolivian miner: your hand.
> Chilean cowboy: your hand . . .
> Unity. Unity brothers!
> So that reaction can't dominate us.*

At other times it has been immediate and material, as when blood, supplies, and medical teams were flown to Peru

---

* For the complete poem and the original citation see "The Cuban Revolution: Enemies and Friends," in David J. Finlay, Ole R. Holsti, and Richard R. Fagen, *Enemies in Politics* (Chicago: Rand McNally, 1967), pp. 201-202.

to aid victims of the 1970 earthquake. But always the message is the same: Were it not for the divisions imposed upon us (Latin America) by imperialism, capitalism, and their domestic allies, the latent brotherhood and unity of the hemisphere could assert itself and flourish.

For obvious reasons, the mass organizations of the Revolutionary Government provide the most propitious setting for experimenting with and implementing the politics of unity. Whether intended for youth, women, farmers, workers, or the neighborhood in general (Committees for Defense of the Revolution, CDRs), the mass organizations have always been inclusive rather than exclusive.* The consequences of this organizational philosophy can be seen most dramatically in the CDRs where by 1965 one out of every two adult Cubans held at least nominal membership. Speaking in 1961, on the first anniversary of the founding of the Committees, Castro emphasized that anyone could belong, young and old, men and women, students and housewives, workers and pensioners, intellectuals and peasants. The only test would be one's disposition toward the Revolution. After all, he continued, the Revolution is "the grand union of all honorable persons, of all useful persons, of all studious persons, of all worthy persons, of all persons who produce for the populace." It was indeed a long and inclusive list, excluding only those "enemies of the people, enemies of the masses, parasites, exploiters, slackers, and those who don't work, those who live off the work of others." The criteria by which one's contributions to the revolutionary effort are evaluated are by no means agreed upon in all settings by all concerned. Nevertheless, in the context of the mass organizations, the notion of "the grand union of all honorable persons" has been interpreted very generously. Harmony has been sought in this instance by bringing into the organizational structure every individual will-

---

* This is true even for the Communist Youth, the only mass organization which does not automatically accept any applicant possessing the appropriate demographic qualifications and some minimum reputation as a good citizen. In settings like specialized schools, membership in the Communist Youth may reach 90 percent of the student body. Thus, despite a partially competitive selection process, the organization seeks the widest possible membership.

ing to join and not actually tarred with the brush of overt opposition to the revolutionary government.

As might be expected, the search for a politics of harmony is put to a special test by the regime's relations with artists and intellectuals. To the extent that the government had an official cultural policy during the 1960s, it was promulgated in 1961 in a speech in which Fidel asked and then answered the following question: "What are the rights of writers and artists, whether revolutionaries or not? Within the Revolution, everything: against the Revolution, nothing."* In architecture, graphics, and to a great extent in cinema, this dictum has been interpreted broadly; and the buildings, posters, stamps, and movies done in Cuba are in general colorful, innovative, and tasteful. The visual excesses of socialist realism are pleasantly absent in Cuba—except for the remnants of an earlier period of heroic muralism still evident in and on some public buildings. In literature, however, agreement between the regime and the writers has been achieved much less easily, and in many cases not at all. In writing of all kinds the problem is particularly difficult, for Castro's formulation does not provide an operative guide or boundaries to permissible domains of critical thought. It is quite one thing to allow and encourage color, innovation, and taste in visual representations that carry messages clearly supportive of the Revolution. It is quite another thing to allow (much less encourage) written expression which explores the contradictions, ironies, difficulties, and joys and tragedies of a revolutionary period. In a variant of the classic "emergency" argument, Cuban leaders have in effect said that "we cannot

---

* Fidel Castro, *Palabras a los Intelectuales* (Havana: Ediciones del Consejo Nacional de Cultura, 1961), p. 11. This brief quotation does not do justice to the position on cultural expression developed by Castro on this occasion (June 30, 1961, at the end of a three-day seminar with artists and intellectuals). See also the exchange between Castro and Lee Lockwood in the latter's *Castro's Cuba, Cuba's Fidel* (New York: Macmillan, 1967), pp. 126-131. In April 1971, at the same time that the poet Heberto Padilla was released from confinement and made the self-criticism that aroused so much attention in international literary circles, the Cubans were conducting the First National Congress on Education and Culture. The final declaration and resolutions of the Congress, published in *Granma,* Weekly Review (May 9, 1971), contain by far the most important recent official statements on cultural policy.

at this historical moment allow the writers to ask difficult questions, for the masses are not yet ready or able to answer such questions or to defend themselves from the consequences of doubt."* Thus, the search for a politics of unity leads in this instance to restrictions on those who would introduce additional uncertainty into a system already belabored by a multitude of problems and challenges.

Finally, official attitudes toward black nationalism in Cuba illustrate yet another consequence of the search for a politics of unity. Although the socio-cultural and economic place of the black man in both pre- and post-revolutionary Cuba is a subject of great complexity, at least one aspect of the current situation is clear: After moving with dramatic speed and effectiveness to end institutionalized manifestations of racism (if not prejudice) on the island, the revolutionary government has steadfastly resisted any temptation and all pressures to identify blacks as a group warranting special attention or programs.** To the extent that blacks are found disproportionately among the most disadvantaged social sectors, they of course benefit greatly from revolutionary programs designed to bring health, education, employment, and participatory opportunities to those sectors. But the notion of "special" opportunities for blacks in the revolutionary context would strike the Cuban leadership as profoundly violative of norms of egalitarianism and national unity. In related fashion, what murmurings there are of an indigenous (or imported) black cultural nationalism fall on deaf ears in leadership circles. Why should the Revolution encourage

---

* In 1966, I had an impassioned discussion about these matters with a *comandante* in the Revolutionary Armed Forces, a highly articulate man of relatively humble origins. After we argued at length about possible benefits that might accrue to the Revolution through the public airing of some of the issues raised in private by many writers, artists, and journalists, he grabbed me by the shirt, despairing of ever making me understand and said, "Coño! We are not a nation of professors!"

** Only recently have the complexities of this situation begun to be aired in a sympathetic yet critical way. See, for example, the insightful reportage of Elizabeth Sutherland in "Colony Within the Colony," a section of her *The Youngest Revolution* (New York: The Dial Press, 1969). Sutherland tellingly points out that most of the visual and written material to which Cubans are currently exposed under-represents and sometimes ignores black elements and contributions to Cuban society.

or support movements, the leadership asks, that tend to re-fragment the population into racial groups when the very purpose of the revolutionary effort is to forge a new Cuban identity and nation that are above distinctions of race, class, and region? Furthermore, the argument continues, however necessary such sub-cultural nationalisms may be in the hostile environment of racist societies, the destruction of the institutional framework of racism in Cuba has obviated their value here. Thus, although there are official ethnographic and folkloric programs to discover and preserve Afro-Cuban religious and cultural forms, no encouragement is given to those who would kindle a Cuban movement of Negritude. In fact, those who agitate for recognition of the unique problems of blacks in Cuba, whether black Cubans or visiting Americans, are reminded in no uncertain terms that to do so is to set oneself against the mainstream of revolutionary theory and practice, to create differences where none need or should exist.

The Search for Appropriate Political Forms

"Our task," Che Guevara told an interviewer in 1961, "is to enlarge democracy within the revolution as much as possible.... We feel that the government's chief function is to assure channels for the expression of the popular will. What forms this will take, we cannot say yet. This will depend on the political system to be elaborated."* The political system of which Che spoke was still very much in the process of being elaborated a decade later. Not only were the channels through which the popular will might be expressed still in the embryonic stage, but, in addition, no specific doctrine of the relationship between leaders and led had ever been articulated, much less put into practice.

Yet it would be wrong to dismiss Che's vision of a revolutionary polity responsive to the masses as merely verbal camouflage for authoritarian and hierarchical practice. It is certainly true that the Cuban search for appropriate political forms has not to date led in the direction of critical popular debate on

---

* From an interview with Maurice Zeitlin, quoted in Zeitlin, "Cuba's Workers, Workers' Cuba, 1969," in *Revolutionary Politics and the Cuban Working Class* (New York: Harper Torchbooks, 1970).

national alternatives and policies. As one basically sympathetic observer has noted, "the Cuban revolutionaries have so far done little to establish institutions that will guarantee that competing points of view can be heard within the revolutionary socialist consensus; that meaningful alternatives are debated; that policies are initiated, as well as implemented, by the citizenry at large."* The search for a politics of unity, under conditions of both external and internal threat, has subordinated the always fragile tendency of the earlier years to let the revolutionary political process be "a school of unfettered thought." But counter to this trend runs another, more supportive of the democratic vision although usually less noticed because of the setting in which it is manifested. Specifically, there is in Cuba—and there has been from the outset of the Revolution—what might be called a subculture of local democracy.

The reasons why this local subculture has received relatively little attention are not difficult to discover: In the first place, the conventional wisdom about political democracy directs attention to the national level, particularly to the means by which citizens are heard, represented, and able to hold their leaders accountable with respect to the main issues of public policy. Moreover, Cuban rhetoric has reinforced this national focus of attention by claiming in somewhat mystical fashion that Fidel and other leaders understand and interpret the popular will through mechanisms that—despite the oft-used image of "dialogue"—remain shadowy and informal in the extreme. Furthermore, although rank-and-file members of the Communist Party, the most truly national political institution, are selected in open assemblies by their co-workers, the party in practice represents the government *to* constituencies rather than the other way around. Nor do most mass organizations, although critically important in strengthening citizen identifications with the state and aiding in the mobilization of developmental resources, contribute significantly to the leverage exercised by the governed over their national leaders. Thus, while national politics absorb the attention and critical interest of Cubans and outsiders alike,

---

* *Ibid.* See also the critique in Chapter 11 of Leo Huberman and Paul M. Sweezy, *Socialism in Cuba* (Monthly Review Press, 1969).

when tests of responsiveness or accountability are applied to national institutions and practices, they are almost always found wanting.

Therefore, in order to understand the nascent subculture of democracy in revolutionary Cuba we must focus on activities that are of small scale, institutions and practices which involve citizens in decisions directly tied to problems of the neighborhood or place of work. The most fully developed such local institution is the *tribunal popular* or people's court. The first *tribunales populares* were organized in 1966 in rural areas and they soon were established in the cities as well. Designed to speed the adjudication of minor quarrels and transgressions, demystify and popularize the law, involve and educate citizens in revolutionary justice and morality, the tribunals have strongly democratic and participant characteristics.* Not only are the three judges all laymen, selected from among citizens of the *zona* and only then trained for the job, but the trials themselves are usually well attended and open to public debate and discussion. Although the entire system is subject to the guidance of *asesores*, professional personnel from the Ministry of Justice who also handle appeals, there is a strong element of community control over the day-to-day operation of the tribunals. The egalitarianism of the revolution here finds expression in an adjudicating mechanism that not only works to make all equal before the law, but also to decentralize justice, to make its administration more responsive to local conditions, and to involve the local community in interpreting and applying revolutionary statutes.

Although nowhere else as visible as in the tribunals, elements of decentralization, popular participation in decision-making, open debate of issues, and sensitivity to local problems and considerations are very much a part of the Cuban style. Whether a discussion about dormitory rules in a youth encampment, consultation to determine who should receive the new fishing boats

---

* See the article by Jesse Berman, "The Cuban Popular Tribunals," *Columbia Law Review* (December, 1969), pp. 1317-1354. Berman's observations, based on research conducted in Cuba in 1968, reinforce mine, based on much more cursory experience with the system a year later. All those who have seen a tribunal in operation seem impressed with the particular blend of humanity, fairness, and participation that prevails.

sent to a cooperative, debate in a labor meeting over the causes and cures of absenteeism, or an open meeting of a CDR to distribute community responsibilities, there is an impressive amount of participatory activity going on in Cuba in a variety of settings.* In few if any instances are the issues or stakes of great dimension when viewed from afar. In such settings one hears no abstract arguments about liberty of expression, no discussion of the consequences of alternative systems of national governance, no timeless rhetoric about the meaning of freedom. What one hears and sees are workers and citizens wrestling honestly and directly with problems of local importance and immediate consequence. Because this decisional style and the settings in which it is manifested tend to be unstructured and uninstitutionalized, they are easily overlooked in a system in which at other times hierarchical, authoritarian, and bureaucratic forms prevail. But the closer one comes to grass roots decision-making—and by implication the closer one comes to the realities of the vast majority of Cubans—the more frequently this democratic-participant counter-trend is found in operation. In thousands of farms, shops, towns, and villages across the island, politics is precisely the functioning of this subculture of democratic practice. Protected by no guarantees and enshrined in no constitution, it nevertheless acts as a powerful counterweight to hierarchy, bureaucracy, and authoritarianism at all levels.

During the summer and fall of 1970 there was a flurry of attention given to the necessity of extending and formalizing elements of the democratic subculture. As part of the soul-searching and stock-taking that followed the failure to achieve a ten-million-ton sugar harvest, Castro dwelt at length on the theme of popular participation in decision-making. First in his speech

* This aspect of the Cuban revolution has not been formally studied. The examples used here are taken from personal experience. Again and again when local *responsables* were asked how a particular decision had been reached, they responded with some variation on the theme, *"hablamos con los compañeros"* (we spoke with the *compañeros*). This did not seem to be empty rhetoric, as those who have experienced such sessions can attest. For illustrative reportage see Sutherland, *op. cit.*, and José Yglesias, *In the Fist of the Revolution* (New York: Pantheon, 1968), particularly chapter 10.

on July 26, and then in speeches in August and September to the Federation of Cuban Women and the National Council of the CTC (trade unions), he emphasized giving local communities control over their own affairs, substituting consultative procedures for bureaucratic ones, and making officials accountable to the citizens and workers they are supposed to serve.* Speaking to the trade unionists about forthcoming elections in the CTC, he said:

> We must make it clear that any official can be removed at any time. He can be removed whenever another election is called, so nobody should get the idea that simply because he was elected one day he can spend a year doing just as he damn pleases. In three months or at any other time there can be another meeting or election, and out he goes, and somebody else goes in. But all this must be done through democratic procedures. If the workers' movement isn't democratic, then it is good for nothing.

It remains to be seen, of course, to what extent the ideas developed in these and other speeches will be translated into practice.** At least in plant management and the trade union movement, past promises to nurture the democratic subculture have not been realized in organizational or even informal ways. But neither has the Cuban leadership previously been as frank in confessing that the bureaucratic system of command which dominates production and distribution has not worked well. Thus, added to whatever philosophical attachments the leadership has to the democratic subculture, powerful pragmatic arguments are now being acknowledged as well. In short, many feel that because parts of the revolutionary effort have not been well managed and coordinated through methods of hierarchy, bureaucracy, and authoritarianism, increased decisional decentralization and more genuine forms of mass participation ought to be tried. The experience and the philosophy of the

---

* The three speeches are available in full in three issues of *Granma*, Weekly Review (August 2, August 30, and September 20, 1970). These themes have been periodically emphasized in Castro's speeches, but seldom dwelt on at such length.

** During late 1970, elections were held in work centers throughout the island. In those elections, 163,000 workers were selected as leaders of 35,000 trade union locals. See the report by Jorge Risquet, Minister of Labor, published in *Granma*, Weekly Review (October 24, 1971). It would seem that the "translation into practice" has begun.

tribunales populares may thus be extended to other settings in the continuing search for new solutions to old dilemmas.

Human Transformation and the Search for Productivity

The radicalism of the Cuban leaders is nowhere more in evidence than in their determination to create a new society through transforming the common man into a revolutionary man, a man devoid of *egoismo,* guided by *conciencia,* who puts service to society above service to self. Castro's frequently repeated words on the fifteenth anniversary of the attack on the Moncada Barracks capture this attachment to man's socio-political perfectibility with all of its utopian overtones, both Marxist and Christian:

> No human society has yet reached Communism. The paths by which one arrives at a superior form of society are very difficult. A Communist society is one in which man will have reached the highest degree of social awareness ever achieved. In a Communist society, man will have succeeded in achieving just as much understanding, closeness, and brotherhood as he has on occasion achieved within the narrow circle of his own family. To live in a Communist society is to live without selfishness, to live among the people and with the people, as if every one of our fellow citizens were really our dearest brothers.*

Whether in educational programs, the work of the mass organizations, the operation of the Communist party, or the controversy over moral versus material incentives, the influence of this vision—however much attenuated—is felt. A massive, society-wide, and continuing effort at human transformation dominates the revolutionary tapestry, tying together its disparate elements, tonalities, and textures.

As an integral part of this view of the world and of how change ought to take place, problems of economic development are considered to be—in the first instance—problems of human transformation. Although almost all theories of economic development pay homage to the social and psycho-cultural changes concomitant or requisite to economic growth, the Cubans have elevated the issue of human transformation to a central place

---

* *Granma,* Weekly Review (July 28, 1968).

in their development model. In a line of thinking that goes back to the guerrilla experience, conventional impediments to development (lack of resources, capital, infrastructure, installed capacity, markets, etc.) are often played down, while mass participation, determination, selflessness, enthusiasm, and faith are seen as mechanisms and qualities which, if present in sufficient quantity, will enable the economy to move ahead. This is, of course, too gross a characterization to explain the manner in which specific developmental dilemmas have been approached, but a profound general faith in achieving economic progress through the *formación* and utilization of revolutionary man certainly pervades the highest decisional circles.

The key operational focus and test of this doctrine of economic development come in the domain of productivity. If the revolutionary vision of the new societal order is to be viable, the ordinary worker must give generously of his energies and talents, even if not motivated by conventional economic insecurities or expectations of personal gain. It is precisely at this critical point that politics and economics come together to define the central questions facing the revolutionary leadership: Is it possible to engage the best and continuing energies of the population in production without resorting to conventional systems of economic incentive, reward, and punishment? Can the masses be raised to that unprecedented level of consciousness in which work is pledged to the collectivity, personal performance willingly dissociated from personal consumption, and productivity and quality maintained through political but non-coercive mechanisms of discipline?*

Only the most passionate celebrant of the Cuban Revolution would argue that consistently positive answers can at present be given to these questions. On the contrary, the performance

---

* These questions have a special edge in the Cuban setting where much employment is still in semi-skilled and unskilled industrial and agricultural labor that is physically difficult, repetitive, and intellectually unrewarding. The "material versus moral incentives" debate is clearly related to these questions, although it does not exhaust their implications. The degree to which conventional economic sanctions (docking of pay, loss of job, etc.) have fallen into disuse in Cuba is documented in Zeitlin, *op. cit.*, and in the discussions and speeches at the national meeting of the CTC reported in *Granma*, Weekly Review (September 20, 1970).

of the Cuban economy has been mixed and erratic, and it would be relatively easy to dismiss the Cuban experiment in development-through-human-transformation as having been tried and proven a failure. But funeral orations are just as premature as celebrations are unwarranted. Not only is it impossible to isolate the independent effects of the motivational systems being tried from other factors affecting economic performance, but by any historical standard a decade is a relatively short period over which to evaluate an experiment as profound as the Cuban. What can be said with some confidence is that by the end of 1971 the leadership's commitment to economic development through a socio-political strategy of human transformation was undiminished, despite the attention also being paid to conventional developmental variables. Thus, detailed technical concern with low productivity and non-performance in key sectors such as transportation was coupled with a reaffirmation that such problems stem "basically [from] factors of a moral order, factors having to do with awareness."* Similarly, reducing the exorbitant costs associated with high levels of absenteeism through the passage of new legislation governing attendance was seen as essentially a problem in *formación,* a problem in creating legislation "that will be educational, a law that, instead of leading to entire colonies of loafers, enormous jails full of loafers, will accomplish just the opposite."** The tension and irony that inhere in the clash between the harsh demands of economic development (through high productivity and discipline) and the vision of a society organized around more humane and brotherly principles, thus continue unabated. As Castro commented in response to a series of complaints by a public health worker:

Perhaps our greatest idealism lies in having believed that a society that had barely begun to live in a world that for thousands of years had lived under the law of "an eye for an eye and a tooth for a tooth," the law of the survival of the fittest, the law

---

* From Castro's speech reported in *Granma,* Weekly Review (September 20, 1970).

** From a speech by Captain Jorge Risquet, Cuban Minister of Labor, reported in *Granma,* Weekly Review (September 20, 1970).

of egoism, the law of deceit and the law of exploitation could, all of a sudden, be turned into a society in which everybody behaved in an ethical, moral way.*

Not to appreciate the extent to which this idealism continues to fuel the developmental effort in Cuba is to invite misunderstanding. No single aspect of Cuban politics is as important as this commitment to the creation of revolutionary man and the tangled relationship of that commitment to economic development in general. The potential for both tragedy and triumph therein contained must be embraced not only as a guide to understanding the past but also as a harbinger in exploring the future.

* *Ibid.*

We can see the new man who begins to emerge in this period of the building of socialism. His image is as yet unfinished; in fact, it will never be finished, since the process advances parallel to the development of new economic forms. . . . The road is long and full of difficulties. At times the route strays off course and it is necessary to retreat; at times a too rapid pace separates us from the masses and on occasion the pace is slow and we feel upon our necks the breath of those who follow on our heels. Our ambition as revolutionaries makes us try to move forward as fast as possible, opening up the way before us, but we know that we must be reinforced by the masses, while they will be able to advance more rapidly if we encourage them by our example. . . . The change in consciousness does not come about automatically, just as it does not come about automatically in the economy. The variations are slow and rhythmic; there are periods of acceleration, others are more measured, and sometimes there is even retreat.

—Che Guevara, *Socialism and Man in Cuba*

FERNANDO H. CARDOSO
Brazilian Center for Demographic Research

Cuba: Lesson or Symbol?

"The lesson, however, is much more a symbol than a doctrine — Revolution cannot be exported. Historical conditions rarely coincide. When it seems that there is a firm path to follow, what really exists, as always in history, is an experience which, in order to be relived, has to be restated in the appropriate dimension and reflect the peculiarity of each case."

A moment of greatness in the life of a people creating its own history can galvanize an entire generation. Until now, for Latin Americans, Spain's tragic Civil War was the point of reference—even for those who do not belong to the older generation (in any case, how does one define the political limits of a generation?). "To Die in Madrid"* or "La Guerre est Finie"** symbolize, at least for those who are now reaching middle age, a moment of transition. For us, Spain's epic struggle, with all its heroism, is still very much alive. Many of the older ones still find it difficult to accept the cynical realization that the game was played and lost. Every moment of the battle is so strongly etched in their memory—as is the final outcome, that is, "To Die in Madrid"—that they cannot bear to see these episodes even on the screen without being overcome with emotion, blocking out all analysis.

---

* A documentary on the Spanish Civil War by Frederic Rossif, made in France in the early 60s.

** Another French film of the 60s on the Spanish Civil War.

Will it be the same with the present generation?

I don't know. I do know, however, from experience, that the post World War II years in Latin America were not easy: doubt began to cast a shadow on our dreams. The faith of our elders had had to withstand the Moscow trials. For us, the tempests sowed by the Prague trials and the disclosures of the XXth Congress of the Communist Part of the Soviet Union would have been even more disastrous had it not been for one very specific event: the Cuban Revolution.

Cuba was incorporated into the political patrimony of "our America" at the very moment when memory and reality were burying the great Latin saga of the Spanish Civil War, and survival left the younger generation meditating on the disquieting doubt as to the path by which socialism would be constructed. Certainly, in the post-war years, the most heroic efforts of our youth were oriented toward concrete problems as defined by the political consciousness of that period: the anti-imperialist struggle. Petroleum, copper, iron, tin. From these metals and oils the armor and blood of an entire generation was forged. There were martyrs and heroes, there were sym-

A WARNER MODULAR PUBLICATION

M267-2   Fernando H. Cardoso

Copyright © 1973 by Warner Modular Publications, Inc.

All rights reserved. No part of this publication may be reproduced, stored in a retrieval system, or transmitted, in any form or by any means, electronic, mechanical, photocopying, recording, or otherwise, without the prior written permission of the publisher. Printed in the United States of America.

Library of Congress Catalog Card Number 73-5218

10 9 8 7 6 5 4 3 2 1

The Developmental Economics Series is under the editorship of
DAVID P. BARKIN
City University of New York
Lehman College

GEORGE HARPOOTLIAN
Associate Publisher

SUGGESTED CITATION:
Fernando H. Cardoso, "Cuba: Lesson or Symbol?"
Warner Modular Publications, Andover, Massachusetts
Module 267 (1973) pp 1–9

All original publications in this series appear first as separate modules. Most modules will appear in one collection; many will appear in several. To facilitate research use, all modules are numbered serially, and each module carries the same number and folio sequence in all incarnations.

bols: Cardenas, a fragile Guatemala trying to lift itself up; Bolivia of Indians and of a radicalized middle class; nationalist movements, like the campaigns to defend national economies, the "Petroleum Is Ours" movement against Standard Oil. Even the parties and movements, like the MNR (Guatemala) and the APRA (Peru), which later became tarnished or even undeniably rotten, marked paths in their time.

But, after having achieved "national liberation," what is to be done? It was at this point that doubt undermined fervor. China was, then, far away; Yugoslavia, misunderstood or incomprehensible. Could it be that only a bureaucracy would have the strength to implement socialism under conditions of an imperialist encirclement?

Among the young, perhaps by luck or fervor, the struggle against the principal enemy leaves little room for anything else. But not everybody has the privilege of being young or the disadvantage, if they are not, of thinking as if they were. The "What Is to Be Done?" is more than just a famous book or a question to be answered <u>later</u>. It is an ever-present tension in those who have eyes to see, love for ideals and the strength of character not to surrender.

This is what Cuba symbolized for the Americas. A hope and an alternative. Not only an alternative to imperialist exploitation, but also for the construction of a freer society and a more fully developed individual. This is not the best moment to judge Cuba's achievements nor am I using an adequate vehicle to compare hopes with realization. But there can be no hope without facts. And these, Cuba provides for us.

First, a lesson: <u>dependency can be broken</u>. The weight of structures played <u>against</u> such a break not in its favor. Cold "objective" political analysis could only predict failure. But there was victory. In the back yard of the giant, the freedom to differ was affirmed. With facts.

The lesson, however, is much more a symbol than a doctrine—Revolution cannot be exported. Historical conditions rarely coincide. When it seems that there is a firm path to follow, what really exists, as always in history, is an experience which, in order to be relived, has to be restated in the appropriate dimension and reflect the peculiarity of each case.

The lesson which remains, and the symbol which is bequeathed to the Americas, calls neither for imitation nor duplication. It tells us that in history everything is movement, and that the suffocating structural conditions of dependency and of economic exploitation can and should be changed. How to change them is a question that cannot be deduced abstractly, scholastically, from the non-existent "logic" of general and abstract principles of action. Were the failure of Moncada and the saga of the mountains, by chance, postulated in the politcal manual of the good revolutionary? Certainly not. They were produced by the revolt of one part of the middle class, radicalized and intellectualized, by sugar mill workers, by poor peasants, by city workers, by the degeneration of Batista and his regime, by the fusion of this regime with the old style imperialism of plantation exploitation. Could there have been a Sierra without the solidarity of Havana and its underground networks, aided at times by the liberal enthusiasm of opponents to the dictatorship, but always cemented by the reaction of the working classes to that economic exploitation, which in turn was the shame of the national consciousness?

Thus the history of the Cuban revolution is not mirrored Latin American political practice except in a specific country or situation. The variability and force of reality cannot be submitted to the straight jacket of a model (besides, the attempt would be in vain, since life is stronger than the idealistic illusion of voluntarism). It can only serve as an apprenticeship to a method. The lasting message of this method, as I have already said, is that, yes, it is possible to win, although the road to victory is full of twists and turns. It also shows that two interrelated maxims point the way: first, that objective conditions in themselves guarantee neither the permanence of the established order, nor its opposite; second, that if dedicated and firm action is the necessary response to the paradox of the last enunciated principle, this action cannot be disconnected from the context in which it exists. The decisive part of the lesson is that "action" does not mean the voice of command of one person or one group. Action means a voice of command which reflects the articulated desires of real people, and not just the imagery of an ideology. If the leaders are not, at the same time, a little ahead of, but of the same sentiment as, the exploited masses, this handful of braves, isolated leaders without followers, are like flowers falling to the ground. They lack the life that only the continuous reaffirmation of the link of one person to another, of one group to another, of one class with (or against) another, can maintain. For the Cubans, "that's how things are" is replaced by a more or less deliberate and conscious restoration of the social conditions under which they can consciously participate in the construction of their lives.

This method constitutes a difficult lesson. The near martyrdom of Che and the notes that he left of his last sally, demonstrate the ultimate cost of this apprenticeship for Latin America. There is no leader—and the example refers to the most genuine preacher of the Cuban lesson for Latin America—who does not pay the absolute price when there is a gap between the desire to change and the conditions for change. But even in this failure the symbol remains: to change it is necessary to fight.

It would be unfair to Cuba and its revolution to think that it provides only one method, albeit universal. The unique historical contribution of the continuing Cuban revolutionary process has a greater meaning: Cuba designed a new model for the construction of socialism.

For us Americans, China is like the Himalayas: the largest in the world, but the farthest away. Some of its currents are incompatible with the fossilized industrial bureaucratic society of western civilization. Having offered us in the past such sublime utopias as freedom, humanism, and socialism, western civilization now leaves us with mass consumption and its technostructure. But the Chinese model—what little I know of it—is based on a very different cultural history. The Confucian ethic, the bureaucratic decentralization of the Heavenly Empire, the coexistence of the principles of good and evil (the 100 flowers...), the immensity of an agrarian civilization, have little relation to the centralized states of Ibero-America, with the "ethical" pragmatism of our civic culture, with the exclusive categories and Manichean idea of Christian good and evil.

Cuba, on the other hand, is all this and more: the pachanga*, personalism, paternalism, the weight of the State on civil society, and a radical passion which irrevocably separate good and evil, but which, at the first setback, is lost and turns everything to confusion. If only we were not all Latin Americans, (even when we are atheists and

---

* A Cuban dance popular at the time of the Revolution.

descendents of non-Latins), profoundly Catholic in our roots and, therefore, intolerant inquisitors in the same confusing way in which forgiveness and mercy make us prone to forget all and extend our hand to the enemy ... if we were not, in the severe and Protestant judgment of Anglo-Saxons, weak and given to compromise ...

Yet in spite of this, despite the poverty it inherited, or perhaps because of all these things, Cuba proved that it is possible to create a socialist society in which from the very beginning, equality is unquestioned.

The data provided in the preceding chapters of this book demonstrate exactly this. Mistakes, yes, and how many! But the guiding light is equality, not as a long term goal, but in practice, right from the start. Income is equalized. Rationing is strict. In this context it does not make much sense to discuss whether it is better to plant coffee or vegetables in back yards. This will become clear later. But it is decisive to avoid that with either the vegetables or the coffee, the sacrifice and heroism of so many should nurture a centrally planned but hollow society, enfeebled, bureaucratic and with increasing inequalities. And this, Cuba tries to avoid.

Ideologies, they will say, do not fill bellies. No one should know this better than a sociologist whose life has been devoted to the problems of development. But all the available evidence indicates that the regime has popular support. And it is hard to believe that past mistakes, (which I will not deny) could have prevented the majority from attaining a reasonable and increasingly improving standard of living, even though everyone—even in the name of egalitarianism—cannot rise to the same level immediately.

What is new and invaluable is that the Cuban model subverted the well thought out logic of the eternal "objectivity goofs." Cuba marched decisively to give priority to social investments: education, health, housing, culture, were not put off for a later time which never arrived. At the same time, Cuba, instead of suffering from the chronic problem of unemployment, began to experience a shortage of labor (but this is not an innovation because other socialist economies experience the same problem).

Can there be a different path for creating a new socialism which is not merely an ideology to pacify the conscience of comfortably off well wishers.

Here, we touch on the other limits. If Cuba symbolizes a socialist practice that, in this respect, can enthuse all sorts of oppressed people, this symbol cannot be taken only in part. The question of freedom is not a petty bourgeois affectation, it is the other side of the same march toward equality. In the Latin American view where so many countries are stymied by bureaucratic authoritarianism, the strength of Cuba's lesson will pale if the proposed model has the same liberty-killing rancidity as those regimes which reply to demands for freedom with shouts that the GNP is growing. It is like thinking that social advances can be a substitute for the practice of freedom.

The discussion of freedom on one side and planning on the other, or of private interest versus social interest is generally abstract and devoid of meaning. Not so in this case. It is important to examine the forms of political organization and participation which permit control of the decision-making process and which permanently insure that the successes in the direction of egalitarianism and on the social plane are maintained and broadened. It also means assuring the rights of minorities to express themselves and to fight—without sabotage—for their points of view.

This is the challenge the Cuban model faces. It would be pretentious to try to give lessons or indicate possible choices. I believe, however, that the simple fact that it is possible to raise these questions as a specific problem for Cuban socialism—and therefore to suppose that Cuba can resolve them—distinguishes it fundamentally from other regimes and confirms its symbolic function.

It would be asking too much, given the general state of world affairs at this point, and in the specific circumstances of Cuba within the socialist block facing a real external blockade, to have to measure the progress of Cuban society exclusively from this viewpoint. But it is obvious that Fidel's inherent force as a leader and his uniquely constructive lack of discipline, if they were and are indispensible (perhaps even more than any formal scheme of participation from below) in assuring the creative dynamism of the political game, are insufficient to guarantee the permanence of a liberating policy in Cuban socialism. What is to be done?

This "what is to be done" does not belong to us, the rest of Latin America which has not experienced anything like the concrete possibility of thinking in these terms. What we ask, <u>for ourselves</u> and not in the name of the Cubans, for whom we have no mandate to speak, is that Cuba continue to provide the energy for concrete criticism of the freedom killing regimes which oppress us. At this point what is the use of theoretical jabbering about populist charisma or socialistic militarism? These would be empty words, like the analyses that were done to demonstrate, after the Moncada defeat, that the objective conditions of Cuba, subjected to imperialism, made revolution impossible.

Leaving aside Cuba's problem, we must now say something about what Cuba means more concretely for Latin America and also about past errors in evaluating the conditions under which the Cuban experience could be repeated.

......

In the future, historians are possibly going to separate the history of political battles in Latin America into the populist period and the so-called period of armed struggle. Perhaps if they want a point in time, however precarious, to separate the frontiers between the two stages they will say the 1960s was one of "transition." The most brazen will even think that after the inter-regnum of the sixties, the Americas should have been ablaze with rebellion, falling into step with Vietnam, Palestine—the hot wars which followed the Cold War. Yet, history, with its zigzags, mapped the world differently. So little time has passed and already in 1973 Vietnam is an American defeat; but it was negotiated in the chancellaries and at the tables of multi-party discussion. Through what strange and inscrutable channels did the negotiations pass? I do not know. But I do believe that without the patient heroism of many Vietnamese who supported the war, without the impatient agitation of many protests which checked the madness of "bombs-away" Nixomania, there would not even have been negotiations.

So it was in the Americas. The analyses, and especially Regis Debray's synthesis, were erroneous from the beginning. A Latin America in arms against imperialism was more a desire than a concrete practice. But perhaps without these analyses the "politics of compromise," the vision of a national-liberating bourgeoisie, or—who knows?—failing this, the vision of an army capable of fulfilling the functions which ideology attributed to the national bourgeoisie, would have fed with more force and persistence the illusions of a practice that would maintain the <u>status quo</u> rather than transform it. Here too, Cuban policy was an alert. The conscience of those who wanted to align themselves in defense of the majorities began to be tortured by the "no pasarán"* of our time. One, two, three, many Vietnams.....** As in Spain the reaction past. There is not even one more Vietnam. However the patchwork politics, the "Latin" package of compromise and submission ceased to mark Latin American popular movements. And this, <u>even after the defeats</u> of the tactics proposed in the name of Cuba, even after voluntarism, foquismo***, or militarism were seen for what they are: transposed experiences of a concrete situation where they were able to flourish, to other situations, in which they often became mere words, defeats, and personal heroism rather than a political force.

It is in this sense that the sixties mark a break in the political life of popular Latin American movements. Allende's Chile, is acting as if it were at the negotiating table in Paris. Behind the <u>Unidad Popular</u>**** is a history and an apprenticeship. It is not a repetition of the Popular Front of 1938. The Peru of reformist generals, perhaps because they had to confront guerilla warfare, has no relation to the military populism of Peruvian generals of earlier decades. And even Panamanian Nationalism or the Uruguayan impasse can no longer be read or understood in the same way as they would have been during the fifties.

This was certainly not all due to the Cuban lesson. Important structural transformations in the relations between the capitalist centers and the dependent periphery also occurred. And the evaluation of this point was perhaps even more erroneous than the illusion of a possible formal

---

*   Refers to the Republican forces in Spain who coined this phrase—"they will not pass"—during the Civil War.

**   Refers to Che's prediction.

***   Refers to the tactic for guerilla warfare advocated by Regis Debray

**** Popular Unity government elected to power in Chile in 1970 as a Marxist regime.

repetition of Cuban tactics in Latin America. In fact the two processes are related.

The greatest analytical error lay in not realizing that in the mid fifties the plantation economy* was beginning to lose importance as the basic imperialist relation of the entire Continent. At the same time the defenders of only one policy for Latin America did not see that the homogenizing factors of the region (that is, imperialism) were internally differentiated— there was a new and an old imperialism.

Cuba was the result of the old imperialism, as were Bolivia and so many other countries. Everything in them smacked of—and really was—foreign domination and exportation. Cheap labor, tin, and sugar cane, or, in other areas, petroleum and copper, constituted the bottom of the pot to be wiped clean. What did it matter to the American stockholder, or his representative, if the Indians chewed coca or the Cubans wasted away with alcohol and hunger in the fields? Did the consumer market of sugar, tin, or petroleum depend by chance on the buying power of this miserable mass? It was only for humanitarian reasons or in the name of a policy of social integration that these people figured in the economic practice and action of the State. But where in the world have these motives influenced the decisions of rulers? Only when some political menace is fed by hunger. Since misery feeds apathy more than revolt, "social policies," when they existed, were directed more towards integrating the urban middle class, and, in a few cases, some of the more dynamic sectors of workers, into the game of compromise with foreign domination, rather than towards attending to the needs of the great mass of the people. Thus, the interests of those who, because of their political and intellectual condition, could see the exploitation of the majority most clearly were wedded to those who exploited the same masses. The "service sector," the bureaucracy, and the rentier intelligentsia grew, and at times a few crumbs from the imperialistic repast fell to them. Not to all of them, since there always were, in Cuba, as in Bolivia, Venezuela, and Peru, non-conformists within those same acquiescent classes.

But I do not believe we can generalize on this basis, nor that the image always has been true for Latin America, at all times.

The history of Argentina, Brazil, Mexico, Uruguay, Chile and a few other countries travelled over more complex roads toward total and direct external control of agricultural or mining enclaves. In these countries, in some cases from the 19th century, both the local bourgeoisie as well as the nation states controlled an important part of the productive system. Imperialism did not cease to influence and condition the economic and political life of these countries. But its relation, in financial and mercantile terms, (through external loans and control of markets) had different consequences for the formation of social classes and in the definition of the economic and political interests of these local groups. How can the Mexican or Brazilian State and their performance in local economic life be compared with Gomez' Venezuela, Batista's Cuba or the Somozas' Nicaragua?

The historical structural heterogenity of Latin American nations is not limited to this. Beginning in the mid-fifties, and increasingly in the sixties, there were changes in the international capitalistic economy. This phenomenon is obvious in the location of part of the industrial park of multinational corporations within the peripheral economies. This process has two forms, and to confuse them, or simplify them as if they were the same thing, is misleading. In one sense it could appear that this is a repetition of the enclave economy. They would be "plantations" or their industrial "transplants." The factories come to Latin America (to some countries ...) just as they go to Hong Kong, Singapore, or Formosa. They benefit from tax exemptions, from the availability of raw materials, and from cheap labor. Finally, they export the products they manufacture in the periphery to the world centers of consumption. But factories are also established with an eye on the internal market. More than 95 per cent of the production of automobiles, refrigerators, televisions, etc., made in Brazil, Argentina or Mexico are consumed locally. From this we see the economic need of the large monopolies to broaden internal industrial consumption. This is the second form of the industrialization of the periphery of the capitalistic system.

---

*   that is, the intensive and extensive exploitation of the periphery's natural resources, such as land to plant cane and cheap manpower, and the total exportation of tropical products or minerals to consumers in the central countries under the control of imperialist finance capital.

Historically the industrialization process began as a result both of local attempts to break out of underdevelopment by means of industrialization, and of the strengthening of national decision-making centers. In the period between 1930 and the end of the Second World War, Latin American societies were characterized by expansion of the local bourgeoisie, by the extension of the proletariat and the formation of middle classes linked to industrialization. In the fifties the effects of this objective process permitted the growth of ideologies favorable to development and nationalism. The Economic Commission for Latin America symbolized and rationalized policies promoting this approach. Politically, as a consequence of this process, there was popular mobilization of the Peronist or Vargas style. Even on the left the proposed policies were related to this process: "national reformism" and the belief that the Latin American bourgeoisie could repeat the "democratic bourgeois" stage of the social revolution find their roots in the objective existence (but momentary and not analogous to the European or American historical process) of conditions which favored industrial development and the strengthening of nation states.

Imperialistic interests reacted to this first Latin American attempt at industrialization in a stern way: the "rational" international division of labor should be respected. The periphery should produce raw materials and "take advantage" of their natural comparative advantages (climate, land, natural wealth, and of course, cheap labor ...) while the center should dedicate itself to industrialization. However, as I said before, the imperialistic strategy has changed since the mid-fifties. It is not pertinent to the present discussion to explain why the monopolists had to expand into the outside world, by decentralizing production and reenforcing centralized control of the creation of new technologies and financial decisions. For our purposes it is important only to consider the effects of this process. The effects were clear in several Latin American countries: instead of continuing to place obstacles in the way of, or ignoring local industrialization, the international finance agencies, large monopolies and imperialistic diplomacy began to utilize capital to try to control the incipient process of autonomous industrialization of Latin American nations. The phase of "dependent association" was inauguerated.

Beginning in this era the "national bourgeoisie" began to internationalize itself, associating with the large monopolies. At the same time the various States continued to invest in their local economies and required foreign companies to make production, finance, and exporting agreements with State enterprises and international finance agencies or corporations. Distributive populism died, cut down by the "technical" necessity of economic stabilization policies to put the house in order and prepare for the marriage between the delicate local "maidens" and the superdeveloped international monopoly sector. The desire for "bourgeois reformist" automony ceded to authoritarian, State controlled reforms which were economically "liberal" (that is, tied to foreign interests) within a context of growing internationalization and of a new type of dependency (which is presented by the current ideologues as being "interdependence").

Within this changing picture there developed a general acceptance of the idea that the national bourgeoisie and reformism were dead as a viable policy in all of Latin America. Another idea also flourished in this context: the State and the bourgeoisie, incapable of implementing policies for necessary reforms, would hand over a stagnant, exploited and defenseless Latin America to the fury of the trusts and cartels.

At this point confusion set in. The criticism as to the impossibility of national bourgeois reformism was, and is, correct. The resulting expectation of an unviable internationalized capitalist development is falacious. In fact, the national bourgeoisie does not disappear, but changes in content and meaning when it internationalizes itself. The nation states are not weakened when associating with each other, but they do transform themselves. To think that either one of these are paper tigers that will crumple under the first blows of a popular movement is an illusion due to a lack of understanding of the historical structural modifications. These historical structural modifications brought about by internationalizing the economic interest of the bourgeoisie and strengthening the productive structure of the State, created a new platform for the accumulation of capital, permitted a more intense capitalistic dynamism and at the same time, further united the interests of the dominant groups and the imperialistic sectors.

To misunderstand the political effects of this process is to imagine, for example, that everyone considers the local army to be an occupation force. But, just as each state can determine its own goals—even when it is objectively associated with foreign interests in economic affairs—so do the national armies remain, even in the face of foreign interests. It is as if internal and external interests fused together, amalgamating in such a form that it is difficult to recognize the cat's paw of imperialism in the patriotic ardor of those who, wishing to defend national sovereignty, turn upon the "internal enemy" represented by the guerilla. The rebel, in the eyes of the man in the street, instead of combating submission and dependency appears to be undermining the bases for national grandeur. This type of struggle becomes isolated and loses force in countries where dependency coexists with a burst of development and industrialization, associated with international consortiums in the historical stages when capitalist accumulation expands.

Certainly the process is not as mechanical or economically determined as the above lines may suggest. Nonetheless, if the political elan of the local bourgeoisie and the nation states is associated with the impulse of dependent growth, a type of perverted "bourgeois revolution" can result. Conditions give the dependent bourgeoisie the ability to make "revolutions." Instead of the liberal grandeur of the bourgeois revolutions of metropolitan countries, one has repression and authoritarianism; instead of the ideal of equality, growing inequalities not only in fact (income) but as an ideal (as an ideological justification for development).

Nevertheless, in each and every instance where the local bourgeoisie, associated with imperialism, and the nation states, strengthened by authoritarianism and repression, are capable of assuring economic expansion and the partial incorporation of the most active parts of the lowest groups, they will have fused the political counterrevolution with the economic realization of the form of capitalism which corresponds to it—dependent and internationalized. During the initial phase of the implantation of this new, plebian absolutism there will be none of the political elements which characterize the phases of decadence. In the Batista, Gomez or Somoza regimes, corruption replaced efficiency and personal interest took the place of the state's interests. When one does not have a situation of this type in which, as Lenin said, the dominant class is incapable of command and no longer has a viable historical role to play, a hasty diagnosis implying that a drop of heroic blood will destroy the established order is a dangerous illusion. Similarly, it is dangerous to suggest that when the signs of economic stagnation and of political disintegration begin to appear, the lesson of hard struggle is no longer necessary and that the established order will disintegrate with words.

......

It would be simplistic to think that because of the effects of the present form of imperialist expansion, its internal and external difficulties as well as the contradictions and the necessity of struggle would disappear. On the one hand, the processes I described above are not generalized. They apply to some sectors of Latin American economics and societies. On the other hand, the level of capitalism's advance and its history (as I indicated briefly) are also not uniform. And finally, to say that capitalistic growth exists, does not mean that the Latin American populations are benefiting from the process of capitalistic accumulation, which itself takes place precisely at the cost of these same people.

Politically, the problem is to determine how to break the barriers of political and social domination which maintain the many existing contradictions. Within diversity, it is necessary to specify how these contradictions are articulated and related hierarchically in each specific case. When penetrating rural areas, for example, internationalized agrarian capitalism disorganizes old forms of productions, forces people from the land, requires the formation of wage relationships, creates new land-owners and brings former rural workers to the city. All of this creates a tide of contradictory interests. At the same time in the city the heterogeneity of interests, even among the working classes, grows. The worker in a General Motor's factory does not live in the same style as a textile worker in a traditional industry. The possibilities for demanding higher salaries and better working conditions are obviously not the same.

How can these interests be unified? How and when can the conflict between the State and the multinational corporations best be utilized? Is it possible to take political advantage of the desire for more consumption which the emergence of mini-societies of abundance in some Latin nations stimulates among the urban masses but which the highly unequal distribution of income denies for the majority?

Questions of this kind are a challenge for those who want to mobilize broad masses in order to achieve a more profound social change in the future. Political tactics and words of command cannot be deduced from general analysis or from historical revolutionary examples. They have to be discovered in daily practice and transformed into a force which can integrate what appears to be a multiplicity of different, chaotic conflicts and contradictions.

It was in this respect that the copy of the Cuban "lesson" became flawed and rigid. In this case, again, the Cuban experience is more a symbol than a lesson. Imitation without creativity, and the lifeless transposition of formulas and methods became pale and deformed. Rather, the inspiration derived from the example, the analysis of the experiences and, most important, the continually renovating symbolic power of a society which confronts the worst difficulties without losing sight of its goal, aid and fortify popular movements.

Cuba is a symbol leading to action for the people subjected to the double pressure of economic imperialism and authoritarian and technomilitary bureaucratization. It provides the pardigm of a society which, though poor, persists in the search for egalitarianism. A society which, though surrounded, continues to permit constructive disagreements to flourish, and which, most importantly, even knowing that the ideal will not come tomorrow, continues to scan the horizon for it.

It is important to the people for whom the war has not even begun, as is the case of most Latin Americans, to avoid the immobilization resulting from the consciousness that tomorrow will be much like today. It is necessary that they fix their sight on a horizon of vivid symbols which sustain immediate action, without despair, without heroic and useless voluntarism, but also with the firmness that derives from the profound belief that one day things will be different.

This is the symbol which Cuba bequeaths to the Americas. Its transformation into practical policy is a challenge which depends less on the Cubans and more on the creativity and spirit of struggle of each Latin American people.

DATE DUE

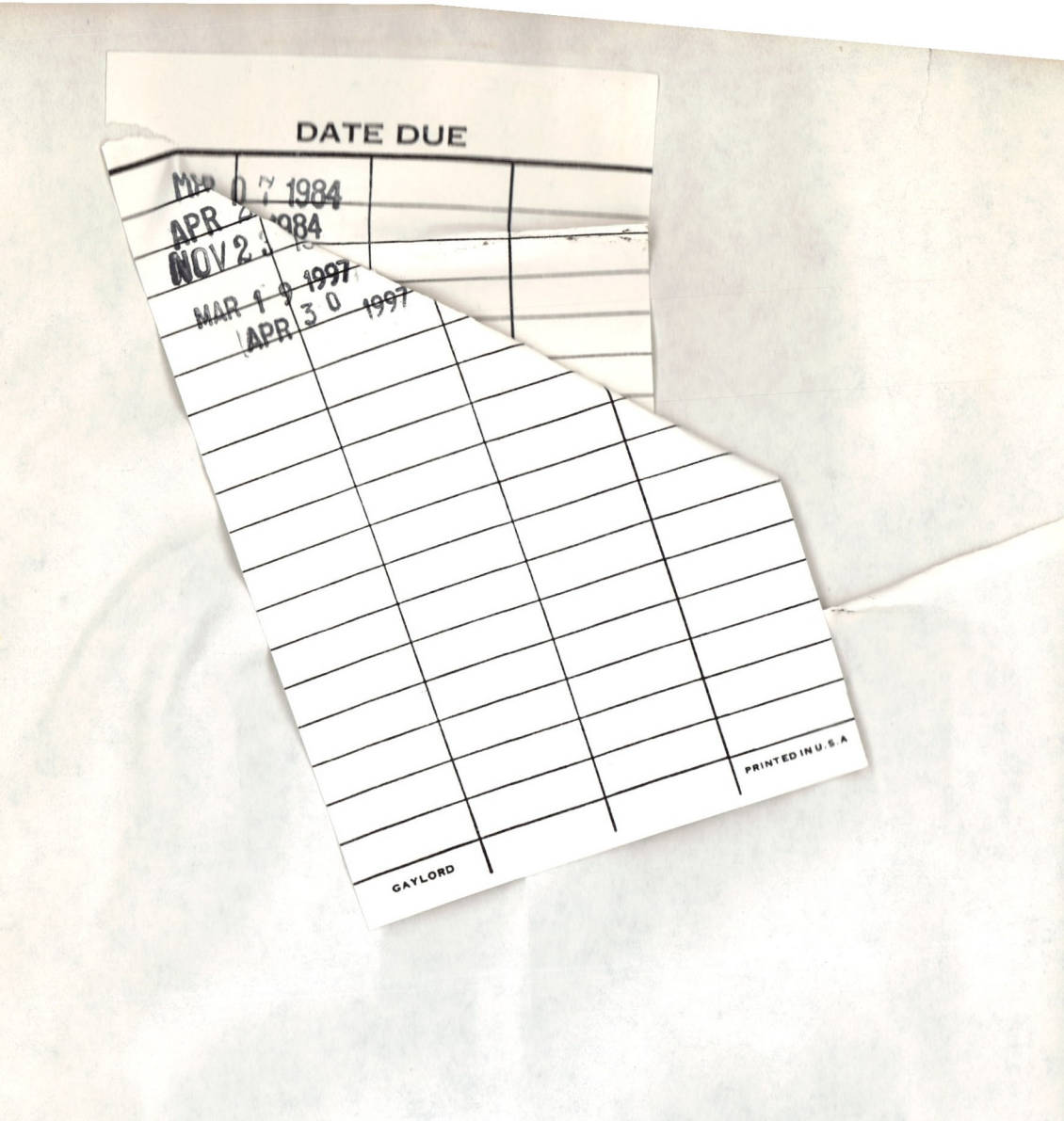

MAR 0 7 1984			
APR 2 1984			
NOV 2 1984			
MAR 1 9 1997			
APR 3 0 1997			

GAYLORD   PRINTED IN U.S.A